A
COLUMBINE
BOOK

A
COLUMBINE
BOOK

WHO. WHAT. WHERE. WHEN. WHY?

C. SHEPARD

~{@}~

Semper Memento Inc.
Phoenix • U.S.A.

This publication is designed to provide accurate and authoritative information regarding the subject matter covered. While all efforts have been made to ensure accuracy and contact individuals involved, the publisher and author make no guarantees with respect to the accuracy or completeness of the contents of this book and assume no liabilities for errors.

Cover and book design by C Shepard
Interior images by C Shepard; Jefferson County
http://www.aColumbineSite.com

Shepard, C.
 A Columbine book : who what where when why / C. Shepard.
— First Edition
   p. cm.
 ISBN 979-8-9916221-0-3 (hc.)
 ISBN 979-8-9870778-2-5 (pbk.)
 ISBN 979-8-9870778-8-7 (ebook)

LCCN: 2024920196

PRINTED IN THE UNITED STATES OF AMERICA

10 9 8 7 6 5 4 3 2 1
First Edition

In memory of
Stephen Austin Eubanks
Theresa Miller
William Erickson

Thanks to...

The Columbine families and everyone who has helped them

aColumbineSite readers

My family and friends

HOPE

The Columbine community

You

A COLUMBINE BOOK series by C Shepard:

PREFACE

Since April 21, 1999, my website www.aColumbineSite.com has presented accurate, unbiased information about the Columbine shooting. For years people have asked me to write a book about it. After 25 years, I finally felt it was time.

Researchers all over the world have wanted to know the "who, what, where, when, and why" of the massacre since the start. This book puts things together in a "big picture" narrative reconstructed from various sources including survivor and witness statements, the Columbine Report and Documents, other official reports, media interviews, forensic analysis, documentaries, and more.

All effort has been made to avoid embellishment or opinion. Descriptions and dialogue come from the people involved. If this manuscript says someone thought, saw, or did something, it is because they said so. I did not annotate the book primarily because the whole thing would be riddled with distracting footnotes. The resources I have used over the years are listed in the back of this book if you wish to fact-check.

Not everyone went public with their experience. As such, some accounts are more detailed than others. Some witness statements contradict others. Individuals might have recalled incorrectly right after the event or years later. Stories have gotten conflated with others. This book tries to weed out misinformation and present the facts as clearly and truthfully as possible. If it doesn't appear in this book, it's either because it is unnecessary to understand the event, or I was unable to verify it.

This is the story of unprecedented tragedy and recovery.

This is the story of the Columbine shooting.

According to the Distaster Center, in 1999, more than 15,522 people were the victims of homicide in the United States.

Thirteen of those murders occurred at Columbine High School.

Stop violence before it begins.

Violence prevention:
https://www.cdc.gov/violenceprevention/about/index.html

Suicide prevention:
https://www.cdc.gov/suicide/index.html

Mental health assistance:
https://www.samhsa.gov/find-help

INTRODUCTION

I'll never forget the day it happened. I was sitting at the computer talking with friends online when the news interrupted the television show my preschooler was watching. I glanced over, expecting to see the President. What I saw what would become an iconic image: People escaping from Columbine High School. I watched in shock as terrified kids scrambled out of a shattered window in the side of the school with their hands on their heads while black-clad men aimed automatic weapons at them.

What was happening? I asked my friends online, but no one had even heard the news yet. I was the closest to the shooting, being only one state away. And that began my quest to piece together what happened and why. My research brought me in contact with several of the Columbine families, counselors, law enforcement, district staff, medical personnel, journalists, authors, students, and even more people worldwide. What I thought would be a couple of days of digging turned into a quarter of a century of study and connecting with people about this gripping subject. Years after the Columbine shooting, the subject continues to attract attention from people of all ages and backgrounds. There's a common need to understand this bizarre tragedy. Most people in the modern world attended school at some point. We can understand potential issues that might lead to something like this, while not condoning it. And most of us have had a moment where we wanted to go berserk on someone who made us feel unwanted or attacked.

But there's a difference between rage-quitting a video game and opening fire on a crowded school yard. There is a difference between fantasizing about violence and actually going through with it. In the film *Falling Down*, Michael Douglas portrays the character DFENS, a man who reaches his breaking point and takes his frustrations out on people who seem at first to deserve it. Arrogant gang members threaten his life because they want his briefcase. He fights back and defeats the thugs. The audience feels a thrill of justice: The villains got what they deserved.

As the movie continues, though, the acts of vigilantism become less justified until the "hero" is blowing up a street where construction workers are just trying to do their job. In the end he's left wondering aloud: "When did I become the bad guy?"

In their amateur film projects, Harris and Klebold portrayed themselves as hitmen for hire who assassinated bullies for picked-on students. But by April 20, 1999, they had shifted focus to treating life like an ultimate game of *Doom* where they were gods, and everyone was a fair target to kill. The only thing that mattered in the end was getting the "high score" – the highest kill count.

Hundreds of questions were left unanswered following the tragedy. Why did they do it? Why did they stop? Did they have help? Did they know their victims? Who suspected something was wrong before the shooting? Why wasn't something done sooner to end the incident? Or to stop it before it even started? The shooting left an indelible mark in people's minds as the world learned about and wrestled with such large-scale violence in a place that should have been safe. Even now, over two decades since the shooting, many questions remain without explanation.

This book exists to provide the most clear and accurate depiction of what happened and why. It is written in three parts: Part one is narrative nonfiction describing what happened that day, part two is an extensive timeline, and part three is an analysis. The narrative covers the day of the shooting minute by minute, in graphic detail. The timeline covers nearly 100 years of history leading up to the shooting, the time of the shooting, and things that have happened relative to the tragedy up to 2024. The analysis looks at the who, what, where, when, and why of it. The conclusions presented are the result of 25 years of studying the crime, first from an armchair detective standpoint and then as a student of Forensic Science, Psychology, and Journalism.

With thousands of people interviewed and witness reliability shaky under the circumstances, there are many versions of any given moment of the tragedy. The most likely scenarios have been presented herein based on where evidence and people's stories line up. All effort has been made to avoid embellishment or opinion. Descriptions and dialogue come from the people involved. I didn't annotate this manual because the whole thing would be riddled with footnotes. It's intended to be a quick way for researchers to digest and understand what has taken a quarter of a century to piece together. To allow the reader to study what happened without spending months scouring the web, reading articles and watching videos. Everything referenced in this book is out there available to the public. The resources I've used are listed in the back of this book for fact-checking purposes. I encourage anyone to do their own research when they have the time.

About the Timeline:

There are several official and unofficial timelines. Like a house with more than one clock, no two agree on what time any given event happened. Witnesses used their own watches to denote the time. Agency clocks weren't synched to each other or the school's clocks, which weren't even set to the same time as each other. You can read more about this discrepancy in the "What" section.

Outreach:

I have tried to reach out to individuals whose stories appear in this book, to alert them to its publication and offer a chance to add to or edit the content. While I've been in contact with some individuals and families, I haven't pushed to engage anyone not receptive to my inquiries or dug up contact information for those who haven't made it publicly available. I don't want to make anyone relive this event if they want to move on.

Not everyone went public with their experience. As such, some accounts are more detailed than others. Some witness statements contradict others. Individuals might have recalled incorrectly right after the event or years later. Stories have gotten conflated with others. This book tries to weed out misinformation and present the facts as clearly and truthfully as possible. If it doesn't appear in this book, it's because it is unnecessary to understand the event, or I was unable to verify it.

If you or someone in your family experienced this tragedy first-hand and you want to share your story or request corrections, you can reach me at webmaster@acolumbinesite.com or http://aColumbineSite.com/contact.html.

WARNING

This book contains graphic descriptions of injury and death.

This is the story of what happened at Columbine High School before, during, and after April 20, 1999. It is not intended to sensationalize the event. It is a painfully honest look at what happened moment by moment, day by day.

This book is a tool to help educators and students, first responders, and researchers by providing an accurate, unbiased, forensic and historical look at the details of one of the worst school shootings in the USA.

If you or someone you care about had to live through this terrible incident, I **strongly** encourage you to NOT read this book. If you are easily triggered, struggle with depression or instability, or have suffered similar trauma, again: Do not read this book.

Though presented with the utmost respect for those whose lives were impacted by the tragedy, this is not a book for everyone.

TABLE OF CONTENTS

SECTION I

4-20-1999 Narrative

APRIL 20, 1999

10:30 AM – HARRIS BASEMENT

"Say it now."

Eric Harris aimed the video camera at his best friend, Dylan Klebold.

Dylan, 17, had his favorite black Boston Red Sox baseball cap on backward. His reddish-brown shoulder-length hair puffed around his long face. He wore a button-down plaid shirt over black battle dress uniform pants— tactical gear known as "BDUs". There were several gym bags on the floor at his feet.

"Hey, mom." Dylan's tone was casual. "Gotta go. It's about a half an hour before our little judgment day. I just wanted to apologize to you guys for any crap this might instigate as far as—"

He turned his head and the camera lost audio. Unaware, he kept talking. The sound picked up again when he looked back at the lens.

"...or something. Just know I'm going to a better place. I didn't like life too much and I know I'll be happy wherever the fuck I go. So... I'm gone. Goodbye." He looked past the video camera at the person holding it. "Reb..?"

1

Eric handed him the camera and they traded places. A skinny young man, he was 5.5 inches shorter than Dylan's 6-foot-2. Eric's brown hair was cropped short in a buzz cut. He wore black military-style BDU pants. The collar of a white T-shirt showed beneath his buttoned plaid overshirt. He had celebrated his 18th birthday just ten days ago.

"Yeah," he said to the camera in an off-handed way. "Everyone I love: I'm really sorry about all this. I know my mom and dad will be just like... just fucking shocked beyond belief. I'm sorry, all right? I can't help it."

"We did what we had to do," Dylan added offscreen.

"Morris, Nate," Eric went on. "If you guys live, I want you guys to have whatever you want from my room and the computer room."

Dylan said they could have his stuff too.

"Susan: Sorry," said Eric. "Under different circumstances, it would've been a lot different. I want you to have that fly CD." He paused for a moment, thinking. Then: "That's it. Goodbye."

Dylan turned the camera around and put his face up close to the lens. It would have been silly if not for the ominous message that came before it. "Goodbye."

Before he turned the video camera off, it captured a glimpse of one last thing—a sign on the wall that bore the letters CHS. Someone had drawn a crude sketch of a lit bomb on it. Written in bold black letters in the corner was one word: CLUE.

—

COLUMBINE HIGH

Among other things, 17-year-old Rachel Scott was an artist. That morning the doe-eyed junior sat in class sketching a rose in a notebook where she kept her art and poetry. She had drawn a similar picture the previous year.

Things had been rough for Rachel. For months she'd been making poor choices. Smoking, fighting with her family, letting her grades slip, distancing herself from her religious upbringing. She'd befriended people who were toxic influences. Wanting to get back on a good track, she made major changes over the past weeks. She quit smoking. She joined the Speech and Debate teams and spent more time doing theatre projects. She was writing a play. Recently she was the lead in a school production, *Smoke in the Room*, written by senior Andrew Robinson. Sophomore Devon Adams helped her trim her brown hair short for the role. Rachel's friends Nick Baumgart and Lauren Beachem were also in the performance. Nick took Rachel to prom last weekend and encouraged her to stop smoking. Rachel was trying to make things better at home, too. A week ago, she'd had a long talk with her father. Their relationship was improving but she was melancholy. Her social life had taken a hit. Some of her friends felt threatened by the changes in her behavior. They teased her about her renewed devotion to religion. Some stopped hanging out with her.

She added a pair of soulful eyes above her rose. The eyes cried thirteen tears on the petals and leaves.

—

Columbine's video announcement system Rebel News Network (RNN) had a "Thought for the Day" which changed each morning. Senior James Davis wrote one that morning that said: "Quit your bitching." Eric Veik, a junior on the RNN staff, didn't think it was appropriate. He changed it to:

"How could you expect us to stay in school on a day like this?"

+ + +

FLASHBACK TO 5:58 AM – OFF CAMPUS

17-year-old Chris Morris was getting nervous. There was no sign of his ride to zero-hour bowling class. Eric Harris should have been there to pick him up at 5:50 a.m.

Chris was 6-foot-4 with short brown hair and glasses. He was a close friend of Eric and Dylan. He was a member of their school bowling team along with their mutual friend Nate Dykeman. When the semester began the Columbine seniors picked their teammates. They were friends and enjoyed bowling together outside of school, so it made sense to be a team. They also worked together at Blackjack Pizza the past year and hung out a lot up until late 1998. Around December, Chris started spending most of his down time with his girlfriend, Nicole Markham, a junior at CHS. They'd been dating since 1997, but things were getting serious. Nate also had a girlfriend, Kristine Epling. The blonde girl was also a senior at Columbine.

Kristi didn't know Dylan that well, but she knew he was like a brother to Nate. She'd known Eric since the 9th grade and thought of him as a good friend. The past four years they took German classes together. They were such a fixture their teacher allowed them to pass notes in class through fall and winter of 1998. In them they discussed weekend plans. Sometimes Eric asked her for advice about girls he liked. In January 1999, she and Eric went on an informal bowling date at Belleview Lanes along with some friends. The date led to a falling out between Eric and Nate, who already expressed interest in Kristi. The guys stopped speaking to each other until she intervened. They made up, but they weren't as close as they once were. In February, she and Nate officially started dating.

The past few months, Chris and Nate's free time was spent with their girlfriends. It wasn't just because of the girls, though. Eric and Dylan had been acting differently. They slept in class and ditched often. Dylan withdrew from friends and family. He was quick to anger. Eric was more aggressive than ever. He picked fights and expected friends to back him up if things got

4

physical. Being put on the spot angered Chris and made Nate uncomfortable. Neither wanted to fight impulsive battles for Eric, so they hung out less with him—and Dylan, as they were usually together. Chris was a manager at the restaurant where they worked. When they rigged an explosive trip wire behind the shop and brought a pipe bomb into the kitchen, Chris had to put his foot down. They forced him to prioritize work over friendship, which drove a bigger wedge between them.

Around Christmas 1998, Chris noticed Eric seemed depressed. His interests changed: He got into German industrial music and read books about Hitler and concentration camps. He talked about guns a lot. As Eric's interests polarized toward the negative, Chris spent even less time with him. But Eric still gave him rides to bowling class.

When 6:00 a.m. rolled around, Chris gave up waiting and drove his own 1985 red Dodge Lancer to school. The old car was prone to overheating. He got to class too late to make attendance or bowl for a grade. He and Nate bowled against senior Mike Paavilainen's team, though Nate was the only one who posted scores. The teacher wrote the other three students' class averages on the roster and circled them to denote their absence.

Eric and Dylan had skipped several bowling sessions recently, so their teammates weren't concerned. But Nate found it odd when Eric also missed the next hour. Eric liked video production class and was rarely absent. Dylan and Eric were also missing from the fourth hour Language Arts class they shared with Nate. They never missed so many classes at the same time.

+ + +

11:10 AM – OUTSIDE COLUMBINE

Eric and Dylan—"REB" and "VoDkA"—arrived at Columbine High School. The "A" lunch hour had just started.

Kristi was leaving campus to meet her boyfriend Nate for lunch when she saw Eric in his gray 1986 Honda Civic, a car

5

distinguished by the Rammstein sticker on the back window. He pulled into the parking lot and headed her way. She honked and waved to him as they passed. He smiled and waved back. Then he parked his car in the southeast junior student lot.

Senior Chad Laughlin was leaving at the same time and nearly collided with Dylan, who was racing into the lot in his black 1982 BMW. The old car had a white NIN sticker on the back windshield. Chad backed up to let him pass, jokingly giving him the middle finger. He had known Dylan since grade school when they were both in the gifted program CHIPS (Challenging High Intellectual Potential Students). Chad ran a fantasy baseball game at Columbine and online. He spoke with Dylan daily about player trades. Toward the end of 1998, Chad and a mutual friend of theirs went to Wyoming. Dylan asked them to pick up $80 worth of fireworks for him since he couldn't go. He was on probation for breaking into a van in January. At the time the request didn't seem strange.

Andrew Beard, another senior, was also heading out for lunch. He was in the same bowling class as Dylan and played fantasy baseball with Chad and him. They'd talked about trades the night before, which they did often. They passed each other as Andrew drove out. Dylan parked in the southwest senior lot, angling his car toward the commons. Eric's car faced the southern doors of the cafeteria. Neither parked in his assigned spot. The spaces they took offered an excellent view of the school's front and side entrances.

As lunch break began, 18-year-old senior Brooks Brown stepped outside for a cigarette. Tall and dark-haired, he and Dylan were close since 1st grade at Normandy Elementary School. Dylan introduced Brooks to Eric in the 7th grade at Ken Caryl Middle School. All three were good friends until the past two years. Eric used to ride to school with his older brother, but when Kevin graduated, Eric rode with Brooks. But Brooks was bad about being on time. One day he slept in, prompting a nasty argument when he called to tell Eric he'd be late. So, Brooks didn't pick him up that morning. When the argument resumed at school, he told Eric he wouldn't give him rides anymore.

Enraged, Eric launched a series of dangerous "pranks" against Brooks and his family which escalated to violent attacks. Things got crazy. He broke Brooks' windshield and posted hateful rants online, making death threats against his former friend. He posted Brooks' phone number on his website and encouraged people to call and harass him. He left lit explosives on Brooks' bedroom windowsill at night. To put a stop to it Randy and Judy Brown, Brooks' parents, filed a police report in March 1998. Eric eventually apologized, but the Browns doubted his sincerity. After that, though, Brooks and Eric stayed away from each other until the start of their senior year when they learned they would be sharing several classes. They couldn't avoid each other. Neither wanted to spend the school year watching his back, so they agreed to let bygones be bygones.

Brooks saw Eric pull into the parking lot that morning and went to talk to him. There had been a major test in philosophy class Eric missed when he ditched third period. Brooks knew it would affect his grade and upset his parents, so he went to talk to him. When Brooks got to him, Eric was messing around with something in the trunk of his car.

"You missed the test," said Brooks.

Eric laughed. "It doesn't matter anymore."

He pulled a blue duffel bag out of his car and set it on the ground. Then he paused and looked at the other teen. When he spoke next, his expression and tone were intense. "Brooks, I like you now. Get out of here and go home. Now."

Eric went around the side of his car to pull another bag from the back seat. Brooks noticed he wasn't wearing his hat. Eric always wore his hat. It was a small detail but combined with the rest of his odd behavior—skipping classes, his paramilitary clothes, their conversation—the situation was unsettling. Uneasy, Brooks crossed the parking lot to head for Pierce Street.

7

+ + +

11:11 AM - CAFETERIA

Columbine's cafeteria was a wide, rounded room. The west wall and south hall that led outside were composed of large windows that let in sunlight and offered a pleasant view of the tree-lined street beyond the parking lot. The serving line and kitchen were on the north side of the room. Several dozen round tables filled the room, crowded with students.

Kyle Velasquez left the table he shared with his friend Adam Kyler. Though Kyle was only 16 years old, the dark-haired boy was 6 feet tall and weighed 230 pounds. He had a sweet disposition. Behind his glasses his brown eyes were often smiling. Others knew him as a "gentle giant", like the pandas he loved. He suffered a stroke as a baby which left him mentally and physically disabled, but he was kind and looked for the good in people. He and Adam, also 16, were both Special Needs students. Kyle had attended Columbine High for three months, only mornings at first. Recently he started staying through lunch. He loved computers and used them frequently at school. He went upstairs to use the library computer lab before he had to leave.

+ + +

11:14 AM – OUTSIDE COLUMBINE

In their journals, Eric and Dylan drew outfits they called their "NBK gear". The abbreviation for the clothes and weapons came from a Tarantino film they were obsessed with: *Natural Born Killers*. It featured extreme violence committed by two people who murdered for no reason. The two teens revered the power the killers had. They could quote the whole film, something even their closest friends found strange.

They left their vehicles and closed in on the school. The duffel bags they carried held homemade time bombs crafted from 20-pound propane tanks attached to gasoline canisters. They'd duct taped BBs and nails to them to make deadly projectiles. The explosives had timers set to go off at 11:17 a.m. when the cafeteria was most crowded according to Eric's notes.

They were outfitted in their "NBK gear": Wraparound sunglasses, black leather dusters, black BDU pants and combat boots. Around their waists they wore BAR belts filled with ammunition. Dylan's black T-shirt had the word "WRATH" in red on the front and he wore his favorite Boston Red Sox cap backward. A Soviet hammer and sickle medallion was clipped to one of his boots. Eric wore his black KMFDM hat, a white T-shirt with "Natural Selection" printed in black on the front, and a tactical ammo vest. He had a box strapped to his ankle with gray duct tape. Both carried knives and had match strikers taped to their forearms.

They were suited up for war.

—

INSIDE COLUMBINE

Campus Supervisor Andrew "Andy" Marton turned off the cafeteria surveillance camera to rewind the videotapes. It was a routine he followed every day. While they were rewinding, he left the room to make a quick phone call. The school had three locations where security cameras recorded during the day: One outside the library, one facing the principal's office, and four cameras that recorded the cafeteria commons. Each morning Marton took the tapes out, rewound them, and replaced them with the previous week's tapes.

+ + +

11:15 AM

17-year-old Daniel Steepleton finished fourth period weight training class with Coach Andy Lowry and headed up to the library. The brown-haired junior had "A" lunch but preferred to spend it with friends rather than go to the cafeteria.

Outside the library he said hi to Crystal Woodman, a junior with shoulder-length blonde bob. She was with her friends Seth Houy, a senior, and his younger sister Sara, a sophomore. They often hung out in the library during "A" lunch with Seth's girlfriend, Erika Dendorfer, but she had to work on a presentation for French class. Crystal needed to study for her Physics test, so she and the Houys headed to the center of the library where they typically sat.

Dan also went in to grab a table with his friends Makai Hall, Stephen "Austin" Eubanks, Patrick Ireland, and Corey DePooter. The juniors sat at a table together in the back near the west windows.

———

Columbine junior Aaron Wright dropped his backpack off in his car and headed back to the cafeteria. On his way he saw Eric, an acquaintance, carrying an athletic bag toward the school. The bag was 18-24 inches in length, about 12 inches wide, black and very heavy as Eric was having to carry it with both hands.

While the security cameras were offline, Eric and Dylan entered the cafeteria and planted the duffel bag bombs. Then they returned to their cars to wait for the big bang.

———

Sarah Slater went to join her friends at a table in the commons near one of the four support pillars. She noticed a large blue duffle bag with a strap across it on the floor. She asked her friends if it belonged to anyone, but nobody claimed it. She tried to push it aside with her foot, but it was too heavy to move, so she stepped over it.

Sarah knew Dylan in 9th and 10th grades. They worked together on lighting in theatre and used to chat on the internet. Dylan and his friend Zach Heckler both had a crush on her, but she wasn't interested in dating either of them. She remained good friends with Zach, but lost touch with Dylan the past year

+ + +

11:18 AM

Supervisor Marton set the VCR to record over last week's tapes. It would take the machines a few minutes to start recording again. In addition to managing the security cameras, Marton worked as an unarmed Security Resource Officer at Columbine High School. He went to join Jefferson County Sheriff's Deputy Neil Gardner in the cafeteria for lunch.

Gardner was a 15-year police force veteran and a School Resource Officer at Columbine who did bike patrol around Clement Park. He and his wife had separated three months ago. It was a rocky time for them and their kids, but they were making shared custody work. During lunch Gardner typically parked his squad car in front of the cafeteria between the junior and senior lots and ate with Marton. That day he was driving the lieutenant's unmarked blue Chevy Caprice. When they learned the meal in the cafeteria was teriyaki, the SROs decided to drive to Subway for sandwiches. They got their food to go and parked next to "Smokers' Pit" at Clement Park northwest of the school. Smoking wasn't allowed on campus, but students could get "pit passes" to go there and smoke. The officers could keep an eye on the kids while on lunch break.

—

OUTSIDE COLUMBINE

Things were not going as planned.

The diversionary time bomb behind the high school exploded on schedule but didn't fully detonate. The device was in an open grassy field three miles southwest of Columbine, and east of Wadsworth Boulevard. Jefferson County Dispatch Center received a 911 call from someone in the neighborhood who heard the blast. Emergency sirens howled toward field between Ken Caryl and Chatfield Avenues. There officers found two backpacks loaded with pipe bombs, aerosol spray cans, and small propane tanks attached to clocks. The pipe bombs and one of the aerosol cans had exploded. The propane tanks were intact. Still, the partial detonation caused a fire large enough for the Littleton Fire Department to dispatch Engine 13. Two pipe bombs planted at Wadsworth and Elmhurst didn't go off. Investigators found them later when they tripped over them.

There was supposed to be a huge explosion inside the school too. The duffel bag bombs were meant to deliver a blast that would bring the upstairs library crashing down on the commons below. There were 488 people in the cafeteria. The death toll could potentially pass 500 according to the headcount Eric took in his notebook. It should have been chaos. Eric and Dylan waited at their cars to pick off terrified survivors who ran from the flaming wreckage. Instead of explosions and screams, though, the only sounds were those of students enjoying lunch in the warm spring sunshine.

The bombs inside Columbine were mysteriously silent.

+ + +

11:19 AM

Dylan and Eric got tired of waiting.

They set the timers on the explosive devices they'd rigged in their vehicles. Then they each grabbed a duffel bag and a backpack that collectively held two sawed-off 12-gauge shotguns, a 9mm semi-automatic Hi-Point model 995 carbine rifle, and an Intratec 9mm TEC-DC9 Mini semi-automatic pistol. Each teen had a single fingerless glove. Dylan was left-handed, so he wore his glove on his left hand. Eric wore his on his right. While testing their firearms at Rampart Range they'd learned protection was necessary. Their sawed-off shotguns were so short, firing them made their hands bleed.

In addition to guns and knives, they carried dozens of homemade explosives and several dozen rounds of ammunition. Heavily armed, they climbed the stairs in the hill outside the cafeteria. It was the highest point on campus. The west entrance was on their left, the athletic fields to the right. The cafeteria's west door was below them. The spot offered a perfect view of the main entryways and grounds, which were popular at lunchtime. The way the school was built into the hillside, they could cover the downstairs and upstairs exits at once.

It was Zero Hour of an event they planned for over a year.

—

Richard Castaldo, a 17-year-old junior with curly dark brown hair, sat with Rachel outside on the grass. They were having lunch together, something they'd started doing every other day. It was Richard's first year at CHS. He transferred from Catholic Machebeuf High at the insistence of a friend who attended Columbine only to find he didn't like being there. He was a quiet kid who never told his family why he was unhappy, only that he was planning to transfer to Cherry High next year. But he enjoyed lunch with Rachel.

Until recently Rachel spent her lunch break at "Smokers' Pit" in Clement Park, which she and Richard were currently facing. She and her younger brother Craig both shared mutual friends with Dylan and Eric, all of whom had spent time at "Smokers' Pit". When Rachel quit smoking, she stopped going there. It was a choice some of her friends didn't like. They thought she believed she was too good for them now. She didn't. She just needed a change.

Rachel knew Dylan since kindergarten. At Columbine, they were both active in theatre, as was Brooks Brown. Brooks had played Frankenstein in the 1998 school production. A year earlier, Dylan was the sound tech for a talent show Rachel was in. There were technical issues with the music during the mime of "Who Nailed Him There?" that she performed to the song

Watch the Lamb by Ray Boltz. Devon Adams was in the sound booth with Dylan and saw him save the act by hooking up a reserve tape deck. In addition to working sound, Dylan also filmed intros for Rebel News Network with the help of Eric Harris and with Rachel's friend Eric Veik. Rachel had auditioned for the role of RNN anchor that morning.

Eric and Dylan made other videos over the past months—"Basement Tapes" the media would later call them. In one they made fun of a girl named Rachel and other Christian girls who were "always talking about Jesus". Though they might have meant someone else, Rachel recently became a born-again Christian which caused her to lose friends according to her diary.

She and Richard were seated between the armed teens and the west entrance.

"GO! GO!"

The shout came from behind them. A loud explosion from a pipe bomb shattered the peaceful morning, signaling the start of one of the worst school shootings in history.

Eric pulled out his rifle. Dylan drew his sawed-off shotgun. They opened fire.

Richard glanced back and saw two guys in long black coats, one with long hair, the other had a buzz cut. He'd seen them around school but didn't know them. That's all he took in before eight bullets tore through his spine, puncturing his lungs and a kidney, and rupturing his spleen. Two more bullets slammed into his left arm. Another hit his right arm. The barrage dropped him instantly.

Three bullets from Eric's rifle struck Rachel in the left arm and thigh. Another bullet punched through her chest, fracturing her ribs and lacerating her lungs and heart. Still conscious, Richard heard her crying in pain, but he couldn't help her. His injuries had paralyzed him.

—

CAFETERIA

Lance Kirklin sat at a table with his friends, stacking dishes like an artistic centerpiece. It was characteristic silly behavior for the 16-year-old sophomore, who kept his sense of humor despite his family issues. His mother Dawn divorced his father Mike in 1993, taking Lance and his younger sister Amanda to live with her. But she got frustrated with Lance's behavior and sent him back to Denver to live with his father when she moved with Amanda to Nebraska. Lance felt abandoned.

Five months ago, his half-brother Nolan committed suicide. Following the death, Lance's dad Mike struggled with alcoholism, too lost in his grief to see how his behavior affected his surviving son. Mike would spend hours at the cemetery instead of working. They lost their apartment but were able to get into another. When they lost that one, Lance leveled with his dad.

"Hey. You've got another son who needs you."

That snapped Mike out of his funk enough to start trying again. Things were getting better: Mike was rebuilding his tree service and was considering other job offers. Nothing he did came with health insurance, but at least they had a home.

Finished with his dish art, Lance wanted a cigarette. He and freshmen Danny Rohrbough and Sean Graves, both 15, left to head to "Smokers' Pit". His friends weren't smokers, but they didn't mind hanging out with him there. The boys went out the west door to the hill and trekked up the dirt path beside the stairs. They were almost to the top when they saw two guys they didn't know in long black coats. One, Eric, stood at the top of the stairway. The other, Dylan, was facing the west doors and running backward. He had his TEC-DC9 in one hand and a curved clip in the other. Eric dug around in his pocket, his rifle in hand. Gym bags littered the ground around him. He popped a fresh clip into his gun.

Sean assumed they were playing a prank. Everyone knew seniors pulled all sorts of shenanigans close to graduation. A week ago, they closed off the junior parking lot as a joke. Each year the graduating class played a game on campus called "annihilation". They wore white T-shirts and "shot" each other with water pistols and paintball guns. Eric was wearing a white T-shirt. The friends headed toward the shooters.

They were easy targets.

Lance heard fireworks. He looked up and saw one of the guys in black coats holding what he thought was a paintball gun. Then Eric pulled the trigger. Bullets pounded the ground in front of the younger boys.

Danny took a bullet in the left leg just below his knee. The weightlifter yelped and stumbled, falling backward. Lance tried to catch him, but Dylan fired his TEC-9. The 9mm ammo ripped through the left side of Danny's chest and abdomen, leaving wounds half an inch in diameter. Blood spread over his green shirt as he fell down the stairs into Sean. A bullet from Dylan's TEC-9 grazed Sean's neck near his ear. He turned to run but he didn't get far before three bullets tore into his back and abdomen. A fourth bullet hit his leg. He lost all feeling in it, dropping to the sidewalk outside the cafeteria door. Lance also tried to run. Pain seared through his foot as three bullets struck his lower right leg. His knee buckled. Another shot lodged in the back of his left knee. A shotgun blast slammed into the right side of his chest, knocking him to the ground.

Lance hollered for his friends, every breath bringing up blood. Sean screamed that his legs didn't work. Danny was silent.

—

Mike Johnson, Denny Rowe, Mark Taylor, John Cook, and Adam Thomas were hanging out on their lunch break about 25 feet from the stairs. The cafeteria was packed, and the weather so pleasant, the friends chose to wait on the grassy hill until the commons cleared. When the shooting started, they also assumed it was a prank.

Freshman Adam heard popping noises and looked up the hill. He saw Dylan and Eric setting off Black Cat fireworks. He didn't know them but had seen them around school. Sophomore Mike had seen them too, but he didn't know them either. He was still seated when something struck the ground around him. Then he felt a sensation like warm water pouring over his left leg. Not sure what was happening, he got up to run.

Mark, another freshman, had been attending CHS for only five or six weeks. He was in Special Ed classes because he had a learning disability which affected his reading skills. The private school he'd been at, Silver State Baptist School, wouldn't issue him a diploma so he transferred to public school. Mark's home life was anything but easy. One of seven kids, his grandmother was fighting a second round of breast cancer and his father, Mark Sr., suffered from diabetes and neuropathy. Despite both parents working, the Taylors struggled with financial problems. Mark was gathering his stuff to go inside, not paying attention to the ruckus. Pain suddenly radiated through his left leg. He looked down and saw blood oozing from his thigh.

"Oh, my God!" he cried in horror. He clutched his leg. "Help me! I've been shot!"

He tried to run, but his injured leg couldn't support him. Then he felt like someone was punching hard in the side as he was shot repeatedly. One bullet tore through his armpit and out the other. Penetrating wounds collapsed his lungs. He went down on the grass, defenseless out in the open. He heard something whiz by above him and saw Mike's face shatter as a bullet went through the right side of his jaw and came out near his nose.

Mike felt a warm sensation below his ear and realized he'd been shot. There was no time to think. He, John, Adam, and Denny ran. Mike saw more bullets hit the ground around them, fired by a guy in a long black coat and a black hat. He didn't even feel the shot that went through his upper right arm.

Anne Marie Hochhalter, a junior who played clarinet in Columbine's wind symphony, was sitting on the concrete near the grassy knoll. She was eating lunch with her friends Jayson Autenrieth and his girlfriend Kim Blair when the sudden noise drew their attention uphill to the armed guys in trench coats. They all thought it was a prank. Even when she saw dark red on the victims' clothes, Anne Marie believed it was paintball paint. Then one boy collapsed, and she knew the shooting was real.

Eric made eye contact with Kim and aimed his rifle at her and her friends. With a loud bang a shot from Eric's gun struck Anne Marie's lower back. She dropped instantly. Pushing herself up, she looked down in horror. Blood covered her chest. She couldn't move.

"I'm paralyzed!" she screamed.

Terrified, her friends ran to the school to seek help.

Freshmen Matt Parsons and Anthony Shoels were close enough to hear Anne Marie. Realizing people were being shot, the friends darted inside. They crawled through the cafeteria, ran out the far exit, and kept running until they reached the park across the street. Even at a distance they could hear the gunfire.

Anthony's older brother Isaiah was still inside the school.

—

OFF CAMPUS

Not far from the school, Brooks had just finished his cigarette when he heard what he thought was a nail gun from a nearby housing development under construction. More loud popping sounds followed. With growing dread, he realized it wasn't hammering. Then he heard an explosion.

Alarmed, he took off running. More sounds, awful sounds, echoed behind him. Something terrible was happening at Columbine.

He stopped three blocks away in a bicycle underpass, second-guessing what he heard. It might be a senior prank. He'd seen Eric messing around with stuff in his car and he knew the senior made pipe bombs. Had he thrown some in the parking lot? Brooks smoked another cigarette to calm his nerves and thought about what he should do. He didn't know his younger brother Aaron was at ground zero of what had become a war zone.

—

LIBRARY

Unaware of the massacre outside, 16-year-old sophomore Nicole Nowlen skipped lunch and went to the library to do geometry homework, something she did often. Spotting an open table in the back near the west windows, the blonde girl carried her dark green backpack over and settled in. Her parents were divorced. Seven weeks ago, she was living with her mother and younger brother in Sioux Falls, South Dakota. When her mother moved to California, Nicole chose to join her dad in Colorado. He was a Columbine graduate. When he enrolled her, he said it was because she would be safe there.

As she studied, she heard a hammering noise overhead. then from the front of the room. The librarians had been working on the library the past week. She reckoned they were still at it.

Across the library, Daniel Steepleton, Makai Hall, and Patrick Ireland sat with their friends Austin Eubanks, a sandy-haired 16-year-old, and Corey DePooter, 17. Corey, a former wrestler, loved to fish. The brown-haired junior was Austin's best friend. They spent lunch together almost every day. At the moment the boys were deciding whether to go fishing after school or play golf. Corey recently got a job doing maintenance at the golf club so he could save up for a fishing boat.

At the north row of computers, their mutual friends Ryan Barrett and Evan Todd were chatting. Ryan, a football player with a boyish face, often spent "A" lunch in the library with friends including his best friend, popular footballer Matt Kechter. Ryan was there to type an essay for Dusty Hoffschneider, another sophomore football player and wrestler. Dusty was paying him ten dollars for the work. Evan had forgotten he and Ryan were supposed to run during their free period. The friends agreed to tell Coach Lowry they did it during "A" lunch. It meant lying, but the sophomores intended to do the run after school. Lowry was a kind-hearted man who preferred to persuade rather than punish so there was little to fear in fudging the details.

Craig Scott, a sandy blond sophomore in a red long-sleeved shirt, entered the library. He'd been running late that morning, which annoyed his older sister Rachel. On the ride to school, she pressured him to be on time so she wouldn't be late. They bickered back and forth. When he got out of the car, he slammed the door. It was a rough start to the day, but he looked forward to spending lunchtime with his friends Ryan, Evan, Corey, and the rest. Craig was also a friend of Aaron Brown, Brooks' younger brother. He spent the night at the Browns' home last year and played basketball there several times.

He paused at the front central table to say hi to fellow sophomores Brittany Bollerud, Josh Lapp, Aaron Cohn, and Byron Kirkland. Isaiah Shoels stopped by, sporting a black polo shirt and dark green corduroy pants. Nicknamed "Bushwick", the 18-year-old was a popular senior on the wrestling team and an aspiring comedian. He was born with a heart defect which required two surgeries when he was little including a Fontan procedure, an operation for people born with only one working ventricle. But he was a fighter who overcame his disability. He played cornerback on the football team with Matt last year, though he wasn't on the team his senior year. He was focusing on his keyboard skills so he could pursue a music career like his father Michael.

He told a few jokes, then he and Craig headed west to the table where their friend Matt was sitting. He was a straight-A student who was typically studying in the library at lunch. The sophomore showed potential for a career in football. He planned to attend the University of Colorado when he graduated, which meant he had to keep his grades up.

+ + +

11:20 AM

17-year-old junior Kacey Ruegsegger was a blonde girl with big blue eyes and a bright smile. She normally left campus for lunch at home with her friend Spike, but Spike didn't show up at their shared locker. It was getting late, so Kacey went to the library instead of going home. It was her first year at the high school and her first visit to Columbine's library.

Over the past year, Kacey lost two friends to suicide and two more to cancer. In need of a fresh start, she had asked to transfer to CHS for her junior year. Her family agreed, hoping she would be happier in a more positive environment.

She sat in a chair near the west windows to read a magazine. A boy she didn't know—freshman Steve Curnow— wandered over, looking lost. She invited him to sit beside her. They read together in comfortable silence until a popping sound outside made Kacey look out the window. Seeing nothing unusual, she went back to reading.

—

Bang-bang-bang-bang-bang!

"Is there construction going on in the RNN studio?" asked staff member Lois Kean.

Kean was head librarian Liz Keating's assistant. Keating left campus for lunch at 10:45 a.m. She lived close to the school and usually went home on her lunch break to let her dogs out. Teacher Rich Long, a computer tech, was in the library to fix one of the computers. He said he didn't know if anything was being worked on. Library tech Carole Weld volunteered to go check.

—

As Ryan collected his papers from the printer and put them in a blue folder, there was a loud explosion outside. Gunfire followed, and more detonations. Students rushed to the west windows, Evan among them. There was smoke out there. People were shouting. Students ran toward the soccer field. All hell had broken loose. Evan shared a knowing smile with Craig who joined him at the window. A major prank must be underway. Then they heard a shotgun blast. Both boys had gone hunting. That shot sounded real.

—

OUTSIDE COLUMBINE

"This is what we always wanted to do!" one of the gunmen hollered. "This is awesome!"

Lance woke on the ground in pain. He could hardly move. Confused, he thought paintballs had hit him and pinched a nerve. But a bullet had severed the femoral artery in his leg. He was slowly bleeding out. A shadow fell over him, and he sensed someone moving toward him. He lifted an arm to signal he needed help.

"Sure," Dylan said, standing over him. "I'll help you."

He put the barrel of his shotgun behind the wounded boy's ear and pulled the trigger. Lance saw blue sky above him. He felt his face jolt as the blast mangled his jaw. Blood pooled in his mouth.

"Look at this fucker's head!" Dylan shouted to Eric.

"This is awesome!" Eric responded.

The day was warm. Too warm to be wearing a leather coat during vigorous activity. He took off his black duster and dropped it near the stairs. Then he reloaded his rifle.

Before Lance lost consciousness again, he saw Danny draw his last shuddering breath.

—

By the cafeteria, Sean heard the shot behind him and looked back. He saw Lance on the ground, his face covered in blood. Bleeding badly himself, Sean went into shock. He couldn't feel his legs. The guns must be loaded with tranquilizers, he rationalized. He dragged himself to the cafeteria's west entrance. The door was closing. His life-threatening injuries weakened him; he couldn't stand up. He wouldn't be able to reach the handle of the door if it shut, so he stuck out his arm to block it.

"Help!" he hollered at the people inside. "Get the tranquilizers off my back!"

—

An athletic equipment shed west of the school was roughly 120 yards from Mike and his friends. They raced toward the outbuilding, running for their lives. Mike collapsed behind it and propped himself against it to check his left leg. A bullet had gone through his outer thigh exited the inner thigh. Blood soaked his jeans all the way down to his ankle.

Denny, John, and Adam reached the baseball field. John ditched his backpack behind the shed and scrambled over the fence. Denny and Adam paused to make sure they were okay. Then they followed the chain link fence west around the football field. They heard shots fired at them as they ran toward Clement Park. Once there they met back up with John and hid in a maintenance shed. Mark was left behind. Incapacitated, he couldn't protect himself when the gunmen shot him in the back. Two bullets lodged close to his heart, missing his aorta by the width of a penny. One tore through his spleen. Two got caught in his spine. His best bet was to play dead, but that was hard to do while trying to suck air into lungs that couldn't hold it. As he lay there fighting for life, he saw Eric go over to where Rachel was struggling to get up. She was crying.

He shot her in the head. The crying stopped.

Down the hill Anne Marie played dead since she couldn't run. She heard the shooters shout to each other, but they were too far away for her to hear what they said. The terrifying sounds of gunfire and bombs echoed across the parking lot as Harris fired on students at the soccer fields. They were out of range, so the gunmen lit and threw homemade pipe bombs onto the school roof. They tossed more explosives down the stairs and at the grassy knoll. One landed near Mark and rolled downhill, exploding as it went. Hot shrapnel cut into his skin. Unable to do anything, he turned to prayer. He prayed to be rescued. He prayed the shooters wouldn't hurt him more. As he grew drowsy from blood loss, he forced himself to stay conscious. He was afraid if passed out, he wouldn't wake up.

Down below, Sean heard the awful sounds of the brutal assault behind him. He tried to scoot inside the cafeteria, but his injuries were too severe. He couldn't haul himself past the threshold. His back hurt. Traumatized, he believed his backpack was causing his pain, so he struggled out of it. There was a bullet hole in it. No exit hole. He thought the bullet must be stuck in one of his books.

It had ricocheted into his back.

———

UPSTAIRS

Carole Weld cut through the magazine room and crossed the hall to the northern conference room. Windows on the north and west walls afforded the widest view of the school grounds. She looked out the west window and saw a student she didn't recognize—Eric—about 20 feet away. He was leaning against the fence beside the library with a gun in his hands. The short weapon had a long handle.

"God damn!" he swore loud enough for her to hear through the glass. "Fuck it!"

It seemed his weapon had jammed. Looking past him down the hill she saw a young man curled in a fetal position on the sidewalk outside the cafeteria. Up the hill, a boy was dragging another student toward the athletic shed to the west. The victim's right leg was covered in blood. It left a dark red trail in the grass visible even at a distance.

Then she saw Dylan. She didn't know him by name, but often saw him in the library. He had never been a problem for her. He was a few feet behind Eric near the west entrance, looking at the doorway. There was a gray pipe in his hands, two to three feet in length. It reminded Weld of the potato cannons some of her friends owned. Dylan inserted an oblong black grenade into the homemade launcher. Were they recording something for the Rebel News Network? The school's broadcasting system had aired student videos in the past which featured gun-toting teens in the school halls. But what she saw now looked disturbingly real. Upset, she hurried back to the library to ask Rich Long to see if it was real.

+ + +

11:21 AM – INSIDE COLUMBINE

Video production teacher Peggy Dodd left her class and went to the library to ask Rich Long for computer file for one of her students. She had a short conversation with him before Weld came back in and asked Long to come see what was going on outside. She was very upset, so Long and Dodd went with her to the conference room. She waited in the hall while they went in.

Dodd looked out the window and saw Dylan about 10 feet away down the hill. She recognized him from her class last year. He was a troublemaker who hacked the computer system and showed up to class wearing tall Nazi boots and a trench coat. A few days ago, he made trouble in the library when she told him to pay for using the printer.

Now, Dylan had a gun in his left hand. He fired it at the south parking lot in a sweeping motion, a smirk on his face. She'd seen kids in the A/V programs film stunts on the school grounds before. She thought it was a senior prank or a bit for a video. Dylan and Eric recently filmed an amateur short *Hitmen for Hire* on campus with the help of Eric Veik and other students. Veik played a bullied student. Dylan and Eric played hitmen hired to take revenge on the boy's tormentor, played by junior Michael Vendegnia. They carried what everyone assumed were prop guns.

Long saw Dylan too. The senior had been in his classes for two years and had helped him as a student assistant. The barrel of his gun was smoking. He fired several rounds, ejected a spent clip, then shoved another one in. Long was an Army Reserve member. He had fired M16s and rifles. He knew gunshots when he saw and heard them.

"This is real," he said, pushing the women away from the conference room. "Get down! Get down low!"

—

CAFETERIA

Jayson and Kim rushed into the commons. Kim frantically searched for her friend Mary Baribeau.

"Anne Marie's been shot!" she screamed when she found her. "Anne Marie's been shot!"

—

OFF CAMPUS

Not far from Columbine, Deputy Paul Magor was dispatched to investigate the explosion on Wadsworth Boulevard. No one off campus knew of the terror unfolding at the high school.

+ + +

11:22 AM – CAFETERIA

The cameras came back online in the cafeteria. In the black-and-white footage, students were starting to notice what was happening outside. Brooks' younger brother Aaron was one of several students crowded at the west windows. Some were still eating as they looked outside. Aaron thought maybe it was a prank or a fight had broken out.

"You have any idea what's going on?" he laughed, looking at his friend beside him.

Behind them, the shooters' duffel bag bombs blended in with the other bags and backpacks scattered on the floor.

—

At a table near the west windows Nicole Markham, Chris Morris' girlfriend, sat with her friends Krista Hanley and Alejandra "Alex" Marsh. They were associates of a group from Columbine known as the Trench Coat Mafia. The "TCM" were outcasts and geeks, several of whom used to wear trench coats to school. Other students had mockingly given them the name, and the teens embraced it. They even used it in a yearbook picture they purchased space for last year. But they had largely disbanded over the summer of 1998. Many of the "gang" had graduated. Those who remained stopped wearing their trench coats. Chris was one of the first to wear a long black coat. He no longer wore to it school as the style had gotten too popular. It wasn't a sign of individuality anymore.

27

Nicole and Krista went to get in the lunch line. Looking out the west windows, Alex saw a boy run by. There was blood on his jeans. She was in the theatre program and assumed it was stage blood. Then she heard popping sounds outside. Gunfire.

Dylan walked by the window with a shotgun in his hands. Alex recognized him. She'd worked with him on last year's production of *Frankenstein*. She knew Nicole, Krista, and Chris hung out with him and his friend "Reb". As Alex watched, Dylan climbed the hill to the north, out of her line of sight. Then he came back. He'd traded the shotgun for a gray canister which he threw into the senior parking lot. A loud explosion followed.

—

STAFF LOUNGE

Earth science and Special Ed teacher Christina "Chris" Redmerski, Coach William "Dave" Sanders, and intervention staff member Judy Greco were eating lunch together. It was something they did every day. They were used to hearing noise in the cafeteria. When they heard a disturbance that day, they ignored it. Then someone pounded urgently on the door. Redmerski went to investigate, glancing out the window as she passed. She saw two students on the ground. Had there been a fight? She opened the door. No one was outside, but she knew something was wrong. Students were looking out the windows with concern and confusion, and there was a boy sprawled in the nearby exit. She hurried over to Sean.

"What are you doing on the ground?" She figured he'd been pushed and might be exaggerating his injury.

"I can't feel my legs," Sean responded.

"What do you mean you can't feel your legs? Did you fall?"

"No. I can't feel my legs!"

28

"Did you have a seizure?" Redmerski was grasping at straws. "Did you trip on something?"

"No," Sean said, annoyed that she didn't understand. "I can't feel my legs!"

"Did somebody push you? Were you in a fight?"

Sean cursed and said again that he couldn't feel his legs.

"Look, I'm confused here," said Redmerski, frustrated. "You're lying on the ground. Why are you lying on the ground, and why can't you feel your legs?"

"I think I've been shot in the back."

Now they were getting somewhere, but it was nowhere good. Redmerski still wasn't sure what was going on. Was it a prank? A fight? Something else?

"Well, who shot you?" she asked.

"Up on the hill. There's a kid in a black trench coat. He shot me."

Redmerski stepped past him and poked her head out the door. Immediately she heard gunshots. She quickly retreated. Sean was too big for her to move on her own. She needed help.

"I'll be right back," she said.

Panic rising, she ran back to the faculty lounge where Sanders and Greco were still eating.

"Help me!" she yelled at Sanders. "A student's been shot and I can't move him!"

Sanders got to his feet. Greco ran to the phone. Redmerski didn't wait to see what they did next. She raced back to Sean.

—

29

Freshman Christopher Markham, Nicole's younger brother, was eating lunch in the cafeteria with his friends when he heard an explosion outside. He ran over to the door next to the staff lounge. Pushing it open he saw Lance, Danny, and Sean on the ground. Sean was right outside the door.

"I got shot," Sean told him.

———

CLEMENT PARK

Over at "Smokers' Pit", Marton and Gardner were finishing lunch when an urgent broadcast came over on the school radio. Custodian Jay Gallentine was calling from the cafeteria on his walkie talkie.

"Neil!" Gallentine was frantic. "I need you in the school lunchroom!"

Gardner radioed back that he received the transmission. He and Marton hurried back toward the school.

———

CAFETERIA

"Get down!" Gallentine hollered at the kids in the commons as he ran toward the kitchen.

"Sean got shot!" Christopher added his shout to the custodian's. "Get the fuck down! Get down now!"

He heard a loud BOOM outside. Looking out the windows, he saw a couple of guys in black trench coats standing by the cars in the parking lot. Though there was smoke and fire out there, the pair were laughing.

Christopher followed his own advice and got down. He huddled in the cafeteria's northeast corner, still holding his sandwich. Several students dove under their lunch tables. Some kids ran. A few remained at the windows, transfixed by the unprecedented scene. Outside, guns went off. Bombs exploded. It wasn't a prank. People were dying.

—

Freshman Anthony Sammauro had been with Lance and the others but stayed behind when they left. He left his hiding spot under his table and crawled over to the south doors. He came across Jayson who told him Anne Marie was shot, and someone was throwing pipe bombs. On his way back to his table, Anthony saw Anne Marie through the west windows. She was sprawled on the ground near a planter. Hearing an explosion above, he looked to the stairs and saw a bunch of kids turn and run back down to the commons. A bomb went off in the parking lot. Smoke wafted up.

Anthony grabbed his backpack and ran out one of the southern doors. Looking back, he saw Dylan heading for the cafeteria's west entrance.

—

Dylan stepped over Sean who continued to play dead. Across the commons, Adam Kyler was hiding under his table with his friends. The dark-haired teen heard several popping shots from the doorway and saw Dylan. He recognized the tall, long-haired senior from unpleasant encounters in November and December of 1998. Adam's facial muscles were disfigured by a disorder that left him with a learning disability. His long features and full lips made him a target for bullies. He attended private school until 8th grade. When he transferred to Columbine, Dylan harassed him so badly, Adam's mother Susan reported it to the school. Staff said they would handle the issue. The bullying stopped, but Dylan was hard to forget when he showed up to Spirit Week with a swastika painted on his face.

The shooter looked around, gun at the ready. The explosives were still there. They just hadn't gone off. He headed

31

to the kitchen where another bomb sat. Then he went back outside, stepping over Sean again, and joined Eric on the hill.

+ + +

11:23 AM – OUTSIDE COLUMBINE

Lindsey Macy, a junior, called 911 from a payphone outside the school. "Someone's shooting a gun out here. Some girl over there, I think she's paralyzed."

—

OFF CAMPUS

As Deputy Gardner drove down Pierce Street to the high school a call came in over Jefferson County Dispatch radio requesting Unit 147 respond. "One female down in the south lot of Columbine High School."

The dispatcher then said the female might be paralyzed. Gardner hit the lights and sirens, fearing a student had been run over. Deputy Paul Magor also heard the call and diverted from his route to the bombed field and headed to the school.

"Attention, south units," dispatch continued over the police band. "Possible shots fired at Columbine High School, 6201 S. Pierce, possibly in the south lower lot towards the east end. Unknown situation."

—

CAFETERIA

Teachers hurried through the commons, trying to sort out the situation. Seeing kids up and moving, custodian Gallentine motioned them back down as he ran to the kitchen. A boy in a white cap who was crouched down out in the open tried to talk to him. Gallentine patted him on the head, encouraging him to get under cover as he jogged by. Jon Curtis, a custodian in a light short-sleeved shirt and a ballcap, took a wary look out the windows. Seconds later Gallentine was at the exit next to the teachers' lounge, instructing kids to flee while they could. A third of the room cleared.

—

UPSTAIRS

Patricia "Patti" Nielson was a part-time art teacher at CHS. Her shoulder-length blonde hair and youthful features made her look younger than her 35 years. Her teaching shift was over, but she had hall monitor duty. Hearing a commotion outside, she went to the west entrance to investigate. The entryway consisted of two sets of metal double doors with large windows in them. One pair of doors was inside the school, the other was outside. They were separated by a small vestibule and flanked by wide windows. Outside a male student was carrying what she thought was a toy gun toward the school. She figured it was probably for a video or was some sort of prank, but it looked too realistic to be appropriate for school.

Down the hall Brian Anderson, a dark-haired 17-year-old junior in a white baseball cap, left the office. He was with his friend's girlfriend, Jenny Matthews, and a boy in a green baseball cap. They were student assistants off to collect attendance from classrooms. As they walked toward the library, they heard shots and explosions outside. Brian saw two guys out there. Despite the paramilitary garb he recognized Eric and Dylan from Film class. A couple of weeks ago they asked him to help locate sound effects for a project about a house under siege by gunmen, but he couldn't find anything.

Eric had a long gun in his hands and was leaning over the chain link fence by the stairs that led from the library down to the cafeteria. Dylan was nearby in a black trench coat. He was reloading a sawed-off shotgun.

"What's he doing out there?" he wondered aloud, with a quizzical look at Jenny.

The students and Nielson got to the doors at the same time.

"What's going on?" the teacher asked in case the kids knew.

"...shooting a movie?" Brian offered as they entered the vestibule. "That's probably a cap gun."

Nielson didn't care if it was a cap gun. She went outside to tell him to knock it off. Eric turned and, seeing the group, gave them a crooked smile. He lifted his gun, aimed, and squeezed the trigger. A bullet whizzed past and struck the window in the door behind Nielson, leaving a huge hole in the glass. She thought it was a BB gun until she saw the damage. That gun was real.

"Dear God!" Nielson yelped. "Dear God! Dear God!"

She scrambled back inside as another shot smashed the window beside the door. Glass and hot metal chunks sprayed into the vestibule. Burning shrapnel struck the back of Nielson's shoulder. She didn't feel the bits that cut into her forearm and knee. Brian, right behind her, was hit with bullet fragments and broken glass. It peppered his chest and ricocheted off his necklace. He fell to the floor, blood seeping through his shirt. Abandoning his backpack, he scurried on hands and knees back the way he came. Nielson dropped to all fours and crawled after him. Jenny and the boy in the green hat followed suit. As soon as they were out of the vestibule, they got to their feet and ran down the hall to the right. The teacher led the way to the library, the closest place to hide. She was out of breath and in a full panic when she burst into the room.

The library was large and crowded. There were over fifty students at twenty tables and other areas. They were all in danger.

"Get down! Get under the desks!" Nielson shouted. "Get under the desks! There's a kid with a gun!"

Many students took her seriously and ducked down. But the library tables were small, not made to hide under. Some kids thought it was a joke or drill and stood up. They looked around the room and at each other, trying to figure out what was happening. Special Needs student Kyle Velasquez hid behind his chair at computer station #10B.

"Help!" Nielson desperately looked around for the adults. "Where's Mrs. Keating? We've been shot! Someone, call 911!"

Not seeing any faculty, she went behind the circulation desk and grabbed the phone.

Bree Pasquale was sitting in the computer lab's south row reading a magazine when she heard Nielson shout. Bree, a round-faced junior with long brown hair, plucked brows and an eyebrow ring, noticed popping sounds earlier but ignored it when she saw nothing amiss in the library. Looking out the west windows now, she saw a guy she didn't know—Dylan—standing atop the hill. He threw a pipe bomb the size of a small aerosol can down into the south parking lot. It exploded. Gray smoke rose from the lot. At the bottom of the hill Bree saw a student— Danny—lying on the sidewalk in a large pool of blood. A dropped can of Dr. Pepper spilled beside him. That would later become the world's first look at the carnage at Columbine.

+ + +

11:24 AM – OFF CAMPUS

Deputy Paul Smoker, a Jefferson County motorcycle patrolman, was writing a speeding ticket on West Bowles Avenue when he heard the dispatch call: *"Female down in Columbine's parking lot."* Since he was close to the school, he radioed he was heading that way.

—

CAFETERIA

Adam was still hiding under his table in the cafeteria when Dave Sanders ran through. Sanders coached the girls' softball and basketball teams. Though he was 47 years old, he had the look of a kindly grandpa: Balding, gentle of face with a salt-and-pepper beard and glasses which framed his expressive eyes. He taught business and computers at Columbine for 25 years. The assault on his home turf had him in action mode. His priority was to protect the kids, many of whom had left their hiding places and were milling about in confusion.

"Get under the tables!" he commanded. "Get down!" Then he ran upstairs to clear the halls.

The students were quick to obey but as soon as Sanders left, a wild stampede began. People threw chairs out of their way and scrambled over the stair handrailing. Some held hands so as not to be separated. They left behind books and backpacks. Shoes littered the floor as kids ran right out of them. The way the crowd surged reminded Christopher of a hurricane. He dropped his sandwich in the trash, jumped over the stair rail, and darted upstairs. Reaching the choir room first, he pounded on the door. Lee Andres Jr. opened it. Andres was a football coach and the vocal teacher. Christopher told him what was going on then continued down the hall toward the front office, banging on doors to alert people there was trouble. Hearing shots ahead, he turned down the south hall and ran out the east exit. He jumped a fence and kept running until he reached Leawood Park.

Hundreds of students poured out of the cafeteria's south and west exits. Others ran upstairs, thinking the danger was only outside. Sean, still alive in the west cafeteria doorway, was trampled as frightened teenagers evacuated the building.

Amidst the chaos, Jayson grabbed Kim's arm to get her attention. "Stay here."

He ran back out the door they'd come in. Despite his instructions, Kim and Mary followed him.

Meanwhile, Alex crossed the cafeteria to get out of Dylan's line of sight. She scanned the kitchen area, looking for Eric. He and Dylan were always together. Not seeing him, she headed toward the bathroom just past the kitchen.

"Alex! Get in here!"

East of the kitchen behind the stairs Andres held the auditorium door open. He ushered Alex and twenty other kids into the auditorium. Most screamed and ran. Alex walked.

———

Sarah Brown, a sophomore with her blonde hair in a ponytail, ran to the auditorium. In her panic she left her purse in the cafeteria though it held mementos of her father who passed away last month. Nearby gunfire was so loud, it sounded like it was right behind her. She passed a girl with shoulder-length brown hair who was wearing a black shirt, black jeans, and an orange and green Miami Dolphins hat. Sarah didn't know Alex; she just knew she shouldn't be walking at such a dangerous time.

"Run!" Sarah screamed at her.

"Shut up, man!" Alex snapped back. "I could kill you." Then, to herself: "If I could kill that girl..."[*]

Shocked, Sarah didn't know how to react. So, she ran. The group she was with flooded through the east exit over to Clement Park. Alex joined the herd who ran to "Smokers' Pit". Senior Zach Heckler helped her over the fence. Though he was one of Dylan's closest friends he was running for his life just like everyone else.

---

[*] Alex told investigators she was walking calmly while others ran. Sarah was interviewed later and described what Alex was wearing that day, along with how she was walking and responded to Sarah's scream. Officials provided a yearbook for her to look through, and she pointed to Alex Marsh's picture. When questioned again after Sarah's interview, Alex denied hearing anyone yell at her and denied saying anything in return.

While others were trying to escape or hide, 18-year-old senior Nick Foss ran outside to see what was happening. The blond athlete saw two guys on the ground bleeding. He ran to the boy curled up near the stairs and shook him. He was dead

Looking up, he saw two gunmen at the top of the stairs shooting at the people below. He recognized Eric from his fifth-period Psychology class. Then Nick felt a shot whiz past his head and realized the danger he was in. He ran back to the cafeteria, through to the staff lounge. His friend 17-year-old Tim Kastle and sophomore Sean Nossaman followed him. As Tim passed the windows he saw the bodies outside. Even from that distance he could tell one victim had been shot in the face.

—

FRONT OFFICE

Senior Jeffrey DiManna was working as a student assistant in the office answering the phone when staff member Judy Greco called from the teachers' lounge and asked for an adult. He handed the phone to Secretary Jan Fiedler. Listening in, Jeffrey learned there was a shooter in the building. As soon as Fiedler hung up, more calls came in from teachers all over the school. It quickly became apparent there were two people shooting up the school. Jeffrey told all callers that office staff knew about the situation and were calling the police.

—

CAFETERIA

Cook Karen Nielsen was serving pizza when she heard someone in the cafeteria shouting at people to get down. Custodian Jon Curtis ran by the serving line. Then there were several shots from the northwest. Kids hit the floor and dove under tables. An ear-splitting explosion followed. People ran.

Nielsen abandoned the serving area. She ran to the faculty lounge and ducked through the open door.

"He's not breathing!" someone shouted outside the doorway.

The cook went back to the cafeteria. Out the windows she saw injured kids sprawled on the ground. One was lying in the west doorway. She rushed over to him.

"I can't feel my legs," Sean told her. Blood pooled on the ground beneath him.

Nielsen hurried back to the lounge. Judy Greco was near the phone.

"Did you call 911?" Nielsen asked.

"No," Greco said. "But I called the office."

Nielsen dialed 911 and told the dispatcher there was a gunman at the school wearing a black trench coat. She had to run back and forth between wounded boy and the phone to provide information about the shooting and Sean's condition.

"So far, they're outside," Nielsen reported. "We've got a student out here...we can get to him, but we're afraid to move him.... We've got another kid shot in the face; half his face is hanging off. We've got another one shot, and he's not breathing."

The 911 operator told her not to move Sean due to the possibility of spinal injury.

———

Teacher Chris Redmerski got back to where Sean was. She crawled to the doorway and put her left arm out to prop the door open. Lying on her stomach, she reached out to him.

"Give me your hand!"

She tried to pull him in, but she wasn't strong enough. Custodian Jon Curtis came over.

Redmerski glanced back at him. "I can't pull him in. He's too big."

Nielsen came running back and, seeing what was happening, yelled: "Don't move him! He might have spinal damage!"

"He already can't move his legs!" Redmerski snapped. "What's the difference? I can't leave him out there! There's shooting outside! He needs to get back into the school!"

Nearby shots shattered the windows beside them. Redmerski saw students outside coming around the corner, unaware of the danger they were walking into.

"Get down!" she shouted at them. "They're shooting!"

Curtis grabbed the injured boy's hand and tried to pull him into the cafeteria.

"No!" said Sean. "I don't want to be paralyzed!"

The window next to the door burst inward. Broken glass rained down on them. In addition to the noise outside they could now hear shots inside the school. Nielsen ran back to the staff lounge to talk to the 911 operator. Curtis yelled at Redmerski to leave. She didn't want to abandon Sean, but the custodian told her he would stay with him. Redmerski pulled her arm out of the doorway. The door swung shut, hitting Sean's head. They had pulled him in just far enough to obstruct the door. There was a huge puddle of blood on the sidewalk where he'd been.

Redmerski back ran toward the lounge and found Judy Greco and two students, Araceli Gaucin and Michelle Huff, huddled near the soda machines.

"You've got to get out here," she yelled at them. "They're in the building!"

They all ran to the kitchen to hide.

Curtis stayed with Sean as long as he could. But when they heard the gunfire in the school coming closer, the teen told him to leave. He didn't want the shooters to discover he was still alive. It was too risky to move him, so Curtis left him. There were more shots and explosions. Out of options and with no one to help him, Sean played dead.

—

OUTSIDE COLUMBINE

Despite the risk, Jayson hurried over to where Anne Marie was sprawled. She was desperately pounding on her legs, trying to get them to move. He grabbed hold of the bloody girl and dragged her toward the cafeteria's south doors. Bullets whizzed past them. A pipe bomb exploded where Anne Marie had been just seconds before.

Mary was lingering with Kim near the entrance and saw a tall teen in a black trench coat carrying a gun. Dylan didn't say anything. He just stared blankly as he looked around for his next victim. Not wanting to be that target, Mary ran back inside and crouched down where he couldn't shoot her through the windows.

He fired his TEC-DC9 at Anne Marie, puncturing her lungs, diaphragm, and liver. Eric's shot had severed her spine so she didn't feel this bullet pass through her body, but she could no longer breathe. Unable to do more for his friend without endangering himself, Jayson left Anne Marie face-down close to the building, out of the line of fire. He went back to his girlfriend Kim and pushed her inside the cafeteria. A hail of bullets ricocheted off the pavement in the senior parking lot.

—

INSIDE COLUMBINE

Normally Principal Frank DeAngelis would be down in the cafeteria or the library during "A" lunch. "Mr. De" to the kids, he liked to be visible to the student body. That morning, however, he was in a meeting with temp English teacher Arthur "Kiki" Leyba. Leyba's contract was up and DeAngelis was bringing him on full time. The happy meeting was suddenly disrupted when DeAngelis' secretary, Susan White, charged into the office.

"There's been a report of gunfire!" she blurted.

The fire alarm went off.

———

Senior Alisha Basore was painting in Art class when she heard a shriek from the hall. She looked over and saw a girl run by, toward the school's exit. Seconds later, the fire alarm went off. A dean came in and announced there was a shooter in the school. The room quickly emptied.

Foot traffic in the smoke-filled main hall slowed to a crawl as students piled out of classrooms. The tight-packed crowd pushed toward the exit, hands on backs. Once outside, kids flooded across the street to the park without even looking for oncoming cars.

Alisha was injured in December when a friend was playing around with a handgun and accidentally shot her in the back. Still recovering from surgery, she couldn't move very fast, but she made it out of the school safely. She knocked on doors of houses until she found someone who let her use their phone to call her dad. The first thing she did when she got home was call her friend Rachel Scott's house to make sure she was okay.

Rachel wasn't there.

———

UPSTAIRS HALLS

Teacher Theresa Miller was on hall monitor duty when sophomore Chris Therrien ran up the stairs, a personal pizza in his hands. Running in the hall and food outside the cafeteria were two "big no"s for a student. As he passed her, the dark-haired teacher yelled at him to stop, but he didn't even slow down. Miller heard a noise behind her and turned to see five or six more students running toward the library. She recognized one, senior John Veigel.

"There are a couple of guys down the hall with guns shooting people!" he told her.

Nearby gunfire scattered the students.

Miller ran to a science room to call the school's head office. A student picked up.

"I need to speak to an adult right away!" said the teacher.

"They know," Jeffrey replied. He'd already taken several similar calls, reassuring faculty that police had been notified. "They're on their way."

Miller hung up and went back to the hall to close the doors in the science wing. Many people were still in class and had no idea what was happening. After all the rooms were shut, she herded kids from the hall, corralling roughly 60 students in classrooms where they overturned tables to hide behind.

Then she called 911.

—

LIBRARY

Weld, Long, and Dodd returned to the library. Long hollered at the students to get down under their tables while Dodd defaulted to fire drill training and ordered them to evacuate.

The library erupted in panic.

Dodd saw Coach Sanders run by the library, heading north. He lifted his hands, motioning at her to stay in the room.

43

She smelled smoke and heard gunfire. She thought maybe some kids had set off some smoke bombs. Just then Brian Anderson ran in and collapsed on the floor. Jenny and a younger boy were with him.

"I've been hit!" Brian said. "I've been shot!"

Lois Kean came out of a side room and, seeing the injured boy, went to help him. Dodd hurried to assist as well. She tried to examine his injuries.

"Eric Harris fucking shot me!" the boy said.

Weld rushed into the workroom/kitchen behind the librarian's desk to call the front office. A student answered and told her help was on the way. Weld hung up and went back to the main room.

Long pushed students near the entrance out into the hall and herded them to the stairs that led down to the commons.

Behind the circulation desk, Patti Nielson got through to 911 dispatcher Renee Napoli.

"Jefferson County 911."

"Yes. I am a teacher at Columbine High School," Nielson said, trying to communicate as clearly as she could in a state of terror. "There is a student here with a gun. He has shot out a window. I believe one student—uh...um...um... I've been— I don't know if it's... I don't know what's in my shoulder, if it was just some glass that went through it or what."

"Has anyone been injured, ma'am?" the emergency operator asked. There was a lot of noise behind her. Dispatch was bombarded with incoming 911 calls.

"Yes!" Nielson exclaimed. "Yes! And the school is in a panic and I'm in the library. I've got—" She noticed people up and moving around. "Students down! Under the tables, kids!! Heads under the tables!!"

Once they complied, the teacher tried to focus on the call again. Gunfire in the hallway was loud, close enough for the dispatcher to hear over the phone.

"Um. Kids are screaming," Nielson went on breathlessly. "The teachers, um, are, y'know, trying to take control of things. We need police here. We need—"

"Okay," Napoli said. "We're getting them there."

"We need police here. We need them fast."

"Who is the student, ma'am?"

"I do not know who the student is. I saw a student outside. I was in the hall—" There was a loud explosion nearby. It shook the floor. "Oh, dear God!" Nielson's next words were an adrenaline-fueled blur. "Okay! I was on hall duty. I saw a gun."

There was another explosion, this time down the hall, followed by a gunshot.

"I said, 'What's going on out there?'" Nielson rattled off. "And the kid that was following me from Video Production said it was probably a joke, and I said 'Well, I don't think that's a good idea.' and I went walking outside to see what was going on. He pointed the gun straight at us and shot and—my God! The window went out and the kid standing there with me, I think he got hit."

"Okay."

"I have something in my shoulder."

"Okay," the dispatcher said. "We've got help on the way, ma'am."

"Okay."

There was a bright flash of light in the hallway and a loud BANG. Smoke billowed into the library through the wide-open doors. There were two more booming gunshots from the hall.

45

The fire alarm went off, adding to the noise. Scared by the violent sounds, several kids got up to find better hiding places.

"OH, God!" screamed Nielson.

"Stay on the line with me," the operator coached. The teacher was her best chance of knowing where the shooters were.

"Oh, God!" Nielson panted.

Over by the counter, Ryan was rightfully concerned. He set the folder of copies he'd made down on the printer and went to join Matt.

"Let's get out of here," Ryan said. "Let's go."

Just then there was gunfire in the hallway. Startled by how close the five shots were, he jumped over the librarian's desk and landed on the floor.

Thinking it was some sort of senior prank, Josh got up and started toward the exit. He heard the popping sounds from the hall and, an avid hunter, he recognized it as real gunfire. He ran back to his table and hid with Brittany underneath it.

Aaron Welsh was at one of the front center library tables. He didn't know what was going on, but he knew it was serious. He ducked under his table and lay face down, his head to the north. When a bomb exploded in the hall, he felt the floor vibrate.

+ + +

11:25 AM – TEACHERS' LOUNGE

Tim, Nick, and Sean N. ducked into the small bathroom attached to the lounge. Faculty Joyce Jankowski, Sue Caruthers, and Amy Burnett were already hiding there.

"Oh, my God!" Nick exclaimed. "I saw some kid's face get shot off! And I got hit!"

He took off his shirt, but Jankowski didn't see any injuries. Just then they heard a lot of noise in the cafeteria. Loud voices and bangs.

"They have shotguns," said Nick.

———

OUTSIDE COLUMBINE

Deputy Gardner and SRO Marton arrived at the school. As they pulled up in Gardner's borrowed car, they saw kids running from the building in all directions. There were several loud explosions. Smoke billowed up from the parking lot's west end. Students near the soccer field were pointing at the school.

A call came in from Columbine's radio. "Neil, there's a shooter in the school!"

The report prompted a flood of responses from other officers and emergency vehicles. There was so much radio traffic, Gardner couldn't get through to say he was on the scene.

———

Still on the phone with 911, Macy reported: "A cop just pulled up."

———

On high alert, Gardner got out of the car. Marton followed. There were shots inside the building, but it was impossible to tell where they were coming from. Neither man was wearing protective gear. Marton didn't even have a weapon. Gardner had on a bright yellow bike patrol shirt and black BDUs. The shirt made him an easy target. Eric fired ten shots at him with his rifle from the west entrance. The deputy took cover behind a white Chevrolet Blazer as bullets pelted two cars behind him. He saw bodies on the ground by the west entrance. With two kids in need of immediate rescue, he took a chance and fired four shots with his .45 Sig Sauer P220 at his assailant from about

47

60 yards away. The deputy had been shot at twice before in his career. This was the first time he had to shoot back.

When Eric suddenly twisted to the side, Gardner thought he hit him, but the gunman was only clearing a jam in his weapon. Eric popped off another fifteen rounds at the deputy. Most flew over the top of the Blazer. Gardner couldn't believe what was happening. He tried the radio again and got through. He told dispatch he was under heavy fire and was returning fire.

—

LIBRARY

"What should we do?" Kean asked.

Weld had a key to the sound booth in the RNN studio which was connected to the library. The door had an auto-lock. When it closed no one could get in. She and Kean decided to hide there under the counter.

Dodd, Brian, Jenny crawled to the nearby periodicals room, followed by Ryan. They closed and locked the two doors. The door to the library had a small inset window and all four walls were glass from shoulder height up. They turned off the lights and Dodd had the kids hunker down close to the wall to make it harder to see them.

Daniel Steepleton's table was in the back west side of the library. Out the window he saw people running past the soccer field, away from the school. He knew from their behavior something was seriously wrong. He ducked under the south side of his table. Makai and Patrick hid with him, along with a dark-haired Asian girl Daniel didn't know, freshman Kathy Park. Austin and Corey grabbed their backpacks and ran to the center of the library where they hid under a table in the back. It seemed safer than the front table where they'd been.

Aaron Cohn and Byron Kirkland were seated from their friends Josh and Brittany at the front center table, which was a clear shot from the door. Aaron and Byron got up and ran to the back of the west section.

Nielson saw them. "Kids just stay down!"

The boys hid under a table near the windows along with Stephanie Salmon and Andrew Fair. They were joined by Bree Pasquale and a couple of other students. There were too many teens packed under the small table, so Bree wedged herself between it and the windows. Cassie Bernall and another girl, Emily Wyant, were hiding under a table directly north. Bree could also see Craig and Isaiah under a table to the east. She made eye contact with Isaiah.

"What's goin' on?" he asked her.

"Someone's outside with a pipe bomb," she said. She told him she thought it might be a former Columbine student, but she didn't recognize him.

Nicole Nowlen noticed the popping sounds earlier but dismissed it as a senior prank. When she saw the other students getting down under the tables, she did too. She looked at the library entrance. The popular girls who'd been seated at the table by the door were hiding beneath it.

—

UPSTAIRS

The gunmen stalked the northern hallway, shooting and laughing. Dylan fired his TEC-9 down the eastern hall as they passed. Bullets ricocheted off lockers and lodged in walls. Smoke choked the air. A crowd of panicked students bolted upstairs, right in front of the shooters. The gunmen fired on their schoolmates as they chased them toward the main entrance.

"I'm shot!" someone screamed.

"Get to the front!" someone else yelled.

Bullets flew above the students, shattering the glass doors ahead of them. Aaron Brown was part of the crowd. He didn't pause or look back; he ran for his life. Aaron and his friends made it outside and kept running until they got to his car. Hopping in, they drove as fast as they could to his house nearby.

—

Principal Frank DeAngelis bolted from his office with teacher Kiki Leyba close behind him. Secretary Susan White followed but fell behind.

"What should I do?" she called after them.

"Call 911!" DeAngelis shouted back, not slowing.

White stayed in the office to call for help while the men raced to the front hall.

At the far west end of the northern hall, they DeAngelis and Leyba someone in a white shirt, black pants, and boots. The person had a gun in his hands.

POP-POP-POP-POP-POP-POP-POP!

The gunman fired off seven rhythmic shots down the hall toward the library. Then he turned and shot at the men. The glass doors behind them shattered. DeAngelis wouldn't remember the screech of the fire alarm, but the sound of breaking glass would stay with him.

Leyba ran to the English hallway to flush students out of the building.

"Shots fired in the building!" he shouted at faculty in the Social Studies office as he passed. "Get out now!"

DeAngelis' focus was on a large group of girls who had just left the locker room. Among them was Danny Rohrbough's stepsister, Nicole Petrone. The girls were walking right into the gunmen's path. Telling them there was gunfire, the principal

50

herded them down the hall. But when they got to the gymnasium the doors wouldn't open. The school was in lockdown mode. DeAngelis had a ring of 35 keys on him. The gym key looked the same as the rest and was somewhere in the middle of the ring. Somehow, he managed to grab the right one on the first try. He opened the door and hid the girls in a storage room.

—

MUSIC ROOM

Fifth hour choir class was getting ready to sing. Senior Brandon Reisbeck excused himself to get a drink from the hall fountain. As he sipped, he heard what sounded like two gunshots. He was about to return to the classroom when a bunch of students ran up the stairs from the cafeteria.

"He has a gun!" one screamed as they passed.

Brandon ran back to class and burst through the door.

"There's a girl who said there's a guy with a gun!" he yelled. "They're shooting! We've got to get out of here!"

The class was instantly abuzz.

"Stay calm," said the choir teacher, Leland Andres. "Sit down. Sit down."

He was the father of vocal teacher Lee Andres Jr. He didn't know it, but his son was protecting kids in the auditorium. Brandon understood the man wanted to know what was going on before letting anyone leave, but he wasn't about to sit down after what he heard. He ran north to the auditorium, away from the gunfire.

Jake Cram saw the flood of kids rush past the classroom door window. He had been in the gifted program with Dylan from 1st to 6th grade, and even went to his house a couple of times. Jake stopped hanging out with him in high school but noticed in his junior and senior years Dylan changed, wearing

51

strange clothes and hairstyles. Looking out the door, Jake saw what looked like the barrel of a shotgun. He dove away from the door as the gun went off with a loud BANG.

Students hit the floor. Some ran to the auditorium. Adam Foss, Nick's twin brother, yelled for everyone to get to the music room office. Jake ran and hid in the office. There were roughly 60 students in the room. When some of the students froze up Adam and a few other boys got them moving. They steered their classmates into the office and barricaded the door. Adam promised them the shooters wouldn't get past him and the others.

Zach Heckler was in the choir room. He was a close friend of Chris Morris and Dylan Klebold, and an associate of the Trench Coat Mafia. He worked lighting in the theatre program and had helped Dylan with sound for the school's production of *Smoke in the Room*. Known as "KiBBz" to his friends, Zach chatted on the phone with Dylan almost every night about school and the game *Quake*. They'd talked just last night. Dylan ended the call early saying he was tired. Unusual, but not alarming. Zach also knew Eric Harris. He was friends with both boys since 8th grade. He used to sneak out with them on their "missions", setting off fireworks and sabotaging neighborhood houses. When the three of them got busted a year and a half ago hacking into Columbine's computer system, Zach's father restricted his association with Eric. But they still bowled together.

He didn't know that the pair were behind the shooting. Just as scared as the rest, he joined juniors Charles Simmons and Jonathan Cohen in the crush of teens who fled to the auditorium. Semi-automatic gunfire rang through the halls. Jonathan found his sister Diana in the crowd. They ran to the main entrance where they saw bullet holes in the doors. Broken glass rained down on them as they ran through the vestibule.

In the hallway senior Emily Stepp and junior Adrian Barcelona broke away from the group and ran to the English office where several staff members were having lunch.

"There's a shooter in the building!" Emily told them, frantic.

English teacher Claudia Abbott thought it might be a senior prank, but part-time educational assistant Jackie Reardon had just seen Principal Frank DeAngelis in the hall. He looked worried. Jason Webb, another English teacher, went to investigate. Discovering broken windows, he phoned the English office from another part of the school and told them about the damage and said they should barricade themselves in the room. English teacher Eric Friesen called 911 while the others shoved a filing cabinet in front of the door. They covered the door window with a poster so no one could see into the room.

The hall fire alarm went off.

—

CAFETERIA

At the cafeteria's southern doors Jayson and Kim encountered two terrified freshmen girls. Jayson directed them to the junior parking lot to run home while there was a lull in the shooting outside.

—

LIBRARY

At the circulation desk, Patti Nielson was still on the phone with 911.

"Do we know where he's at?" dispatcher Renee Napoli asked her.

"I'm sorry?" With all the noise from the hall, Nielson missed the question.

"Do we know where he's at?"

"Okay. I'm in the library," said Nielson. "He's upstairs. He's right outside of here."

"He's outside?"

"He's outside of this hall," Nielson tried to clarify.

"Outside of the hall or outside—"

"He's in the hall."

"Okay."

"I'm sorry," Nielson said. "There are alarms and things going off... There's smoke... My God, smoke is, like, coming into this room. I've got the kids under tables here. I don't know what's happening in the rest of the building."

"Okay."

"I don't know—I'm sure someone else is calling 911."

"Yes, we've got a lot of people on," the dispatcher said. "Okay. I just want you to stay on the line with me, I– we need to know what's going on."

"Okay." Nielson tried again. "I am on the floor—"

"Okay. You've got the kids there?"

"—in the library," the teacher went on, not hearing. The fire alarm was piercing. The gunmen were close to the library, shooting and setting off bombs that shook the room. "And I've got every student in this library—"

In the back of the room, Austin peeked out over his table to see what was happening. He made eye contact with Nielson.

"ON THE FLOOR! You guys STAY ON THE FLOOR!"

Austin ducked back under the table.

"Is there any way you can lock the doors?" Napoli urged.

"Um, smoke is coming in from out there, and I'm a little—"

Nielson broke off as the gunfire moved toward the library. Two loud shots, then three more. BANG-BANG! BANG-BANG-BANG! She didn't have keys to lock the doors. She could try to shut them, but that would risk drawing the shooters' attention.

"The gun is right outside the library door, okay?" she said, her voice trembling in fear. She could barely catch her breath. There were three more shots, even louder now that they were just a few feet away. "I don't think I'm going to go out there. Okay? I've got—I've got three children of my own. Okay?"

There was more gunfire in the hall and screams from downstairs.

John Tomlin was a 16-year-old sophomore with blue eyes, close-cropped light brown hair, and an easy smile. He wore glasses and a dark T-shirt. A Wisconsin native, he moved to Colorado with his family in 1995. Shy and lonely, he found the move difficult until he met Michelle Oetter in his church youth group. They started dating seven months ago and were very happy together. Recently John got his driver's license and bought a Chevrolet truck—his favorite brand. He'd been working for it since he was 14, hauling trees and driving tractors 30 hours a week at a plant nursery. John was a good-hearted, hard worker. He'd even driven all the way to Mexico once to help build a house for a family in need.

He was hiding under the table east of Nicole. She realized if the gunman came into the library, he would see her. She looked over at the popular girls' table. Some were crying.

"Can I come over?" she asked him.

John's table offered better concealment. He looked toward the main doors where the sound of shots came from. When he was sure it was safe, he waved her over. Nicole crawled

55

to his table and ducked under. She drew her knees up to her chest and put her back to the base. John took a similar position facing her. They pulled in chairs to hide behind.

There were more shots in the hall. Closer now. Fear growing, Nicole started to say something, but John motioned her to silence. To comfort her he held her hand. She could see into the hallway through the open doors. A tall guy with long hair passed by. He was wearing a black trench coat, and a backward black baseball cap. Nicole didn't know Dylan, but she could tell by the way he moved he must be one of the shooters. He wasn't trying to hide or run.

"I saw someone in the hall," she whispered to John.

Not far from them, juniors Lindsay Elmore and Rebecca Parker were hiding under a table in the center near the back. Lindsay, a big girl with long brown hair, was hiding on the west side of the table. Rebecca was on the east. When Lindsay squeezed further under the table, she accidentally pushed Rebecca out.

Under a front center table, Brittany began to cry. Josh put his arms around her and tried to soothe her. She could see Dan Mauser hiding under a table to the southeast. A shotgun went off right outside the library. The powerful blast was so loud, it hurt to hear it. Josh pulled Brittany closer and covered her ears. Smoke rolled in through the open doorway.

Nielson grabbed the phone and curled up with it under the circulation desk. She was too vulnerable standing up. She didn't want to give the gunmen reason to notice the room where she, 3 other faculty, and 55 students were hiding.

"Um. I'm not going to go to the door," she repeated into the phone. "He just shot towards the door. Okay? I've got the kids on the floor, um. I got all the kids in the library on the—"

56

She could hear another dispatcher managing a phone call from another concerned caller, assuring him they had fire and police on the way.

"Okay. Okay. It's just that— I mean he's—He's—" Nielson stammered. "I—I can't believe he's... not out of bullets! He just keeps shooting and shooting and shooting!"

+++

11:26 AM – OUTSIDE COLUMBINE

Deputy Neil Gardner got on the police band and radioed for backup after his shootout with Eric Harris. "Shots in the building! I need someone in the south lot with me!"

There was a flood of 911 calls coming in from all over the neighborhood and inside the high school. Dispatch had to direct the officers to take their radio traffic to another channel.

—

Deputy Paul Smoker made it to Columbine's west side. Explosions and gunshots rang out as he pulled up on his motorcycle. He was looking for Deputy Gardner, but another officer found him first. Deputy Scott Taborsky was on the scene. Smoker hopped into his patrol car. It offered better protection than his motorcycle.

Taborsky drove them closer to the school. While they were looking for Gardner, they spotted two wounded students on the ground and headed that way. Smoker got out and walked beside the moving patrol vehicle so he could hear the gunshots better, trying to get an idea of where the shooting was. Taborsky pulled his car in front of Mark Taylor to shield him. Students fleeing the school immediately hid behind the patrol unit.

"There he is!!!" Gardner's shout reached Smoker.

Downhill to Smoker's right, Gardner had his gun out, aimed at Eric. The gunman was back at the shattered double doors of the west entrance. He exchanged fire with Gardner, shooting his rifle at the deputy through a broken window.

Smoker couldn't see what Gardner was shooting at. A fence and a dumpster blocked his view. He had to move out into the open to see the gunman. Eric used the door frame as cover while he shot at fleeing students and law enforcement. Smoker joined the defense, firing three shots at Eric. The shooter retreated into the building, firing more shots inside. Several kids ran from the school and took cover behind the parked police cars.

—

INSIDE COLUMBINE

Eric Veik was in his fifth hour Algebra class taking a test when a bunch of people ran by the door.

"Get out of the school as fast as you can!" a teacher yelled from the hall.

There was a large BOOM. The fire alarm went off. Thinking it was a drill, Eric V. left his backpack at his desk. In it were video tapes he'd recorded with Eric Harris and Dylan Klebold, including *Hitmen for Hire*. The hall smelled of smoke. He was immediately swept up in a wave of people fleeing the building. Outside he ran to the park across the street. He could hear explosions from the school.

—

Science teacher and department head Frank Peterson was giving his students a test when Theresa Miller closed the back door of his classroom. Then she came to the main door and motioned him over. She told him about the shooting. His first thought was that it was a prank because it was close to graduation. He left his class and shut the door behind him. He headed for the stairs.

At that time, Rich Long and his group reached the first landing of the stairs and heard gunfire. They could see people

58

running in the cafeteria, so he steered the kids back upstairs and down the south science hall. They ran into teacher Theresa Miller. Long left his group with her, telling them to hide in one of the classrooms.

Freshman Nathan Epling, younger brother of Kristi, was outside with his friend John Bright when he heard shots from the hill. He abandoned his backpack and went through the first southern door he reached. Unaware that the gunmen were inside, he ran straight through the cafeteria and up the stairs with a bunch of other kids.

Meanwhile, Coach Sanders was clearing students out of the upstairs hall. He ran up the western hallway past the library, stopping when he saw the gunmen in the northwest corner ahead of him. He tried to double back but it was too late. Seeing him, Eric fired his rifle. The coach took a bullet in his neck. Another tore through the back of his shoulder and out his chest just as he rounded the corner. Several kids hit the deck at the sound of gunfire. Sanders stumbled a few steps east down the southern hall and collapsed near the stairs.

Nathan reached the second floor and saw Sanders get shot right in front of him. The boy turned and ran east down the science hallway and ducked into biology class SCI-3.

Sophomore Greg Barnes was in a nearby science room. At 6'4 and 175 pounds, the dark-haired boy was a top player on Columbine's varsity basketball team. He and Matt Kechter were friends. Greg was looking out the classroom window into the hallway when he saw Sanders get shot. Blood flew off the coach and splashed the window as he went down.

"Dave is hit!" someone said.

Dylan fired a shot down the northern corridor then ran south down the western hallway. He passed the library and Sanders who was sprawled on the floor, a wide pool of blood spreading beneath him. The gunman paused near the stairs that led down to the cafeteria and threw a lit pipe bomb at the injured teacher. The bomb went off as he ran back to the library hall where Eric was searching for something in his duffel bag. The explosion was huge. White smoke filled the corridor.

"Dave!" Long yelled. "You've got to get up!"

Sanders pushed himself up, leaving a bloody handprint on the carpet. He crawled a short distance to the corner beside science room 8 and collapsed again. A trail of blood streaked the carpet behind him. Long rushed to help him up, yelling at Peterson to go get help. Peterson ran east down the hall, hollering at kids to get out of the school. Long shouldered Sanders over to Doug Johnson's Biology classroom, SCI-3 where several terrified kids were already hiding.

"Rich," Sanders said with difficulty. "I think they shot me through the mouth."

The coach's shoulder was torn up. He was bleeding badly from his mouth, too. The bullet that entered his neck had come out the far side of his jaw, mangling his tongue and teeth.

"Rich, I'm losing a lot of blood," said Sanders. "I think I'm going to pass out."

He took a few steps on his own and then fell to the classroom floor unconscious.

———

Science teacher Kent Friesen was in the restroom when he heard the commotion in the hall.

POP-POP-POP!

After the rapid fire there was a loud BOOM, the sound of the pipe bomb going off. The fire alarm went off. Friesen left the bathroom and saw people out of their classrooms.

"What is happening?" someone yelled.

Friesen headed toward the library. He met fellow science teacher Doug Kraft at the top of the cafeteria stairs. There was blood on the floor. Friesen called Kraft's attention to it.

"It's not blood," Kraft said. "It's a senior prank."

Just then Jay Gallentine and Jon Curtis came running up the stairs toward them. The frantic janitors said there were active shooters in the building. There was gunfire close by. Kraft and Friesen ran back to their classes to lock the doors. On his way, Friesen gathered students from the hall and herded them into his classroom. He had them crouch down between the sinks in the lab. Then he ducked back out into the danger zone, returning with fire extinguishers.

"There's no way a gunman is coming in here," Friesen promised the kids. "I'll blind him before he comes in here."

Every sound he heard in the hallway, he would grab an extinguisher. He stayed on guard until the noise died down.

—

17-year-old junior Stephanie Munson just started attending Columbine four months earlier. She and her friend Melissa Walker, another junior, came out of a tech lab classroom in the northern hallway to go talk with an A.C.E. teacher. They heard strange popping sounds Stephanie didn't recognize. She'd never heard gunfire before. Science teacher Frank Peterson ran up the hall toward them followed by several teens. He was heading to the front office to get help for the wounded Coach Sanders. On his way he rounded up every student he came across.

"Run!" he shouted at the girls as he passed. "Get out of the building!"

"Why?" Melissa asked.

"People are shooting!" he yelled back.

61

"Oh, my God!" one of the teens with Peterson wailed.

The girls ran with the group through the glass doors into the northern hallway. Melissa glanced west and saw someone down the hall. She had taken a gym class with Eric her first semester and sometimes hung out with him. On April 16, she saw his KMFDM hat and mistook the logo for a radio station. He got defensive about it and told her it was a German band. She didn't recognize him now. All she saw was a boy in black who wanted to kill her. She and the others ran for the main entrance.

The gunmen chased and shot at them the whole way. The crowd scrambled to the front lobby where Peterson broke away to dash to the administration offices. He needed to tell the other staff members to get out. Dylan fired his TEC-DC9 at the fleeing students. The rapid bursts were so loud, they hurt Melissa's ears. As they passed the front office Stephanie felt her left ankle explode. It was like a firecracker went off in her shoe. There was a burning sensation and a pop, then her foot went numb.

"I can't feel my foot!" she cried as she passed through the first glass doorway.

Melissa grabbed her arm and pulled her along. Rapid shots followed them. On their way through the second set of glass doors Stephanie felt something strike her upper right arm hard enough to bruise it. Outside, she paused by the bike racks just beyond the entrance to look at her foot. It was covered in blood.

"You've got to keep running!" Melissa was hysterical, afraid the shooter would see them. "You've got to keep running!"

They ran east to Leawood Park across the street where the injured girl took off her blood-filled shoe and sock. There was a hole in her jeans and two holes in her leg, one in her shin and one in her lower leg. Entry and exit wounds. She'd been shot.

—

A girl in the lobby was on a payphone talking to her mother when the crowd ran past her. Peeking around the corner she saw the shooters coming her way, chasing after the kids. Dylan opened fire on them. The girl dropped the phone and hid in a nearby restroom. Just in time: The gunman stopped right beside the bank of phones. The frightened girl hid in the bathroom until he ran back toward the library. As soon as it seemed safe, she crept back to the pay phone and picked up the dangling handset.

"Mom," she whispered. "There's a shooter in the school. Come pick me up."

She dropped the receiver and ran out the main exit.

—

Custodian Curtis headed back to the kitchen where he met up with Gallentine and social studies teacher Eric Kritzer. The men urgently discussed their plan of action then Kritzer crossed the room in the direction of the staff lounge. Gallentine went upstairs. The janitor had just reached the top when Theresa Miller ran up to him.

"Jay! Dave Sanders has been shot!" the teacher said. "Call an ambulance!"

As Gallentine reached for his walkie-talkie a look of terror come into Miller's eyes. Here attention was on something behind him in the direction of the library. Turning, he saw a student in a long black trench coat down the hall. He was holding a gun and had what looked like a long-barreled grenade launcher in a sling strapped to his shoulder. Gallentine leapt from the top step down to the first landing below as gunshots rang out above him.

—

LIBRARY

"Okay," said dispatcher Renee Napoli. "We've got a police officer on scene.

"—I went out to talk to him," Patti Nielson continued. "I thought it was —"

"Just try and keep the kids in the library calm," the dispatcher told her.

"Yeah."

"Is there any way you can block the door so no one can get in?"

"I—I do—I do not—"

There was another loud shot in the hallway.

"Okay," said Napoli.

"I... yeah. I guess I can try to go but, I mean, like, he's right outside that door. I'm afraid to go over there."

"That's okay."

"That's where he is."

"Okay."

"I'm afraid to go there. Okay?"

"That's okay."

As the sound of gunfire moved away from the library, Nielson calmed a little. "Okay. I told the kids to get on the floor. I told them to get under the tables. All of the children are on the floor under the tables. Um... um... Yeah, they're all under the tables."

"Okay. As long as we can just try and keep—"

" And— and I just— everyone is staying calm. No one is saying a word."

"Okay," said the dispatcher. "As long as we can keep everyone there as calm as we can..."

"I hear some yelling out there going on right now," Nielson said.

"Yeah, we've got alarms going off now as well."

"Yeah. There's alarms. This room is filled with smoke."

"Okay."

"Okay."

"Keep everyone low to the floor," said dispatcher Napoli.

"Yeah," Nielson said. "Yeah. Everyone's...yeah. Everyone, stay on the floor! Stay on the floor. Stay under the tables. Um... I... I don't know... I..."

"Okay. I know. Just..."

There was nothing the dispatcher could say to help.

$+ + +$

11:27 AM - CAFETERIA

Gallentine came down off the stairs. Curtis followed. Teacher Eric Kritzer joined them. As the men started toward the kitchen there was a thud on the floor behind them.

The shooters had thrown a pipe bomb down the stairs.

The device exploded. It shook the walls and blew out the windows of the school store Rebel Corner. The force of the blast rattled the library floor above. Kritzer dove forward over scattered chairs and landed hard on the tile. Curtis and Gallentine scooped him up as they ran to the kitchen. A blanket of smoke filled the commons and whited out a nearby security camera for several seconds.

"Where the hell is Jefferson County when you need them?" Curtis exclaimed.

Students in the cafeteria bathroom took a chance and escaped. Adam Kyler abandoned his hiding spot and ran to the kitchen. He left his backpack and wallet behind in his panic. Another bomb exploded right before he reached the serving line. An airborne chair struck him in the chest, either thrown by someone or sent aloft by the violent detonation. It knocked him off his feet. Dusty Hoffschneider paused to help him up. They ran to the kitchen and hid in a storage room with several others.

The powerful blasts were recorded by the cafeteria surveillance cameras and shook the library floor above. Students hiding under tables right over the explosions felt the massive impact through the floor like they were being hit. The custodians warned kids in the kitchen to stay in the storage area, but several, including Dusty, insisted on leaving. He and his friends crawled along the cafeteria's west side. On his way out, he hit the fire alarm. He stepped over Sean who was still lying in the doorway.

———

When the store windows exploded, Kim and Jayson fled the commons and ran to the senior lot. They darted down the center row and hunkered behind a light blue van. There was another explosion in the school followed by almost continuous gunfire.

"Hurry!" SRO Marton shouted from the senior lot. "They're coming back! Hide!"

Jayson and Kim weren't sure if he was calling to them or not because right then Dusty came out of the cafeteria. He ran across the parking lot past Marton to the west athletic shed. When he reached the fence, he scrambled over and kept running.

———

UPSTAIRS

When it was quiet Kent Friesen went back out to the science hall where he discovered a trail of blood on the floor. He followed it to the corner and saw the two gunmen in the hallway near the library. They were facing away from him, reloading their weapons. Friesen recognized the tall guy who was loading a double-barrel shotgun. Dylan had been to his house to visit his son Cory several times with Chris Morris. The boys shared cases of Coca-Cola and played pool. Friesen didn't see the other shooter's face, or he would have recognized Eric too. He had been to Friesen's house many times with Dylan and Chris. The teacher retreated unseen.

Entering a chemistry classroom, he came across Theresa Miller and science teacher Caprice Wyatt. Miller was looking for someone who knew first aid to help Dave Sanders. Wyatt, Friesen, and a junior they recruited, Eagle Scout Aaron Hancey, followed Miller to Doug Johnson's classroom, SCI-3.

Once there they rushed to the fallen man's side. Friesen took off his shirt to use as a compress to slow Sanders' bleeding Aaron Hancey and fellow Eagle Scout sophomore Kevin Starkey administered first aid. Blood kept filling Coach Sanders' mouth, so they had him lie down on his stomach and urged him not to talk. Other students called 911. Emergency dispatch said help was on the way.

Five freshmen ran in, yelling about gunmen shooting up the school. Johnson had all the students huddle against the cabinets. They would be less visible from the hall that way.

—

OUTSIDE COLUMBINE

Deputy Gardner radioed in a Code 33: Officer needs emergency assistance. He also requested medical help at the school's west side.

67

On Pierce Street, Deputy Magor set up a roadblock at the southeast corner of the student parking lot. He was immediately approached by a teacher and several students who told him about a person at the school with a gun. He added his report to those on the police radio about perpetrators using guns, hand grenades, and bombs.

—

TEACHERS' LOUNGE

Those hiding in the lounge bathroom discussed climbing up into the ceiling to hide or possibly escape the school. They also tried to guess who the shooter was.

"It's the kid in the next class that wore glasses," Nick said. "Dylan."

Dylan wore glasses in the past, but he wasn't wearing them now.

Tim recalled a conversation he had earlier that day with Nate Dykeman. Nate told him Dylan and Eric weren't in several classes that morning. He knew they were up to something as they never missed so many together at once. Tim had been friends with Dylan for three years. They shared at least one class every semester since Tim's second one at Columbine. Dylan went to his birthday party last year. They played fantasy baseball. Dylan, a Red Sox fan, had chatted with him Sunday about trading player Adam Sands for Roger Clemens. They shared fifth hour philosophy class with Eric. Tim was in video production class with him last year. This year he shared fourth hour video production with Dylan, who spoke to him and teacher Tom Johnson almost every morning.

Eric kept to himself, though it wasn't a secret he was upset when he didn't have a date for prom on April 17. But he had an at-home date that night with senior Susan DeWitt who worked in the same shopping center as him. Eric asked her to the after-prom party, but she declined. Eric went and hung out until

68

nearly 3 a.m. He and Dylan, who took Robyn Anderson to prom, seemed to have fun. There was no indication they were plotting such a violent attack. Despite his friendship with Dylan, Tim was in just as much danger as anyone else.

—

CAFETERIA

Another powerful bomb went off in the commons, shaking the walls and the security camera near the stairs. Smoke billowed across the ceiling, completely obscuring it and the camera near the kitchen.

+ + +

11:28 AM – TEACHERS' LOUNGE

Karen Nielsen was still on the phone with 911 when she heard the explosion. She hung up and ran to hide in the staff bathroom with the others. The last one in., she feared they would be like fish in a barrel if the shooters entered the lounge. But it was better than being out in the open.

—

OUTSIDE COLUMBINE

Deputy Rick Searle pulled his patrol car up onto the grass on the school's west side and drove to the concrete shed where Mike Johnson was sprawled on the ground. The boy was badly wounded and bloody but still conscious. As Searle started first aid Mike said he thought the shooter's name was "Ned Harris". The deputy had no paper, so he wrote the name on the side of his vehicle. He radioed the information in as soon as he could.

Officer Bob Byerly arrived at Columbine's northeast side. It was the only unsecured entrance left. Exiting his vehicle, he took cover where he could see the northeast entrance and the east windows. Three other law enforcement officers joined him. Gunfire echoed in and around the school.

—

Seeing more law enforcement arrive on the building's west side, Eric ducked back inside to join Dylan.

—

LIBRARY

"I don't know," Nielson stammered into the phone. She was still hiding behind the circulation desk. "I didn't... I said, 'What has that kid got?' He was outside at the time. And— and— and— um... I was on hall duty. A student c—"

There was a loud explosion in the hall.

"Oh, God!" Nielson yelped in fear. Then she soldiered on. "And he was crying, he was like, going 'woo-hoo-hoo!'—"

"Mm-hmm. I know," the dispatcher said over the teacher.

"—are getting shot off," Nielson went on. "I do not know who the student was. I don't even think I saw him—"

There was a thunderous shot nearby.

"He was wearing black. He didn't look very large. Um. Male student. Um. He was out there shooting. It looked like he was climbing out shooting and somebody—" Nielson faltered. The gunfire was close. Right outside the open doors. "I said 'What is that?'."

"Mm-hmm," said the dispatcher.

"I said 'What's going on out there?' Well, it's a cap gun. Probably a video production, you know? They do these videos..."

"Right."

Evan was hiding behind a support pillar beside the desk where Nielson was. Peeking out, he saw Eric in the hall. He recognized the senior. He saw him almost every day at school.

70

Eric had a sawed-off shotgun in one hand and a lit pipe bomb in the other. He tossed the device right outside the library.

"And the kids..." Nielson said to dispatcher Napoli. "Well, I said—Well. That's not, you know—a play gun, a real gun... I was goin' out there to say 'No.'. And I went walk—"

BOOM! The noise from the pipe bomb was tremendous.

"Oh, my God!" Nielson yelped into the phone. "That was really close! That just rattled me."

"Okay," said the operator.

In the hall, one shooter said to the other: "Are you still with me? We're still gonna do this, right?"

—

INSIDE COLUMBINE

Freshman Robin Carroccia was in the 2nd floor wrestling room when Principal Frank DeAngelis ran in. He told the class to get to the gym. He took the 15 kids to the gymnasium where he hid them in a closet.

At the same time, English teacher Kiki Leyba was trying to flush students out of the main hall. He was met with resistance. Many assumed it was a prank or drill and didn't want to be bothered, but Leyba's frantic insistence finally got them moving. After clearing the hallway, he ran to the teachers' lot near the front entrance. He got his cell phone out of his car and dialed 911. Busy signal. He hung up and tried again. Still busy. It occurred to him that standing near the glass doors of a school under siege wasn't safe. He jumped into his car and drove over to Clement Park. Seeing kids returning from lunch, he hopped out and rerouted them away from the school. When officers arrived, Leyba told them what he witnessed.

—

71

LIBRARY

"GET UP!" Dylan bellowed from the library entrance loud enough to be heard on the 911 recording.

Evan peeked around the pillar again. Eric was right in front of the open doors. They made eye contact. The gunman chambered a round. Not trusting the pillar to protect him, Evan dove behind the copy counter north of the circulation desk. Eric fired a shot at him. It hit the counter, driving splintered wood into Evan's back. Eric fired again. More splinters flew.

Patti Nielson was silent for a few seconds, too scared to speak to the 911 operator. She was under that counter. Finally, she said in a small voice: "Oh, God. I'm really... frightened." She said something more, but it was incoherent. Then, softly: "I think he's in the library."

Under her table Nicole tried again to say something to John, but he frantically waved her to silence. From where he was, he could see the doors to the hallway—and the shooters.

"What's your name, ma'am?" Dispatcher Napoli tried to keep the teacher talking.

"My name is Patti Nielson." Her words were barely a whisper.

"Everybody, get up! NOW!" bellowed Eric. He and Dylan entered the library.

"Patti?" the operator repeated.

"He's yelling 'Everybody get up right now'," Nielson murmured, almost too low to hear.

"Stand up right NOW! Or we'll blow your fucking heads off!" Eric shouted.

No one stood up.

Brittany peeked out and saw a guy in a black trench coat and combat boots. He reached into his coat and pulled out a long gun. She hid her face against Josh's chest again.

"Fine!" shouted Dylan. "I'll start shooting then!"

Spotting Kyle behind a chair in the north row of the computer lab, he blasted the 16-year-old with his double-barrel shotgun. Pellets lodged in and went through the chair. Three pellets tore through Kyle's right shoulder and out his back.

"He's in the library," Nielson murmured into the phone. "He's yelling everybody get up right now."

As Kyle went down, Dylan shot him in the head.

"WOOHOO!" the gunman hollered.

+ + +

11:29 AM

Evan had a clear view of the computer lab from under the copy counter. Seeing Kyle die, he moved behind the administrator's desk. It was a wise choice: The shooters went to the south row of computers and set down a blue backpack full of ammunition. They would have seen him if he'd stayed put.

"So, this is a library," one of the gunmen said in a mocking way, as though he'd never been in one before.

"Where are all the people? Where is everyone?!"

"Everyone's afraid. Look at the scared people under the tables."

"This is for the four years of bullshit you've put us through! We've been waiting our whole lives to do this!"

The armed teens strode past the computer lab, throwing explosives and shooting furniture as they went. Dan could see them from under his table. He didn't know either of them, but it seemed Eric was taking the lead. The killers walked with a bounce in their step. They were having a great time.

"The pigs are here," Eric said.

He hurried to the west windows for a better look. Dylan was right behind him.

In the magazine room, Brian tugged some shrapnel out of his shirt. Moaning in pain, he wandered around the room. Afraid he would attract attention, the others started to get angry. They tried to get him to lie down and be still, but he was in shock.

"It's Eric and Dylan. I have to get out of here, Brian," whispered teacher Peggy Dodd. "They hate me. They're going to kill me!"

The size of the group had Dodd on edge. They made a larger target together. So, she left the group to hide between the magazine racks, flattening herself on the floor. She was a safe distance from the huddled students but could still see them.

In the main part of the library, Eric knelt and shot the windows with his sawed-off shotgun. Glass sprayed outward. He took aim at the deputies below who were evacuating people.

"Cover me. Cover me," he said to Dylan.

Dylan knelt beside him and fired his shotgun out the broken window too. Law enforcement returned fire but neither side scored a hit. Bullets ricocheted off tables and lodged in walls. The gunmen cheered and laughed, enjoying themselves.

"YEAH!" one yelled.

———

OUTSIDE COLUMBINE

Anyone leaving the school was a target for the shooters. Survivors ran for their lives, taking cover behind the first thing they could, including Deputy Taborsky's patrol car. The teens told him two gunmen were in the school armed with Uzis and hand grenades. Deputy Smoker radioed the information in. Dispatch advised him the shooter could be carrying a shotgun.

Deputy Gardner was finally able to make radio contact. "All units are under fire."

LIBRARY

"All you jocks stand up!" Dylan yelled. "Everybody with a white hat, get UP! We're going to kill every single one of you!"

Wearing a white hat at Columbine was a symbol of being in the athletic clique. Jocks, a subset of the athletes, were notoriously rude and aggressive bullies. The shooters knew that athletes and popular kids hung out in the library during lunch. Several were hiding there at that moment. Dylan and Eric hated popular kids, jocks, evangelicals, and anyone not like them.

Pat, Dan, and Makai—all athletes—were under a table nearby along with Kathy Park. Pat was best friends with Sean Graves and Danny Rohrbough. He didn't know they had been shot outside.

"You! With the white baseball cap on! Get up!"

"That's Dylan," Makai said.

He knew him from French class the previous year. Dylan had told him about making pipe bombs at his home. The tall guy had a bad temper and often disrespected the teacher, Catherine Lutz, but he and Makai never had any problems. They had even worked on projects together.

Dan was wearing a white baseball cap. The table he was under had no chairs to shield him and his friends. He thought the gunman had seen him. He didn't want the others to get shot, so he started to get up.

Makai held him back. "Don't move."

He was pretty sure Dylan wouldn't shoot him if he knew he was under the table, but he wasn't going to test the theory.

The room was full of hazy smoke. It set off the fire alarm, adding to the clamor of the one in the hallway. The noise was shrill, loud, and piercing. The alarms weren't installed with the idea that people would be listening to them for long.

—

Across the room, Jeanna was hiding with her friends, fellow seniors Lauren Townsend, Diwata Perez, Valeen "Val" Schnurr, and Lisa Kreutz. They were "popular girls" at Columbine. Jeanna was freaking out about her little sister, Kathy.

"I have to get to my sister!" she insisted. "I have to get to my sister!"

She tried to get up, but Diwata held her down, telling her that Kathy was with Jessica Holliday, a senior, who would take care of her. But Jessica wasn't with Kathy.

Jessica was best friends with Lauren. Both were regulars in the library and often spent "A" lunch there with their friends. During fourth hour Jessica was a student assistant in Al Cram's chemistry class, but he didn't need her that day. Lauren had fourth hour free, so she and Jessica went to the library together and sat at the popular girls' table. Jessica was going to ask Lauren to help her with physics but another friend, senior Amber Huntington, caught her attention. Jessica went to the center of the room to talk with her. Amber was a student assistant in the library. She hadn't wanted to go to school that day and felt a strong urge to talk to Jessica. They met up right before Nielson came in and told everyone to hide. Then they heard shots. Jessica thought it was firecrackers or a prank, but Amber grabbed her hand and pulled her under the nearest table.

When Dylan entered the library, Jessica recognized him from a Government Econ class they shared last semester. He sat directly in front of her. She'd always been friendly with him, though they didn't socialize outside of class. She knew Eric too. He had been to her house for dinner with some other friends two years ago. She hadn't seen him in her senior year. Val was in the same Government Econ class and regularly spoke to Dylan. Robyn Anderson was also in that class. It would come out later that she purchased some of the guns the shooters were using.

+ + +

11:30 AM

The gunmen left the windows and returned to the computer lab to reload. Dylan turned and, seeing Dan hiding nearby, he smiled. He lifted his sawed-off shotgun and pulled the trigger. BOOM! Kids hiding in the room screamed.

"Yahoo!" Dylan whooped.

Dan felt his knee get warm and realized he'd been hit. Makai was, too. The 00 buckshot shredded the black-haired boy's leg. The shot missed Pat, but he played dead anyway, holding his breath.

Under the circulation counter, Nielson was terrified. She tried to speak but her words came out as panicked breaths.

"I have him in the library," Dispatcher Renee Napoli reported to officials. "Shooting at students and the lady I have in the library on the phone."

Nielson began to whisper the Lord's Prayer.

"Okay. Try and keep as many people down as we can," the dispatcher said to her. "Do you know who he is?"

"No. I don't think so," said Nielson very quietly.

"Okay."

"I've gotta go," the teacher murmured. She said something more, but the rest of her words were inaudible.

There was another loud shot nearby. Nielson dropped the receiver and crawled under the desk as far back as possible.

Dylan shrugged off his trench coat. Eric returned to the computer lab next to the west windows. The way the tables were set up created a 3-sided cubby beneath each computer. Steve Curnow, Kacey Ruegsegger, and Amanda Stair were hiding in three of the cubbies. Kacey had pulled a chair in front of her when she curled up under the second computer.

15-year-old Amanda's brother Joe Stair was a founding member of the Trench Coat Mafia. He graduated from Columbine in 1998. Lately Amanda had been struggling with depression. The sophomore was tempted to skip school that day, but she had an appointment with her guidance counselor. Not wanting to be rude and miss it, she went to school. She wore a black T-shirt with the print: "Can't sleep clowns will eat me" on the front. With time to burn between her last class and the meeting, she chose to spend it in the library.

When all hell broke loose, Amanda hid under a table south of the computer lab but felt exposed there. Right before the shooters entered the library, she moved to the cubby east of Kacey. Steve was under the table west of Kacey. He was a 14-year-old freshman, and a major *Star Wars* fan. He loved soccer. Being a player and a referee was his outlet for dealing with his anxiety issues. His favorite color was green because it was the color of the soccer field. His skills weren't strong enough to play on Columbine's team, but he was a player and part-time referee in the Colorado Rush soccer organization where his dad refereed. Eric was a member of Rush and played soccer until fall of 1998.

"Die, motherfucker!" Eric's shout was so loud, it was picked up on the 911 recording.

Steve had no chair to shield him from the shotgun. The close-range blast destroyed his neck and shoulder, killing him instantly.

"Woo!" Dylan cheered.

They both laughed.

"This is so much fun!" one gunman said.

"Isn't this the best time of your life?"

Kacey didn't know Steve. They just shared the misfortune of being in the same place at the same time. She didn't know the killers either. She did know Dan, who they shot right in front of her. They shot the boy next to her. Kacey knew she was next.

Eric moved in front of where she was hiding, and Kacey screamed for him not to shoot her.

"Quit your bitching!" he yelled as he jerked the chair aside.

He pointed his gun at her. She put her head down. She'd plugged her ears with her fingers when he shot Steve to protect them from the painfully loud sound of the blast. She kept them there now. It was her only defense when he pulled the trigger. Kacey felt her body jolt. She saw her right arm fly up from the force of the close-range shot which tore through her Hard Rock T-shirt. She thought her arm might have been blown off. Her head struck the interior of the cubby, and her breath rushed out with an audible, involuntary groan: "Oh!"

"It's merely a flesh wound!" Eric sneered.

Dylan laughed hysterically. Kacey went limp and pretended to die.

—

OFF CAMPUS

Chris Morris had attended his second and third classes earlier that morning. He ditched fourth period Acting to go to Cory Friesen's house near the school, arriving around 10:45 a.m.

An original member of the Trench Coat Mafia, Cory was friends with Chris for years. He took the photo of the TCM for the 1998 yearbook, though he graduated from Columbine in 1997 and had stopped hanging out with most of them by then. Cory's father Kent Friesen was Chris' second period science teacher. They'd seen each other just a couple of hours earlier. The boys had rented a computer game last night from Video City. While they were there, they visited employee Chuck Phillips, a friend and former Trench Coat Mafia associate now grown up. Chris stayed at Cory's house until midnight playing the game. Now they were back at it.

The phone rang. It was Cory's mother Laura. She told him about the shooting and asked if his father had come home or called. Cory said he was with Chris, and he hadn't seen or heard from his dad.

—

OUTSIDE COLUMBINE

Deputy Searle evacuated students from behind Deputy Taborsky's patrol car. By the time he came back, there were more hiding there. He had to make three trips to transport the traumatized survivors, some of whom were injured. He took them south to Yukon Street and Caley Avenue, which became the first triage site for Columbine's wounded.

Deputy Walker arrived. There were now six Jefferson County deputies on the scene. Walker provided cover fire for people fleeing Columbine's lower level. Deputy Neal Schwieterman and several Denver officers joined Searle in transporting survivors to the makeshift triage area. They set up an inner perimeter around the school to cover the east, south, and west sides in case the shooters tried to escape. Securing a crime scene as large as Columbine was a daunting task.

Dispatch was overloaded with 911 calls and had to use an emergency command system. They brought in additional operators to deal with the overwhelming number of reports. The fire department was sent to the school. The first units to arrive thought they were dealing with a drive-by shooting and were unprepared for the war-like situation they found.

—

UPSTAIRS

Kristi Epling's brother Nathan was barricaded in the science room where Coach Sanders was slowly bleeding out. What was taking so long for help to arrive? The students turned on a television set with the sound muted, hoping for some information. The news wasn't much help.

Desperate, science teacher Doug Johnson wrote a sign: "1 BLEEDING TO DEATH" and handed it to freshman Michael Rotole, who put it in the window. Another freshman, Deidra Kucera, held it in place. Spotting Deputy Kevin Walker down below, she pounded on the glass to get his attention. Unfortunately, the surface was too reflective. The officer couldn't see her or the sign. He did catch a glimpse of one shooter in an upper-level window of the school's southwest corner. He gave dispatch a description of a gunman wearing a white T-shirt with some kind of holster vest.

Farther away, another officer saw the plea for help.

"There's a sign in the window that says: Bleeding to death," he radioed in. "They need to get a team up there."

But Command didn't want to send anyone in. It could be a trick, they reasoned. They claimed they had no idea who posted the sign, even though several 911 calls had been made from that room. Critics would later argue that if it were a trap, officials would know exactly where to find the suspects and could go in and deal with them. But no one did.

—

OFF CAMPUS

At Leawood Park, math teacher Terry Havens found Melissa Walker and Stephanie Munson. He looked at Stephanie's bleeding leg and said she'd been shot.

"Someone, call 911," he told the gathering crowd.

A female teacher found a cell phone to call for help.

—

CAFETERIA

The fire alarms and bombs were so loud, emergency operators could barely hear some of the calls from the school. Sophomore Matthew Depew called 911 from Columbine's kitchen. A wrestler and football player, Matthew was son of local police officer Wayne Depew who was not yet on the scene. The lines were jammed so the teen called the Denver Police Department, hoping to reach his dad. Officer John Lietz took the call. Matthew told him he saw Danny Rohrbough get shot. Lietz contacted dispatch and told them there were 18 people trapped near the cafeteria where there was an active shooter.

The kids trapped there, including Sarah Slater, wrote their names down so Matthew could relay them to Lietz.

—

OUTSIDE

Deputy Gardner radioed in a request for an ambulance to stand by. Deputy Taborsky advised dispatch there was a person down on the building's southwest side. Deputy Searle saw smoke coming from the school and radioed it in.

+ + +

11:31 AM — LIBRARY

Cassie Bernall was a 17-year-old junior with straight, long blonde hair and a sweet face with eyes that were serious beyond her years. Like many teens, she struggled on her road to self-discovery. Rebelling against her upbringing, she tried the Goth scene and dabbled in witchcraft. She experimented with drugs and alcohol. When she was 15, her mother Misty found notes Cassie and her best friend wrote about killing their parents and teachers. Her parents transferred her to a private school. Cut off from her friends, she spiraled into depression and wrote poems about suicide. Her parents insisted she attend church youth programs where she made new friends. She became a born-again Christian in 1997. That fall her parents let her transfer to Columbine. She was doing well in her classes. She got into Shakespeare and photography. She wanted to be an obstetrician. Things were improving... until she found herself hiding under a library table with sophomore Emily Wyant.

Emily was friends with Craig Scott, Josh Lapp, and Aaron Cohn. The blonde girl hadn't gone to the library to see them, though. She was supposed to be in science class taking a test. She'd been out sick recently and was unprepared, so her teacher Frank Peterson sent her to the library to study her notes. The table the girls were under was directly across from where Eric shot Steve and Kacey. Cassie had her hands over her face and was praying quietly.

"Dear God. Dear God. Why is this happening? I want to get out of here," she whispered. "I just want to go home."

Eric closed in on their table. For a tense moment it seemed like he might pass by. Then the combat boots stopped right beside Cassie. He slapped the table twice and bent down, keeping his left hand on the surface.

"Peek-a-boo," he said.

He shoved the barrel of his shotgun under the table and shot Cassie in the head at point-blank range. The gun kicked back hard. The butt slammed into his nose, breaking it.

Bree had a clear view of the violence. She watched in horror as Eric shot Kacey then Cassie. Blood darkened Cassie's light green shirt and smoke curled up from her head. Terrified, Bree crawled under the table with Aaron, right on top of him. Though fear moved her, she hid the baseball shirt he wore.

Aaron's backyard was separated from the Harrises' by a fence. He rode to school with Eric more than once and waved to him often when he saw him out driving. He knew Dylan too: They were in weight training class together. And now the seniors were laughing as they shot and killed people. To Aaron it sounded like they were having the time of their lives. Quietly Bree asked him to hold her hand. She couldn't tear her eyes off Eric. He was right next to their table.

The gunman ejected a spent shell from his weapon. He took a couple of steps and then crouched down, squatting on the balls of his feet. His shotgun rested across his thighs.

"Dylan, I got myself. I hit myself in the face."

He was looking at Bree when he said it, but he was talking to his partner in crime.

Dylan laughed. "Why did you do that?"

Eric lifted his gun and swung it back and forth, pointing it at one person and then another under Bree's table.

"Do you want to die?" Eric demanded of Bree, aiming the shotgun at her head.

"No!" she cried in terror.

"Do you want to die??"

"No! No! Please don't shoot me! I have a family and a fiancé! I don't wanna die!"

Blood began to pour from the gunman's broken nose down over his mouth. Several students who saw him would later tell investigators it looked as though he'd been drinking blood.

Eric laughed at her. "Everyone's gonna die."

"Shoot her!" Dylan encouraged.

"No," said Eric. He was still pointing the shotgun at her. "We're gonna blow up the school. You'll all be dead soon anyway."

"How about you, big boy?" Dylan said to Aaron as he came over. "You want to get shot today?"

Aaron looked left and saw a shotgun barrel less than a foot from his face. He was a hunter and knew how deadly the weapon was.

"Why don't you get up?" said Dylan.

Aaron didn't dare move. Amazingly, the shooter passed him by. Then Dylan suddenly fired his shotgun at someone to the south.

Though the killers were still active in the room, Pat had crawled around the back of his table to provide first aid to Makai. He wanted to put pressure on his friend's injured leg to control the bleeding. When his head came into view above the tabletop. Dylan shot him. Pellets also struck Makai and Dan.

"Die!" yelled Dylan. "Down on the floor!"

The long-haired gunman shot Pat again when he tried to crawl back under cover, hitting the back of his head and his foot. The blast knocked off one of his sneakers. He fell to the floor unconscious. Dan and Makai played dead so they wouldn't be shot again.

While the shooters were distracted, Kacey risked opening her eyes. Blood pooled on the floor all around her nearly an inch deep. Her blood and Steve's. The slug from Eric's shotgun had gone through her shoulder and out her collarbone, injuring both of her hands in the process. There were burns on her throat where the wad passed between them. Blood gushed from her mutilated right thumb. If the angle of the shot had been slightly different, she would be dead.

"Are you alive?" whispered Amanda from the cubicle next to her.

Amanda and Kacey didn't know each other. It didn't matter.

"Yes," said Kacey.

"Are you okay?" Amanda asked quietly.

"No."

"Where'd you get shot?"

"In the arm."

Amanda was afraid the gunmen would come back and kill her. She thought about her life and how if she died, she wouldn't get to go to an anime convention she'd heard about. Though she'd wrestled with thoughts of suicide before, when confronted with the reality of dying she realized how much she wanted to live.

"We're gonna be okay," she whispered to Kacey. "We're gonna get out of this. We'll be okay."

At the table north of Makai's, Isaiah was hiding with his buddies Matt and Craig. Seeing other kids get shot, Isaiah tried to scoot further under his table. The motion attracted Dylan's attention.

"Reb," he called, heading that way.

86

"Yeah?"

"Hey, man," said Dylan. "Look what we have here. There's a nigger over here. He doesn't deserve to live. It's that little fucking nigger Isaiah." Then, to Isaiah: "What's so funny, nigger?"

Eric got to his feet and went over to the wrestler's table. The shooters knew him. They'd clashed with him in the past.

"I want to go home and see my mom," Isaiah said in desperation.

"Oh, look. It's a nigger," sneered Eric. "Shoot 'im!"

"SHIT YEAH!" whooped Dylan.

He grabbed Isaiah's arm and tried to haul him out from under the table. "I don't like you fucking niggers!"

"No! No! No!" Isaiah fought to stay under cover. "Mom!"

Dylan couldn't force him out, so he let go and retreated. The gunmen flanked the table on the east and west sides, shotguns ready. Eric's single barrel pump-action Savage-Springfield 67H 12 gauge could fire four rounds before needing to be reloaded—five if the shotgun was "ghost loaded". He could fire it as fast as he could pull the trigger, ejecting spent shells and chambering new rounds automatically. He'd cut the stock and barrel down so the weapon was only 26 inches long. Dylan had a side-by-side double barrel Savage Arms Stevens 311D 12 gauge, sawed off to 23 inches long. It could shoot two rounds before it needed reloading.

Eric fired his shotgun three times as fast as he could under the table. Dylan fired both barrels of his gun. The discharges were so loud, Craig thought his ears would bleed. One of Eric's close-range shots hit Isaiah in the left arm. The lead slug went through his chest and out his right armpit, shredding the heart doctors had worked to save when he was a child. A slug from Dylan's shotgun struck Matt in the left shoulder and chest.

It went through his abdomen and out his neck. The blast fractured his spine and ribs, and ripped through his jugular vein, left carotid artery, and his right lung.

"Woohoo!" crowed one shooter.

When the gunmen stopped firing, Craig was miraculously uninjured. Shellshocked, he looked at his friends. Isaiah was lying in a widening pool of blood, facing away from Craig. Matt was slumped against a nearby chair beside Isaiah with his eyes shut. Blood poured from both of his ears. A gaping hole in his middle was smoking. There was blood everywhere. So much blood. Scott put his head down and silently asked God to take away his fear.

"Is he dead?" demanded Dylan. "Is he dead? Tell me if that nigger's dead. I want to know if that nigger's dead."

"Yeah. He's dead," Eric confirmed. "Wow. Dylan, man, look at this nigger's brains. Isn't it awesome how they splatter across the desk?"

"Yeah. We've never seen nigger's brains before."

There was a pause, then Eric said: "Let me see your knife. I've always wanted to do this. It'll be fun."

There was another pause. Then: "Oh! That's gross."

"I can't believe I did that," marveled Harris. "Cool!"

Craig didn't know what they did. He didn't want to know. He played dead and prayed for strength as his friends' spreading blood warmed the carpet beneath him.

"Who's next?" one of the shooters demanded in the main portion of the library.

Andrew Fair panicked and tried to crowd into the closed end of the table he was hiding under. He was aware of how his legs stuck out in plain view. The other kids under his table were in the same predicament. There just wasn't room to hide.

Striking a match on a nearby tabletop, Eric lit and threw a homemade bomb he and Dylan called a "cricket". The device consisted of a CO_2 cartridge with shrapnel duct taped to it. A bundle of matches was taped around the wick for easy lighting. The bomb bounced under the table where Makai, Dan, Kathy, and Pat were. It landed on Dan's thigh. The fuse was burning but he was afraid if he moved, the gunmen would shoot them again. Makai grabbed the device and threw it toward the south wall. It exploded midair with enough force to shake the floor. White-hot shrapnel pelted the carpet, melting the fibers.

Eric didn't notice. He was jumping on the bookshelves, shaking them back and forth, trying to knock them over. Books tumbled to the floor. When the shelves refused to fall, he shot them. Jessica was close enough that she felt pieces of destroyed books hit her legs.

The fire alarms continued to shriek. Gun smoke hung thick in the air making it difficult to see far. It smelled like fireworks.

Moving to the front of the room, Dylan fired his TEC-DC9 at the trophy case near the hallway doors. A glittering hail of broken glass hit the floor in front of where Diwata, Jeanna, and Lisa were hiding. Lisa screamed. Diwata hugged her and tried to calm her down.

Lauren—Lulu to her family—was a good friend to the girls she hid with. Born two months premature, the brown-haired senior had a 4.0 grade average and was anxious to get out into the world to help animals and the environment. Compassion was in her nature. She was lying under the table next to Valeen. Val had her hands over her ears and was praying silently. Trembling in fear. Lauren put an arm around her friend and hugged her.

"Everything's going to be all right," she whispered reassuringly to Val.

Coming around the shattered display case, Dylan saw Mark Kintgen hiding behind a chair under a nearby table. Mark was a junior. His twin brother Mike drove him to school that morning. Mike was in Algebra class. Mark had fifth hour free, so he went to the library like he usually did. The gunman headed his way, switching to his sawed-off shotgun. He stopped beside Mark's table and fired a single loud shot at him. Splinters flew as the blast ripped through the chair between them. Pellets slammed into Mark's shoulder and head, knocking his glasses off. He fell to the floor unconscious.

"Oh, look at that!" Dylan exclaimed. "Look at all that blood!"

He turned to the popular girls' table. The frightened teens had pulled chairs in around them for protection. Lauren and Val were praying. The gunman closed the distance, switching back to his TEC-9.

"Oh, my God! They're coming!" one of the girls cried.

Dylan fired eight rounds under the table as fast as he could, POP-POP-POP, then fired one more shot. Bullets sprayed Lauren from behind, riddling her shoulders, back, and thighs. Blood soaked her blue top and jeans. She pulled a couple of labored breaths and died.

"WOO!" her killer shouted.

Lauren's mother, Dawn Anna, was a volleyball coach at Columbine. She'd taken the position to be close to her daughter who was on the team. Dawn Anna transitioned to coaching after serious health issues forced her to step down from teaching math. Despite having close ties with the school, it would be over 24 hours before she would hear her daughter was dead—and it would come from the news, not from officials.

Dylan used his shotgun to fire an .00 buckshot round at the girls, hitting Jeanna, Val, and Lisa. Jeanna was shot in the right knee and left foot. Diwata had been hugging her, but the force of the blast knocked Jeanna out from under the table. Lisa was struck in the wrist. She was surprised by how little it hurt. Val fell to the floor screaming and clutching her side. Blood spread through her clothes and over the carpet.

Dylan went to join Eric beside a table near the central bookshelves.

"I've wanted to do this all my life!" one killer gloated.

They were right next to the table where Patti Blair was hiding. Patti normally had lunch downstairs with her twin Kim, Anne Marie Hochhalter, and Anne's brother Nathan. That day, however, Patti had plans to meet her friend, Heather Jacobson, who was hiding under the table with her.

"Oh, my God, Patti!" whispered Heather. "They have bombs!"

"Be quiet!" Patti said. Then she started to cry. "Please, please, God," she prayed under her breath.

Dylan bent down and looked at them.

"Pathetic," he dismissed and straightened back up.

"I want to blow up the fucking library," said Eric.

The shooters paused to reload their weapons. Under the popular girls' table, Jeanna and Diwata sobbed. Lisa and Valeen were screaming. In shock, Val tried to get up, clutching her bleeding middle.

"Oh, my God!" she shrieked in terror. "Help! Help me! Oh, my God! Please, God! Save me!"

Attracted by the girl's hysteria, Dylan went back over to her. "Do you believe in God?" he said as he reloaded his weapon.

"Please," Val begged. She rose to her knees but didn't dare turn around. "I don't wanna die!"

"Do you believe in God!" the gunman demanded again.

Val whimpered in pain and fear. She didn't know what the right answer was. "No," she managed to get out. Then, faintly: "Yes."

She glanced back and saw both shooters behind her. She quickly faced forward again.

"Why?" Dylan said. "God is gay."

"My parents taught me," she said. "And I believe."

She crawled under the table, wadded her shirt up against her injured stomach for compression, then pretended to die.

+ + +

11:32 AM – OUTSIDE COLUMBINE

The first reporters called the Jefferson County Sheriff's office seeking information about the shooting. More would soon call. They would also call 911 for interviews, tying up the lines for more than 6 hours. Media crews were already in the area hoping to dig up something new on the JonBenét Ramsey case. As soon as they heard about the shooting they descended on the school. Close to 400 news personnel showed up. To get as close as possible, media vehicles jumped curbs and parked on the grass, heedless of traffic laws and public safety.

Deputy Magor radioed for mutual aid. A city-wide response was underway as officers all over Denver headed to CHS. The whole world seemed to converge on Pierce Street. Close to 1,000 officials of all ranks rallied from 35 law enforcement and 11 EMS and fire agencies. Littleton Fire Department Chief Bill Pessemier was there. Columbine was in his jurisdiction, so his department oversaw fire and EMS on the scene. Fire Department Division Chief Chuck Burdick was also there. He and Pessemier took over management of medical issues such as setting up four triage and coordinating victim rescues.

Denver Police Department Division Chief Gerry Whitman and DPD Captain Mike O'Neill were there to deploy the hundreds of Denver police officers who mustered at Columbine. They aided the Jefferson County Sheriff's Office in rescues, gunfire, SWAT, perimeter, and traffic control. Later they would assist with explosive ordinance, investigation, and interviews. Colorado State Patrol Major John Wise helped wherever he could. CSP dealt with traffic control and setting up perimeters. Though they closed the streets, traffic near the school was so chaotic that arriving motorcycle officers had to swerve between cars. Police cruisers were forced onto the grass just to get to the scene.

—

CAFETERIA

Custodian Curtis ran to check on Sean while there was a lull in the shooting downstairs.

—

SCIENCE ROOM 3

Students in SCI-3 were in contact with a 911 operator and wanted to know if there was more that they could do to help Coach Sanders. Could they break a window and lower him down to rescue workers? The dispatcher told them they couldn't; it wasn't safe. They would have to wait until help arrived.

—

LIBRARY

When John heard Dylan bully the critically injured Valeen, it was more than he could take. "Don't you think you've done enough?"

Eric went over to where John and Nicole were hiding. The gunman didn't say anything. He just shoved his sawed-off shotgun barrel under the table and pulled the trigger. Pellets hit

93

one of the chairs between him and his victims, spraying them with foam padding and sharp wood chunks. The loud blast knocked Nicole out from under the table. At first, she didn't realize she'd been hit but she quickly felt it in her abdomen, right side, and shoulder. The shot grazed John's chest. Eric fired under the table again. Anticipating it, John sprang out. He landed on his stomach near Nicole. Dylan came around the table and stood over him. He shot the prone boy once in the back with his TEC-9 then fired three bullets into his head. John's legs were touching Nicole's. She felt him go into convulsions. Then he stopped.

"Do you think we've done enough?" Dylan laughed. He moved back around to where Nicole was. "Are you still breathing?"

She had her eyes shut and wasn't sure if he was talking to her. To be safe, she lay still and pretended to be dead. She soon lost consciousness.

Eric moved around the table, back to where Val was also playing dead. The girl prayed silently, struggling to stay awake. She told herself if she went to sleep, she would die for real.

Nearby, Kelly Fleming hunkered down on the floor. She was out in the open because there was nowhere to hide. She and her family moved to Littleton eighteen months earlier. Dressed in a black T-shirt and jeans, she was a quiet writer who loved Halloween. She was born with a jaw that was too small and other complications that made it impossible to breathe through her nose. She was always behind her age group physically. Just a few months ago, she had several surgeries to start correcting the problem. Her braces made her self-conscious, but Kelly told her mother just two months earlier: "Mom, I'm not shy anymore."

Eric shot her in the lower back. The shotgun was so close, the shell's plastic wad lodged in the left side of her body along with the pellets. She died near Lauren, her blood spreading in a large pool beneath her.

94

Jeanna tried to play dead, but every gunshot made her jump. Half her injured body was beneath the table. When she thought the gunman walked away, she slowly tried to slide the rest of the way under. She got her head under cover when Eric randomly fired his shotgun, not aiming. Jeanna never saw who shot her. Pellets seared into her shoulder, and she blacked out. Pellets hit Lauren's pelvis and Lisa's left shoulder, right wrist, and right ankle. One entered her flank and exited her inner thigh. The force of the blast shoved her up against Diwata. Blood splattered the underside of the table and the carpet.

The shooters walked away from the carnage, looking out the southern windows before moving to the library center. Beneath the popular girls' table Lisa said she was bleeding. Val said she was dying. Jeanna didn't say anything.

+ + +

11:33 AM

"I'm out of shells," Dylan announced. "I gotta go reload."

Heading toward two tables in the back center section, he aimed his gun at the teens hiding under the one to his right.

"Who should we shoot next?" he said as he moved the barrel from person to person. "Who should we shoot next?"

He stepped up to the south side of the table where Jessica was hiding with Athena Lagos and Amber Huntington. He had to straddle Jessica's legs to reach the table where he set one of his guns down. The weapon hit the wood with a solid clunk. A sleeve attached to his shotgun made it easy to reload quickly, freeing him from hauling around the heavy ammunition backpack.

"I lost a clip," Eric said from the north side of the table. "Give me one of yours." Then: "You know what else I've been waiting to do?"

"Yeah. Stab someone!"

95

"I wonder what's it like to use a knife on someone," Eric mused. "I've always wanted to kill somebody with a knife. I need to cut 'em. I've never done that. It'd be fun."

Athena knew who Dylan was. She had been in the CHIPS program with him when they were younger. Crouched down under the table, she listened to them happily discuss which clips they had run out of and what ammo they wanted to use next. As they reloaded, they analyzed the carnage and laughed about how their victims looked while they were dying.

"Where's the bag?" Eric said loudly. "Do you have the bag?"

The one he wanted was over by the computers. He crossed the room to reload from the blue backpack then returned to where Dylan was.

"All right," said Eric. "Let's go kill some cops."

Just then he spotted someone he thought he recognized under a central table just north of where Jessica was. Moving closer, he squatted down and shoved the barrel of his rifle under it. The person in a blue sweatshirt and jeans scooted away. Eric pointed the gun at him again. The guy scooted away again.

Straightening up, Eric shouted: "Who is under the table? Identify yourself! Or prepare to die!"

"It's me! John!"

"Are you John Savage?" Dylan came over, his TEC-9 in one hand and his shotgun in the other.

"Yeah!" said John.

"Oh. We know you."

John was a senior with a stutter. Other students nicknamed him "Screech" because he reminded them of the character on the show *Saved by the Bell*. When he heard the explosions downstairs, he thought of the Oklahoma City bombing. Seeing two people he knew at the center of the attack was a shock.

John had been a Trench Coat Mafia member a couple of years back but quit hanging out with them in his junior year when he got involved with theatre. Columbine was a place where people could blend from one peer group to another in various programs regardless of clique or age. Dylan and John met in the theatre stage crew and worked together the past two years. Dylan usually manned the soundboard. John and Dylan shared a second period class. Wherever he was, Eric was. They fed into each other's behavior. John often heard them reciting Rammstein lyrics together. All three were friends with Brooks Brown, who was also active in theatre and shared Philosophy class with John and Eric. John knew Rachel and Lauren, too, but wouldn't know until later they were both dead.

"Hi," said Dylan.

"Hi, Dylan," John said. "What are you doing?"

"Oh. Just killing people," was Dylan's casual answer.

"Are you going to kill me?"

Dylan looked at him for a moment. "No, dude. You've never done anything to us. I like you. We'll let you live. Just get out of here. Run." His next words were cold. Deadly serious. "We're gonna blow up the school. Go. Get up! Run!"

"Thank you," John said. "Thank you!"

Then he ran.

He bolted out the east doors into the smoke-filled hall. It was a hellscape. Fire alarms were blaring. There was a puddle of blood on the carpet as wide as the stairway. A trail of blood led from the spot, but John couldn't tell which direction the injured person went. He didn't stop to investigate. He just kept running. The cafeteria surveillance tape picked up his frantic escape. He practically flew down the stairs. It took him four seconds to make it down two flights of steps. He leapt out of the nearest exit. Moving with more caution outside, John stayed away from the library windows in case the gunmen changed their minds.

———

"Oh, look at the fucking nerd with glasses," Eric sneered. He'd noticed a boy hiding under the library table beside him. "Hey, four-eyes. Nice glasses."

Daniel Mauser was a 15-year-old in a tan shirt and blue jeans. A skinny blond boy with window-pane glasses, he was a shy, gentle soul. Like many of Columbine's students, the sophomore attended Ken Caryl Middle School before high school. It was the same school the shooters went to. During the period last year when Brooks stopped associating with Dylan and Eric, he mentored Daniel in Debate.

A chair was the only thing between him and the gunman.

Eric aimed his rifle and fired. The 9mm bullet went through Daniel's right hand, grazing his ear and head. The near miss spurred the boy into action. He shoved the chair at his attacker and tried to leap on him. Eric shot him in the face. A stray bullet struck the chair, imbedding splintered wood in Daniel's arm as he fell to the floor dead.

"Did you see that?" Eric boggled. "He jumped up at me."

"Was he trying to jump you?" said Dylan.

"Yeah. Did you see? He, like, jolted. I can't believe that."

Under the center table to the west, Crystal Woodman was hiding with Sara and Seth Houy. She saw Daniel die. Trembling in fear, she took her bubble gum out of her mouth, afraid she would choke on it.

Seth was Cassie's friend, but he couldn't see her table. He recognized the shooters from his "zero hour" bowling class, though he'd overslept that morning and missed it. He'd always thought of Eric as being a quiet kid. When the gunmen called out jocks, Seth had taken his white hat off and hid it between his legs. Holding his sister and Crystal close, he tried to reassure them and quietly told them to pray to God to protect them. They did, over and over. He wouldn't let Crystal look up. He didn't want her to see the horror so close to them. Sara hugged the other girl's legs. It was all she could reach. One shooter shoved a chair in as he passed them. It bumped Crystal's arm. She didn't react.

+ + +

11:34 AM – CAFETERIA

Downstairs, Gallentine left the kitchen to go evacuate more than 50 people from the auditorium while he had the chance.

—

LIBRARY

Before the gunmen entered the library, 17-year-old junior Jennifer Doyle couldn't find a spot near Val, Lisa, and her other friends so she ran to the back to hide. Peter Ball was already under the table when she, Corey, and Austin arrived. The blond boy didn't know any of them, but he knew who the popular kids were, and Corey and Jennifer were among them. Corey hadn't seen his close friend Brian come in injured nor did he or Austin know that their friends Pat, Dan, and Makai had been shot. They couldn't see them from where they were.

Jennifer recognized Dylan from Governor's Ranch Elementary School. They had both been in the CHIPS gifted program. Austin recognized both killers. He often saw them together in the halls. As they closed in on his hiding spot, time seemed to slow down. He noticed Dylan was unshaven and neither gunman was wearing a trench coat. Strange. The pair always wore their dusters to school.

"Everything's going to be okay," Corey reassured him.

99

Dylan yanked a chair away and fired his shotgun at them. Eric shoved the barrel of his carbine under the same table, swinging it back and forth as he popped off round after round. Bullets from Eric's rifle pierced Corey's neck and chest, tearing through his back and arm. Dylan switched to his TEC-DC9 and shot Corey once in the side. The bullet came out his neck.

Jennifer screamed and screamed. Realizing what she was doing she forced herself to stop. She didn't want to attract the gunmen's attention. She felt pins and needles in her right hand. She'd had it on Corey's shoulder when Dylan shot him. Her hand was mangled and bleeding. Her ring finger was crushed. She wrapped her hand in Corey's shirt. There was a lot of blood flowing out beneath him. Putting her head down on his back, she played dead with her eyes open.

Bullets from Dylan's TEC-9 struck Austin's hand and grazed his knee. The close-range shots temporarily deafened him. He didn't even feel the pain of his wounds until the gun stopped firing. Seeing Jennifer and Corey covered in blood, he put his head down on his best friend's backpack and played dead. Peter somehow escaped injury. To his right, Corey moaned in pain. Blood trickled out of his mouth. All around the library there were sounds of people suffering. Despite being uninjured Peter curled up in a fetal position and pretended to be dead. It seemed the best plan for survival.

"You all better get the fuck out of here!" Dylan yelled over the fire alarms as he and Eric headed back to the computer lab. "We're gonna blow this whole fucking place up!"

Eric laughed. He lit a Molotov cocktail made from a chemistry flask filled with orange liquid and threw it. Nothing happened. There was clanging of metal on metal next. A bomb went off in the library fifteen seconds later. The detonation was so strong it made decorative rocks on the roof jump and clatter like hail. It knocked down lights and parts of the ceiling. Shrapnel sent wood furniture chunks flying.

100

The shooters headed back to the circulation counter. Eric paused beside sophomore Heidi Johnson's table south of the computer lab and peeked underneath. She was too terrified to make eye contact with him. After a moment, he moved on. He went behind the librarian's desk, taking the east side. Dylan went around the west side, ending up next to Patti Nielson. She was crowded far up under the desk, her knees pulled to her chest.

"Oh. Look what we have here..." The taller gunman had spotted Evan crouched behind the counter.

Evan saw Dylan around campus every day. Seeing him now in this situation was strange. The lanky teen's long, frizzy hair puffed out under his backward baseball cap. To Evan, it made him look like a clown—except this clown was armed. Dylan pointed his TEC-DC9 right at the sophomore's face.

"What?" said Eric, coming over.

He was dizzy from the blow to his nose, his step wobbly. He had to catch his balance. Blood was smeared on his face.

"Just some fat fuck," Dylan said. Then, to Evan: "Are you a jock, fat boy?" He still had the gun trained on the younger boy.

"No."

"Well, that's good. We don't like jocks." He paused. Then: "Let me see your face."

He may have been talking to Eric, but Evan took off his hat. Tipped his head back so the shooter could see him better.

Dylan looked Evan dead in the eyes. "Give me one good reason why I shouldn't kill you."

"I don't want to get into trouble," the boy blurted in terror.

"Trouble?" scoffed Dylan angrily. He leaned in close. "You don't even know what fucking trouble is."

101

"That's not what I meant!" said Evan. "I mean, I don't want—I don't want trouble. I don't have a problem with you guys. I never will and I never did!"

+ + +

11:35 AM

Dylan stared at him for a bit longer, then looked away. "I'm gonna let this fat fuck live. You little fucking fat piece of shit. You can have at him if you want to."

Eric wasn't paying attention. "Hey. Hey. Let's go to the commons."

Dylan finally moved the muzzle of the semi-automatic pistol away from Evan. He fired it into the staff break room as he passed, putting a hole in a television in there.

"Let's do it then."

"Reb, ya ready?"

They gathered their stuff and headed toward the exit.

"Wait," Dylan said. "There's one more thing I always wanted to do." He grabbed a chair and smashed it down on the computer at the circulation desk, right above where Nielson was hiding. Then: "Let's get down to the commons."

The pair left the library, walking backward and sweeping the room with their guns like they expected an attack. No one moved. At the doorway to the hall the shooters turned and ran out, Eric in the lead. Seconds later there was more gunfire and thundering explosions in the hallway. Fearing they would change their minds and kill him if they returned, Evan cut through the break room to hide in the Rebel News Network broadcasting room under the desk.

Out of 56 people in the library, 34 escaped physical injury. In just over seven minutes, 12 people were wounded and 10 more were killed

+ + +

11:36 AM — CAFETERIA

Curtis and Gallentine met up near the kitchen then headed to the stairs but saw one of the gunmen at the top—and he saw them. The shooter opened fire on them, making a small mushroom cloud of smoke where the ammo struck the floor. The men ducked and ran back to the kitchen. Seconds later, a bomb hit the floor and went off, causing a massive explosion. It shook the security camera over the stairs and sent sparks flying. Shrapnel hit the metal serving line door. Thick smoke billowed across the cafeteria, temporarily obscuring the camera above the stairway.

—

Officer Lietz, still on the phone with Matthew, repeated to 911 dispatch there were 18 people trapped in the kitchen who needed help.

+ + +

11:37 AM – OUTSIDE COLUMBINE

Deputy Searle spotted a man in a red, white, and blue striped shirt up on the school roof.

A/C repairman Chris Clark, who worked for ECS HVAC, was on a service call to fix a leak in the roof above the girls' locker room. When the assault began, he thought kids were playing with firecrackers. It wasn't until a bullet ricocheted near him that he realized a shooting was in progress. He used a pair of vice grips to clamp the roof access hatch shut then he hid behind the air conditioning units to avoid bombs and gunfire. At one point he tried to lower himself to the ground with a yellow rope he had, but it wouldn't hold his weight. So, he stayed on the roof.

Sergeant Phil Hy arrived on the scene. He previously worked as the SWAT team support supervisor and quickly set to sorting out the flood of radio communication. He pieced together what he could from the overlapping reports. The broadcasts were conflicting: The shooters were in the library, in the science rooms, in the cafeteria. There was one gunman, and he had hostages in the auditorium. There were two gunmen holding prisoners in the kitchen. Three gunmen. There were eight terrorists in body armor. There were snipers on the roof. They were in the office, the halls, the choir room. The suspects were armed with shotguns. Uzis. Hand grenades. Napalm. They wore black clothes. White clothes. Ski masks. No masks.

It was chaos.

—

INSIDE COLUMBINE

In the cafeteria, Curtis and Gallentine crawled through the kitchen to hide under a large industrial oven.

—

Dylan and Eric prowled the science hall upstairs, looking through several classroom windows. They saw people hiding but didn't try to enter most of the rooms. They threw another bomb down the stairs to the cafeteria. The huge explosion sent sparks everywhere. It was heard and felt in the library. A blanket of smoke crawled across the ceiling, blinding two security cameras.

The gunmen shot up fixtures and lockers in the upstairs halls. They set boobytraps with improvised explosive devices (IEDs), tripwires designed to cause shrapnel-laden blasts when the doors were opened—like the one they rigged behind Blackjack Pizza months ago. They planted a bomb outside the west school entrance and rigged another on one of the library doors. The trap was made of a quart of homemade napalm attached to a "cricket" set to ignite if the door opened. Fortunately, it, like many of the shooters' bombs, was a dud.

After rigging their IEDs, the shooters wandered the halls aimlessly trying to find a way to blow up the school.

+ + +

11:38 AM – LIBRARY

The absence of gunfire and explosions left a strange void in the library. The fire alarms were still blaring. The wounded moaned and cried out in pain. Yet, after the deafening discharges and ruthless taunts from the gunmen, it sounded eerily quiet to those who survived the bloodbath. For a long time, no one moved, spoke, or even dared to look around.

Finally, Josh got up from where he'd been hiding. He grabbed Brittany's hand.

"Let's go," he said.

"Don't let go!" pleaded Brittany.

They ran out the back door together. They were the first survivors to escape the library.

Seth crawled out from his hiding place and saw the devastation. The library was an unfamiliar wreck, the air fogged with smoke. He ducked back under the table and grabbed his sister and Crystal. The girls didn't want to move.

"We're leaving," the dark-haired boy insisted, pulling them both to their feet. "Let's go."

The three teens ran for the west exit. Seth heard bullets zinging over their heads as they raced for shelter behind a nearby police car.

Next to the west windows in the library, Bree waved Emily over to her hiding place. The traumatized girl moved away from Cassie's body, crawling on hands and knees to join Bree and her group.

"Are they gone?" Andrew whispered to Byron under the table right behind Bree's.

"Be quiet," Byron said.

"Are they gone?" Andrew pressed.

"Be quiet!"

Andrew looked around. He saw a student sprawled on his back beneath a nearby table. Smoke rose from his stomach. He was rocking back and forth, moaning in pain.

Under their table, Jennifer tried to say something to Austin, but he shushed her. He checked on Corey. There was blood on his friend's gray shirt and jeans. His backpack sat in a huge puddle of blood on the floor. Austin searched for a pulse at Corey's wrist. He couldn't feel anything.

"We've got to get out of here," Austin said.

He and Jennifer backed out from under the table. They stuck close to the walls as they escaped.

Makai looked around. Seeing people leave, he said to those under his table: "Let's go." Despite shrapnel wounds and a bullet lodged in his knee, he got up and hobbled for the exit. Dan wanted to help Pat but was badly injured himself. Austin and Jennifer made it to that part of the room. Austin saw Dan and helped the injured boy up. They followed Jennifer along the west wall to the northwest exit.

—

Peter heard the other kids from his table leave. No one got shot. He pushed himself up. Corey moaned, one of many who were audibly suffering. Peter was afraid but he knew it could be his only chance to get out alive. He came out of hiding and joined a small group that scurried for the exit. They had to pass the lifeless body of Steve Curnow, and the gravely injured Kacey Ruegsegger who was lying in a large pool of blood.

Kacey couldn't move. Shock prevented her from feeling pain, but her injuries were too severe for her to even push the chair out of her way. Her right arm wouldn't move. There was a hole in her shoulder the size of a half dollar. The crushed joint was showing, and blood was gushing down her arm.

"Somebody, help get me out!" she called, surprising herself with the strength of her voice.

Craig crawled out from under his table and looked around. His clothes were stained with his friends' blood. Spent shotgun shells littered the floor. Heidi crawled out of her hiding spot and saw him.

"We should go," she said to Craig.

He felt the same way. "Let's GO!" he shouted to the room.

Craig saw Amanda under the computer row. "Are you okay?"

"Yeah, I'm okay," she said. "But the girl next to me is hurt."

Craig moved the chair so he and Amanda could help Kacey up. There was no time to be squeamish about her ghastly wound. Draping her good arm around his neck, he held her close and supported her injured arm. They headed north through the library. Near the emergency exit Amanda ducked into an office to sit down and catch her breath. A flood of students rushed past the door, pushing and shoving and shouting. Amanda soon followed them. Craig and Kacey were separated in the crowd. Unable to find the injured girl, Craig ran. When they made it out of the school, he and the other kids raced across the grassy knoll outside the west entrance to the emergency vehicles.

Craig unknowingly ran past his sister Rachel's dead body.

—

Hearing the noisy stampede, Brian, Jenny, and Ryan left the periodicals room. Dodd was afraid she couldn't move as fast as them, so she chose to stay hidden between the magazine racks.

—

Bree saw the other students escape and decided to make a run for it. "Come on, guys. Let's go!"

Students hiding with her told her not to go but she'd made up her mind. She got to her feet. When she wasn't shot, the others cautiously came out. Andrew almost put his hand down in a puddle of blood as he crawled out of hiding. Bree started toward the emergency exit and saw Isaiah's body. Blood pooled around his head in a wide stain. He wasn't moving.

—

CAFETERIA

Matthew Depew, still on the phone with Lietz, heard Gallentine and Curtis were in the kitchen at the time. When the teen heard the custodians' keys and walkie talkies, he thought the sounds were coming from the gunmen. He told Lietz the shooters had keys to the kitchen and walkie talkies with them. This info was passed on to dispatch.

"Is anybody at the command post aware of what's going on in the cafeteria?" Lietz demanded of the dispatcher.

—

UPSTAIRS

As soon as he thought he could safely do it, Principal DeAngelis went with two gym teachers to release the kids from the gymnasium closet. Leading the kids out of the building as fast as he could, he instructed Robin and the others to run. DeAngelis tried to go back into the school for more students, but Jefferson County Sheriff's officer Jeff White stopped him. He told the principal that officials were securing the perimeter. No one was allowed inside. Mr. De would have to wait outside and listen to the nightmarish rampage continue.

—

OUTSIDE COLUMBINE

SWAT commander Lieutenant Terry Manwaring arrived at Pierce and Leawood Streets and declared the area the SWAT staging area. The Littleton Fire Department positioned itself at Pierce and Weaver. Gathering his tactical gear, Manwaring saw teens gathering in groups along the sidewalk. Some seemed to be in a daze. Many were hysterical. Others were trying to comfort them.

Lieutenant David Walcher was the third official to arrive at the command post on Pierce and Leawood. He parked behind Manwaring's vehicle. While Walcher strapped on his tactical gear, Manwaring and Sergeant Phil Hy brought him up to speed. Walcher was fully SWAT trained, making him uniquely qualified to assume incident command. He had been with the Jefferson County SWAT team for seven years, ending just one year ago. The second highest ranking officer on the scene, he used an Incident Management System to oversee the event.

Off duty Captain Vince DiManna was driving home from the store with his wife when his pager went off, alerting him about the shooting at Columbine. DiManna, commander of the Denver SWAT team and a police officer since 1972, went straight from his home to the school still wearing his blue jeans. He had reason to hurry: His youngest son Jeffrey was a senior at CHS. DiManna and three other SWAT officers joined Manwaring and Lieutenant Pat Phelan at the command post.

—

A pipe bomb exploded in the cafeteria, shattering the southern windows. Deputy Walker radioed dispatch to report the blast. Several students ran from the commons to where his patrol car was parked on the grass. To protect them from the gunmen who were shooting at them from the school, he provided cover fire. Once they were hidden behind his vehicle, Walker contacted dispatch to tell them he had a bunch of kids with him and no safe way to get them to the parking lot.

As the gunfire continued, Kim and Jayson gave up hiding behind the van. Staying low, they moved further west. When they ran out of vehicles to hide behind, they scrambled to the far west end and took cover behind a maroon SUV. They heard a big explosion from the cafeteria and screaming up the hill. Kim saw roughly 30 people run from the west entrance and take cover behind a squad car parked there.

—

LIBRARY

Nicole woke to the piercing sound of the fire alarm. That's all she heard. There were no explosions or gunshots nearby. As she lay there, she eventually heard shots, but it sounded as if they were in another part of the building. Terrified and in a great deal of pain, she tried to decide what to do. Sounds of people moving in the library reached her. She saw a couple of kids get up and run away. More soon followed.

"Help me!" she yelled.

More students fled. None even looked her way. She called out several more times, but no one came. With effort, she grabbed the table and pulled herself up despite the agony. Then she saw a girl she didn't know standing by the bookshelf northwest of her. The girl was staring at her.

"Help me," Nicole pleaded. "Help me!"

Patti Blair just stood there in shock. Though she didn't help, Nicole sensed the girl was waiting for her. She struggled to her feet and saw shotgun shells scattered on the floor.

Under a nearby table Mark Kintgen regained consciousness. Seeing Patti, he also called out to her.

"Help me."

The traumatized girl didn't hear him. She waited until Nicole made it to her then led the way to the door. On her way out, Patti saw a boy she didn't know—Isaiah—dead on the floor. The fatal shotgun wounds to his head and side were still smoking.

Mark crawled out from under the table and followed the girls. Evan was part of the mass exodus from the library and saw Mark jostled by the crowd. Evan picked him up and carried him to safety behind the first patrol car they saw, joining Steve Greenwood, Dan, Makai, and Crystal. There were roughly 20-30 people behind the police car. The frightened survivors told law enforcement what happened and how many shooters they saw. Deputy Smoker instructed the boys to use their shirts as bandaging and compresses for those who were bleeding. Patti used one of her socks to help a boy who had been shot in the leg. Peter did his best to help others who arrived with injuries. He used shirts to control their bleeding and talked to them to keep them from panicking or passing out.

Ryan and Evan were reunited behind the patrol car. The boys were sent to hide behind the nearby athletic shed. Evan carried Mark. Lindsay Elmore arrived and recognized the injured boy. She knew his twin brother Mike. She kept him company while they waited to be rescued.

Evan turned his attention to his friend Mike Johnson who was lying on the grass. He was badly injured and covered in blood. Evan and Ryan talked to him to keep him alert.

111

"My feet are going cold," Mike said. He'd lost a dangerous amount of blood.

Evan held his hand. "You're going to survive."

+ + +

11:40 AM – SCI-3 CLASSROOM

Coach Sanders was bleeding out and close to death. Kent Friesen decided to go for help. He tried to leave but David Batchelder, a legally blind student, was lying in front of the door crying. He wasn't intentionally blocking the way. Being unable to see during such a crisis was terrifying. With Theresa Miller's help Friesen moved the anguished teen to a safe spot behind a desk. Then he went out to the hall. The science teacher saw a flash at the corridor's end. The gunmen were coming his way. He ducked back into the science room.

Shortly after, Miller saw Dylan through the window in the door. She recognized him from her Chemistry class the previous year. He was an angry young man who scored D's and F's in her class and often slammed her classroom door on his way out. Scared of being seen, the students in the room hid. They left Sanders on the floor out in the open hoping the gunmen would see him, think he was dead, and not bother with the room. Dylan tried to open the door but found it locked. From where she was hiding, Miller could see he had a gun on a strap over his shoulder. He was carrying something in both hands. Moments later, an explosion rattled the door. He had planted a bomb. Despite the blast, the door held.

Undeterred, Eric and Dylan went to the supply closet at the end of the hall where chemicals and lab equipment were stored. Hoping the toxic combination of substances would cause an explosion if set on fire, they taped a Molotov cocktail to the door and lit it.

"That ought to do it," one said.

Anticipating a fireball, they ran back up the hall.

Once they were out of sight, several teens crept back to Sanders' side. They applied pressure to his wounds to slow the bleeding. Greg Barnes fished out the coach's wallet and showed him pictures of his family. The students encouraged him to stay alive for his kids and grandchildren.

The gunmen went into SCI-8, a laboratory at the hall's northeast corner. The worktables had built-in gas spigots. Dylan and Eric turned them all on and retreated to the doorway. Still trying to set off an explosion, they threw a lit pipe bomb into the room and ran. The bomb went off, but it didn't ignite the gas.

Eric went back and fired his gun into the room. Bullet casings littered the floor. Still there was no explosion. Thwarted, the two killers headed to the stairs. Miller peeked out into the hallway. She knew teacher's aide Elizabeth Schneider was hiding in the science office. Miller wanted her to join them in Johnson's classroom where she might be safer. She hollered for Schneider and then noticed dark liquid on the floor near the storage room. Then she saw the fire. Thinking fast, she used the classroom access door in SCI-3 to enter the storage area. She put the fire out with one of the extinguishers she and the other faculty members had gathered to defend themselves with.

—

OUTSIDE COLUMBINE

Dispatch received reports that 30 people escaped through the school's west exit and were hiding behind patrol cars. Deputy Walker reported he could hear explosions in the school moving east. Deputy Taborsky radioed that one shooter might be named "Ned Harris" and was possibly wearing bulletproof gear. Officers gave DeAngelis a dry erase board to sketch a map of the school. Someone suggested putting him in a bulletproof vest so he could turn off the fire alarms, but superiors said no. They weren't letting anyone into the school before the SWAT team. Time ticked by. The police got restless and then angry. They were trained to save lives and wanted to stop the shooting. Some had children inside. A few hinted they should break rank and go in against orders.

Seeing more police arrive on the field's far side, Smoker came up with a plan to shuttle the students to safety using the additional patrol cars.

———

Kristi went back to school after lunch only to find the way barricaded by police. Assuming there had been a traffic accident, she tried to approach the school from another direction. Every way she tried was blocked off.

Senior Jen Harmon was also trying to return. She was Mark Taylor's cousin and his ride home after school. Her boyfriend John Reffel IV, a senior baseball and football player at Columbine, was with her. They found themselves in a line that was being shunted back the way they came. Police had barricaded the entrance and were shoving students on foot into random cars to evacuate them. They put four girls in Jen's back seat including Terra Oglesbee, who told them what was happening. Jen turned her car around, pulling alongside Nate Dykeman's battered white Ford F-250 truck. She shared Video class with Nate. They both had their driver's side windows down.

"What's going on?" he asked her as they passed.

"Two kids in trench coats are shooting up the school," she said.

"Oh, my God," Nate scoffed in disbelief. "I can't believe they actually did it."

Jen had known Nate for years. He and Dylan were her neighbors. She also knew Eric since the 8th grade. His older brother Kevin was big into playing sports. She got the impression Eric's parents expected him to be like his brother and he wasn't. He played baseball and soccer but quit recently. In his junior year he started wearing a trench coat, as did Dylan. Jen

114

had several classes with all three boys. Dylan shared cookies with Jen, Nate, and Eric in Judith Kelly's creative writing class. Jen had acted in one of Eric's class projects, a video about people kidnapping the President. Eric played one of the kidnappers. Jen played one of the people who shot Harris and rescued the President.

When looking through her yearbook a few days earlier Jen saw the Trench Coat Mafia photo and recognized junior Pauline Colby. Jen worked with her at the school store. Pauline had the "A" lunch shift. Jen took over during "B" lunch. Seeing her in the picture, Jen was curious.

"You were in the Trench Coat Mafia?"

"Yeah," said Pauline. "Last year."

Jen had asked her if there was a specific way to get in.

"No. It's just for outcasts."

Pauline said she got out of the group because they were saying "really weird things" which scared her.

Pauline attended the D.E.C.C.A. banquet then left around 11 a.m. to go change her clothes. She was supposed to return to work at the store, but she didn't come back. Pauline never missed her shift until then. She'd called her dad from the banquet and said she was sick. He scheduled a 3 p.m. doctor's appointment, but she called him again at 11 a.m. and asked him to pick her up. At 11:11 a.m., he signed her out. Jen later saw Pauline on the news saying she was out sick from school during the shooting.*

Kristi saw her boyfriend Nate in his rusty old truck at a nearby intersection. She followed him back to his house where he told her there were two gunmen in the school wearing black

---

* Choir teacher Leland Andre Jr. saw Pauline during first period. When he asked her how she was, she replied: "Strange. Very strange."

trench coats. She immediately thought of Eric and Dylan. They wore their long black coats a lot. She also thought of Chris Morris, who used to wear one. Nate did too but he was with her. She would have been surprised if Chris were involved, but she could imagine Dylan and Eric shooting at the school.

"It can't be my friends," Nate fretted.

+ + +

11:44 AM – CAFETERIA

The gunmen trudged back down the cafeteria stairs to check on the bombs, Eric in the lead. Gone was the spry energy from earlier. Reality was beginning to weigh on them along with the heavy gear they toted.

Dylan scoped the room, his TEC-DC9 ready in his left hand. Eric dropped to one knee on the landing of the stairs, aimed his rifle, and popped off a few rounds. His target was a duffel bag on the left which held one of the 20-pound bombs he and Dylan constructed. Despite hundreds of bags and backpacks scattered around the room, he knew exactly where to aim. He knocked some things off the table but couldn't detonate the bomb.

—

OUTSIDE COLUMBINE

Receiving reports that a suspect may have left the school, deputies radioed in their locations to confirm a perimeter was set up. Deputy Bob Byerly and members of the Colorado State Patrol were by the tennis courts with a clear view of the north side and northeast doors. Deputy Rick Searle was on the northwest side, transporting survivors. Deputy Neal Schwieterman was beside the west athletic shed, taking students to triage. Deputies Scott Taborsky and Paul Smoker were southwest, sheltering survivors who escaped through the west side. Sergeant Ken Ester and Deputy Paul Magor covered the southeast, assisting survivors and diverting traffic away from the area. Deputy Kevin Walker was on the south side, evacuating people from the school grounds.

+ + +

11:45 AM – LIBRARY

Patti Nielson cautiously slipped out from under the circulation desk. Peeking over the top out at the smoke-filled library she saw a pair of white tennis shoes under a nearby table. She didn't see any movement. Horrified, she crawled to the break room and hid in a cupboard.

Under the popular girls' table, Diwata looked around. There was blood everywhere. Lauren wasn't moving. Valeen tried to wake her, but she didn't react. They needed to escape. The girls tried to get Lisa to go with them, but she was too injured to move. Jeanna tried to rise, and everything went black. She collapsed. Badly injured herself, Val couldn't help them. Diwata couldn't do it on her own. They had to leave their friends behind. The choice would haunt Diwata for years to come.

The 11:45 bell went off. "A" lunch was over.

—

OFF CAMPUS

When he heard the gunmen were wearing trench coats, Chris made the dreadful realization Eric and Dylan might be involved. He called 911 from Cory's house but got disconnected while he was being transferred.

—

CAFETERIA

His rifle under his left arm, Eric drank from a cup he took from a deserted table near the kitchen. He set his shotgun down on the table.

117

"Today the world's going to come to an end," one gunman said. "Today's the day we die."

Dylan crossed the room to mess with the duffel bag bombs, spreading flammable liquid between them. Then, backing up, he threw something at the bomb on the left. Students ran by the southern doors, distracting him. He ran over to shoot at them.

—

In the staff lounge bathroom, Nick was tired of hiding. He wanted to do something proactive. Teacher Jankowski opened the door to the lounge and the group peeked out. Through a nearby window, they could see two bodies on the ground outside. Teacher Sue Caruthers said it wasn't a good idea to run that way. They could still hear gunfire though. If they stayed put, the shooters might find them.

They considered going up into the ceiling, which was made of acoustic tiles that were easy to move. Nick boosted Tim up. Jankowski went next, using Nick's head and shoulders to reach the ceiling. Tim pulled her up. He accidentally knocked a ceiling tile loose then moved west, crawling along a metal heating duct to a pipe suspended by wires. He knocked down more ceiling tiles as he went. Reaching the west wall, he heard footsteps below. He looked back and saw a head poke up through a hole he'd made above the kitchen bathroom. The person was about 20 feet away. Tim couldn't see their features in the dim light, but he thought he recognized Dylan's Boston Red Sox hat. The person aimed a shotgun at him. Tense seconds ticked by. Then Tim kicked the tiles out of the ceiling beneath him. He fell 18 feet down into the teachers' lounge, landing on the floor near the window. Not sure where the gunman was, he took a chance. He ran through the cafeteria and out of the school to hide behind a nearby police car.

Jankowski crawled west too, thinking there was a vent there that led outside. She made it as far as the lounge before she fell through the tiles. She dropped to the floor and quickly scrambled back to the bathroom to hide.

118

Nick also went up into the ceiling and fell through. Landing on a table in the lounge, he picked himself up and ran from the school. Sean followed him, as did two staff members from the bathroom. Nick didn't know it, but his twin brother Adam was still barricaded in the choir room.

+ + +

11:46 AM – OFF CAMPUS

Denver Police Sergeant Dan O'Shea was off duty and driving to pick up his daughter from school when he heard the news on the dispatch. He wasn't in uniform, but he radioed back and told them to show him en route to Columbine.

—

CAFETERIA

There was a spark in the duffel bag bomb on the right, then something exploded on the side of the bag. More sparks ignited the fuel between the bombs. Fire engulfed a large portion of the room. The flames forced students om the commons to flee. Dylan jogged back to the stairs. Eric grabbed his shotgun as the fire swept close and ran to join him. They hurried up the stairs, away from what they hoped would be a huge explosion.

Custodians Gallentine and Curtis saw the blaze from the kitchen. Smaller containers of gasoline and other flammable liquids that were attached to the propane bomb on the floor burst under the intense heat. People hiding in the kitchen closet heard the explosion. The small room was packed, so Gallentine retreated to the walk-in cooler while Curtis hid in the freezer.

—

Officer Lietz reached the end of his patience. He could hear gunshots in the cafeteria and knew Matthew and the others were in danger.

119

"Have you guys made any attempt at the school yet all?" he demanded of the dispatcher.

"Not that I believe," the dispatcher responded. "I think we've just got a perimeter set right now. But I don't know that for sure."

"Let me know when you make entry," said Lietz. "I gotta be honest with you, pal… these kids are scared shitless. You guys are going to have to do something fairly quick. We're going to have a major bloodbath."

—

Jankowski and Caruthers heard a loud noise right outside the staff lounge bathroom. There were voices and the sound of something metal being moved. When the commotion stopped, Jankowski cautiously peeked out. The window she'd seen the bodies through earlier was broken. The Venetian blind had been pulled down.

The faculty debated if they should try to escape. They had to cross the cafeteria to leave the school through a door, something neither liked. They were still discussing it when a student's head popped out of the ceiling above them. He told them to make a run for it. He was a Special Education student who took it upon himself to tell everyone to escape while they could. The ladies needed no further prompting. They ran. Soon they were reunited with Tim outside behind a patrol car. He was giving his statement to the deputy.

A few more students in the commons escaped. Several of them stepped on Sean on their way out. The critically injured boy was still lying prone in the west doorway. He heard some say, "Don't leave him!" but no one stopped. He prayed and waited. As he started to lose consciousness, he heard sirens.

+ + +

120

11:47 AM – OUTSIDE COLUMBINE

Deputy Walker was on the school's south side when the cafeteria windows suddenly flexed out and sucked back in. An enormous fireball lit up the commons. The windows burst, spraying glass everywhere. The duffel bag bomb on the table had partially detonated. The blast radius covered nearly half the cafeteria. Flames surged up to the ceiling and over a quarter of the room for several seconds. The intense heat melted the plastic seats of chairs.

Spray paint cans and bottles of flammable liquid in the bag exploded but the propane tank was still intact. The other bomb on the floor and the one in the kitchen didn't go off at all. If the tanks had blown up as planned, the combined force potentially could have destabilized the walls and support beams.

The force of the partial detonation slammed into the floor of the library above. The impact was so enormous, it knocked people off their feet upstairs and those in the parking lot felt the ground shake. It also started a large, persistent fire. 911 calls from neighbors all around the school reported hearing screams, gunfire, and explosions. Teens ran from the cafeteria and took cover behind the parked patrol cars.

"Are we gonna die?" one hysterical girl asked Deputy Walker. "Are we gonna die?"

"No," the deputy assured her. "You're not going to."

Walker, a former member of the bomb squad, radioed in what he witnessed. He also told dispatch he had six students with him but no safe way to evacuate them. Dispatch advised him there might be shooters on the roof, so he had to watch the south exit, west windows, and the roof as well.

—

121

Denver KMGH-TV Channel 7 aired the first reports of shots fired at Columbine High. Families with loved ones at the school who hadn't contacted them yet began to worry.

Roughly 30 students were behind the police cruiser outside the school. Most were victims from the library. Students tended to the injured Makai and Kacey.

+ + +

11:48 AM - CAFETERIA

The huge flames in the cafeteria licked the ceiling and set off five sprinklers which briefly subdued the blaze, bringing it down to campfire size. Another small explosion made it flare back up to a bonfire before the water tamed it again. The spray couldn't entirely douse the fire. It kept burning on the table, filling the commons with black smoke.

+ + +

11:49 AM – UPSTAIRS

Eric and Dylan invaded the front offices where Principal DeAngelis' secretary Susan White and Campus Supervisor Syd Keating were hiding. Both were on lengthy calls to 911 when the gunmen came through. Firing randomly, they put bullets in windows, doorjambs, and the ceiling. They shot telephones, televisions, and monitors and threw pottery against a window. It damaged the blinds and broke the pot but not the window.

—

OUTSIDE

Sergeant Ken Ester reported the SWAT team were on the scene, at the school's east side.

+ + +

11:50 AM – CAFETERIA

The cafeteria floor flooded as the sprinklers continued to fight the flames from the partially detonated bomb. The blaze was stubborn. It wouldn't go out, but the water kept it from spreading.

+++

11:51 AM - LIBRARY

After several seconds of dead air, dispatcher Renee Napoli ended Patti Nielson's 911 call.

+++

11:52 AM – OUTSIDE COLUMBINE

Deputy Byerly reported shots fired on the east side. The Littleton Fire Department radioed that the sprinkler system in the cafeteria was activated. Jefferson County Undersheriff John Dunaway, a man with 30 years of police experience, arrived on the scene. There were kids running. Police, fire, and other agency personnel arrived from all directions. Traffic was completely jammed. He authorized the SWAT team to enter the school.

+++

11:53 AM – COLUMBINE OFFICE AREA

The shooters pushed over computers and a postal shelf, scattering mail on the floor. They fired into almost every room. They only missed the Counseling office. Shell casings and bullet fragments littered the floor in their wake. Secretary White told the 911 dispatcher she could hear the shots where she was at.

Eric and Dylan went out into the Art hallway, still shooting as they headed back to the cafeteria.

—

OUTSIDE COLUMBINE

Officer Bin Tran radioed into dispatch. "There are a bunch of kids down on the west side."

"Maintain cover until we can get a rescue team in," Sergeant Dan O'Shea responded over the radio.

On his way to the school, Jefferson County Sheriff John Stone contacted JeffCo Commissioner Patricia Holloway to inform her that shots were being fired, there were wounded students, and possible hostages. Deputy Searle reported Denver Police were at the storage shed armed with long guns. Dispatch confirmed a live bomb was found in the field behind Columbine.

"Repeat: A *live* bomb at Chatfield and Wadsworth."

+ + +

11:54 AM

"Stand where you're at," Sergeant O'Shea told Officer Tran over the radio. "Don't go in."

+ + +

11:55 AM

Paramedics in Ambulance 5 transported Stephanie Munson from triage to Littleton Hospital, the first of many victims to arrive. Her younger sister, 14-year-old freshman Jennifer, was in the cafeteria when the shooting erupted. She made it out safely and was found at Leawood Park.

+ + +

11:56 AM

Television news broadcasts announced there were two shooters at Columbine High. Deputy Smoker reported to dispatch there were four people down on the west side who needed to be evacuated.

+ + +

11:57 AM - CAFETERIA

The shooters returned to the cafeteria, moving much slower than before. They came down the stairs and looked around, visibly frustrated. Eric stopped at the bottom landing. His gun dangled in a loose grip at his side. He waved his other hand at the low flames in the center of the room like he was coaxing them higher.

They both studied the scene for a few seconds. Then they picked their way across the trashed room and entered the kitchen to check on the bomb in there.

—

OUTSIDE COLUMBINE

Sergeant O'Shea told dispatch he'd entered the inner perimeter on Columbine's northwest side near the air conditioning units. Denver SWAT officer Henry Bloodworth Jr. and his partner Tommy O'Neal arrived with O'Shea. Deputy Walker reported shots fired inside the school.

Deputy Schwieterman radioed that an ambulance had arrived on the school's south side. The emergency vehicle was responding to Deputy Gardner's call for medical assistance. Another ambulance arrived. Having two rescue vehicles on a hot scene was not protocol. Usually in an emergency, fire and rescue didn't enter an area with an active shooter. Not even in the North Hollywood shootout of 1997, when officers and civilians were down and dying. But they did that day. They didn't know the scene wasn't secure yet.

+ + +

11:58 AM

Deputy Schwieterman reported there were five victims on the school's southwest side near the shed. He gave directions so rescue crews could quickly find them. Littleton Fire Department drove their Rescue 11 and 13 Type I ambulances to where injured kids were sprawled on the ground. The crews jumped out. Seeing officers behind cover with their weapons out, one EMT mouthed: "Is it safe?"

"NO!!! It's not safe!!!" officers responded emphatically. "Get 'em and go!!! Get 'em and go!!!"

At the same time, the Littleton Fire Department announced it had set up a command post at Leawood and Pierce.

+ + +

11:59 AM – CAFETERIA

The gunmen left the kitchen, splashing through the standing water, their shoulders slumped in defeat. Holding their guns loosely at their sides they stomped back up the stairs taking them two at a time.

+ + +

12:00 PM – OFF CAMPUS

Television news agencies aired uninterrupted coverage live from the scene. First local then national stations cut into their regular broadcasts to play the dramatic footage.

—

Fearing the worst, Nate called the Klebold house. Dylan's father Tom answered. He hadn't heard about the shooting yet— Nate was the first to tell him about the gunmen in trench coats at Columbine. When Nate asked him if Dylan was home, Tom got a bad feeling. He put the boy on hold and went to check Dylan's closet for his coat. His son shouldn't have needed it, as pleasant as the weather had been lately.

He opened the closet. Dylan's coat wasn't there.

—

Kristi called home to check on her younger brother who was a freshman at Columbine. Her parents hadn't heard from him, and, at their worried request, she and Nate headed back to the school to see if they could find him.

—

OUTSIDE COLUMBINE

The Channel 7 news helicopter was up in the air. Dispatch asked the news station to land and pick up a sheriff's deputy to do aerial surveillance of the high school. Dispatch also sent out a request for an armored unit since the scene was "not safe for medical".

Meanwhile, Channel 7's ground crew interviewed anyone who escaped the school. Sophomore David Mesch told reporters he was in the cafeteria when the shooting started. When they asked him if he knew the Trench Coat Mafia, he said he knew of them but never heard the members make threats. Freshman Justin Woods said he was on the soccer field when he saw two gunmen dressed in black coats and black hats shoot three boys. Reporters also interviewed cafeteria worker Karen Nielsen, who shared her harrowing experience.

Channel 9's reporters were there too, talking to Kathy Park who told them she was hiding under a library table when the gunmen came in and started shooting people including her sister. Evan Todd, Alex Marsh, and Bree Pasqual were also interviewed.

"And we heard, like, popping," Bree tearfully told a CBS reporter. "And we didn't know what it was. And then I looked out the window and there was this guy throwing, like, a pipe

127

bomb at all the cars. And then he came in the— they started, like, blowing up and shooting everyone in the cafeteria and then you could hear him laughing and running upstairs and they were shooting anyone of color, wearing a white hat, or played a sport." She sobbed and continued: "And they didn't care who it was, and it was all at close range."

Her emotions overcame her. She smudged away tears with the side of her hand.

"What did you see?" the reporter prompted. Then: "You have blood on your hand."

Bree looked at her hand and sobbed again. "Everyone around me got shot. And I begged him for ten minutes not to shoot me." She cried harder, the trauma still fresh. "He just put the gun in my face and started bleeding everywhere and started laughing, saying that it was all because people were mean to him last year."

A friend of hers put a supportive arm around her shoulders.

"Who were those people?" asked the reporter.

"I don't know!" Bree cried.

"You saw other people get—"

The reporter couldn't finish the horrible sentence, but Bree understood and nodded.

She lifted a shaking hand to smear away more tears. "He did it right in front of us."

—

Sergeant Richard Euchler of the Arapahoe County Sheriff's Office called Investigator Archie Singleton from the Justice Center Detention Facility, returning the man's urgent page. Singleton told him to head to Columbine High School in a full bomb squad response.

—

Psychology teacher Thomas Johnson and social studies teacher Rick Bath had gone to 7-11 on their lunch break to buy a lottery ticket. When they tried to return to Columbine, they found the way blocked by police and fire vehicles. Bath steered the car off Coal Mine Avenue, took Pierce Street north to Walker Avenue only to find it blocked too. Heading west down Walker, they saw Brooks walking in the opposite direction of the school. The teen flagged them down. He had been going door to door trying to find someone who would let him use their phone. He was visibly upset and shaken as he told them he encountered Eric Harris at the school and that he was carrying a "weird looking" duffel bag into the building. Brooks told Johnson there might be a shooting taking place and Eric had said to him: "Brooks, I like you. Get out of here.".

—

Officer Henry Bloodworth Jr. saw what looked like an automatic weapon or a rifle sticking out of the west entrance. He couldn't see who held the gun, but he opened fire anyway, popping off three to six rounds with his Steyr Aug rifle. He was afraid the gunman would shoot at the officials or the injured kids on the ground near the shattered doors.

+ + +

12:02 PM

The Denver SWAT team commandeered a bright green firetruck, Littleton Engine 11, to use as cover. Together with officers from Jefferson County they started toward the school using the firetruck as a shield. Deputy Del Kleinschmidt, a JCSO K-9 team member assigned to the SWAT, volunteered to drive.

The sprinkler system in the cafeteria finally put out the fire. The whole room was flooded. Hazy smoke hung in the air as water hissed down. Sean, unconscious in the western doorway, came around when two emergency workers grabbed him by his belt and the collar of his shirt. Moving quickly, they hauled him up and away from the school. Sean saw his arms and legs dangling below him as they ran. Bullets hit the concrete around them, sending up little white puffs of smoke. The gunmen had seen the rescuers and were firing on them from the library.

Firefighter paramedic Monte Fleming saw his fellow crew members struggling to get the boy into Ambulance 13 and hurried over to help. They had no time to be gentle. As soon as they got him loaded up, Fleming saw another injured boy lying on the hill. The teen made eye contact with him.

"Help me," he said.

Fleming couldn't leave him there. He ran over, scooped up Mark Taylor, and draped him over his shoulders. Then he ran back down the hill and dumped the young man in the rescue vehicle. Bullets pinged off the ambulance roof as it sped away.

+ + +

12:03 PM

The news reports announced the school was being evacuated, information they gleaned from a police scanner.

Law enforcement dropped students off near Clement Park on the far side of the school's track field. Reporters from Channel 7 and other stations came down Rebel Hill to interview survivors from the library, including visibly distraught Crystal, Lindsay, and Rebecca.

"We were all in the library," Crystal told CNN, her mascara streaked from crying. "We started hearing shots in the hall. And then they came in and—they all told us to get under the desk and we all got under the desk and—" She gasped for breath, becoming more upset as she verbally relived the experience. "And then they just started coming in the library and opening fire and shooting off bombs…" She pushed a trembling hand through her blonde hair, sweeping it back from her face.

"Bombs," Rebecca echoed.

"The commons is right below," Lindsay said. She was calmer than Crystal but emphatic. In the background, one of the other girls wept. "And you'd just feel it shake, and plaster would fall, and the books would fall, and they came in here and they shot some and then they went back out and—"

She shook her head, trailing off. The camera moved to Crystal.

"People were getting shot all around me!" she exclaimed. She started to cry harder, curling one hand over her mouth. Rebecca hugged herself and cried too.

Lindsay continued: "There was one boy under the table right next to us—"

The camera swung back at her. "What's that?" the reporter prompted.

"There was a guy at a table right next to us—next to me and her," she motioned to Rebecca. "And they just shot him and then walked away and then he was just sitting there in a pool of blood."

"Soooo many people," Crystal sobbed, clutching her head.

Not far from them, ABC7 trained their camera on Brian Anderson. There was blood on his shirt where he'd been hit with shrapnel. He was out of breath and upset. Disgusted, even.

"…screaming after they'd shoot up something they'd go 'WOO!'… was just a pleasure for 'em. That's all it is."

The media let the students borrow their cellphones so they could call their families. Lindsay contacted her mother and then walked to a triage location nearby.

+ + +

12:04 PM

Paramedics John Aylward, Mark Gorman, and Monte Fleming, and emergency medical tech Jerry LoSasso scrambled to get victims loaded into ambulance 11 while the gunmen shot at them from the broken library windows. For LoSasso, a military veteran, it was like being back in Vietnam. Shattered glass rained down from above as the crew scrambled to reach the fallen victims. Aylward thought he was being hit with fire.

Anne Marie could smell her blood curdling in the hot sun as she lay helpless on the concrete. A rescue worker scooped her up and hustled her to an ambulance. She and Sean would need wheelchairs following life-saving surgery. The rescuers checked on Danny too, but determined he was dead and left him behind. They couldn't risk their lives for someone beyond help.

Lance saw someone rush by him. He was reluctant to move since he got shot the last time he did. But he decided to risk it and put his arm up.

"Help." It was all he could say. The left side of his face had been blown off and he was exhaling blood with each breath.

Fleming saw him and hurried over. Seeing his condition, the paramedic lifted the injured teen and ran. Lance tried to tell him to put him down, that he was fine, but Fleming tossed him into the back of the ambulance. Under fire, the paramedics hurried to check on Danny Rohrbough as well but left him where he was when they discovered he was dead. It was time to leave. The rescue workers put in frantic reports to dispatch that they were being shot at.

Deputy Walker saw a muzzle flash from a library window and targeted it, returning fire. Deputy Gardner fired three shots. From the cover of the grassy hill, Sergeant O'Shea, who had no prior shooting incidents, provided suppression fire with his Heckler-Koch 9mm submachine gun. While deputies exchanged fire with the shooters, the SWAT secured positions on rooftops of neighboring houses. Once the ambulances left, the gunfire from the library windows ceased.

+ + +

12:05 PM

The Channel 7 News helicopter started aerial coverage of the shooting.

At the Brown home, Brooks and his younger brother Aaron were reunited. While Aaron spent time on the phone asking people if they knew anything, Brooks watched news about the shooting. He saw a body near the outside stairs wearing clothes like he'd seen Rachel wearing earlier.

—

Arapahoe County Sheriff's Captain Bob Armstrong worked with the Jefferson County School District to have school buses transport evacuated students to Leawood Elementary. His office was also involved with explosive ordinance, perimeter control, response to local hospitals, and the investigation later. Littleton Police Department commander Bob Brandt coordinated the SWAT teams and deployed other SWAT members as they arrived. He asked Littleton Police Department Sergeant Bill Black to assist him.

+ + +

12:06 PM

When the hail of gunfire from the library stopped, Deputy Gardner turned his attention to the group of 15 students huddled behind a vehicle one car away from him. He evacuated them one at a time down the line of parked cars, over to the furthest from the school. As more people escaped, officers "leapfrogged" them to Gardner and other deputies to be rescued.

Triage at Caley Avenue and Yukon Street reported they had a victim who had been shot in the head. Rescue Squad 11 radioed that it was en route to the Swedish Medical Center with Anne Marie Hochhalter.

The first SWAT team, a group of 12 men led by Lieutenant Manwaring, arrived at the school on foot behind the commandeered firetruck. They reached Columbine's southeast side where Manwaring split the team in two.

+ + +

12:07 PM

Denver Police Sergeant Eugene Orton radioed Officer Greg Romero. "Is that body down by the door conscious or just staying there?"

"He's gonna stay there," Orton radioed back. "The one in the corner there that I can see."

"The one in front of the silver car, wearing a green shirt," Romero replied. "Yes."

They were talking about Danny Rohrbough.

—

LIBRARY

After nearly an hour of hiding, Carole Weld and Lois Kean left the RNN sound booth. Weld used her staff key to let them out of the studio into the kitchen. She crossed to the Audio-Visual room and saw a red shotgun shell on the floor. From the doorway to the library, she could see right through the destroyed trophy case. Beyond it a student was sprawled on the floor with a

134

hole in their back. She didn't know whether they were male or female, but she could see they were badly injured or dead. She went back to the kitchen and met up with Kean. Both women grabbed their purses and returned to the safety of the sound booth. Once they were locked in, Kean asked Weld if she knew Patti Nielson was hiding in the kitchen.

—

HALLWAY

Concerned about potential booby traps, Simmons' team stopped just outside the closed doors to the science hall. They released approximately 20 students from classrooms.

+++

12:08 PM – LIBRARY

The gunmen returned to the torn-up room. Their plan to blow up the school had failed. At the unsatisfying end of their suicide mission, they set a Molotov cocktail on a table in the southwest section and lit it. Then Eric sat down on the floor with his back to a bookshelf and put his sawed-off shotgun in his mouth. Dylan stood nearby with his TEC-DC9 pointed at his own head.

With two final shots, they died.

The Molotov's fuse burned hot enough to break the bottle. Flaming liquid spread over the tabletop. The small fire set off a smoke alarm directly above it and damaged the table's surface. Then it, too, died.

—

Patrick Ireland woke on the library floor to ringing in his ears. The fire alarms were going off. Alarm strobe lights flashed. He heard a male coughing somewhere to the east. There were no other sounds in the room. The coughing stopped.

135

Pat tried to crawl to the exit. Badly injured, he could only use his left arm and leg. He didn't get far before he passed out.

+ + +

12:10 PM – OFF CAMPUS

Captain Sandoval took command of the outer perimeter using Channel 5A. Captain O'Neil commanded the inner perimeter using Channel 5. Medical triage was officially established southwest of Columbine at Caley Avenue and Yukon Street, at the south entrance of Clement Park. Law enforcement had already taken several students there when they were evacuated from the school's south and west sides, so it made sense to stay there. First responders set up a second triage area on the school's east side after Command was informed remaining victims would be brought out that way.

—

INSIDE COLUMBINE

Teacher Theresa Miller had student Aaron Hancey call home to tell his mother he was okay. A few minutes later, Aaron handed the phone to her. His father had connected the call to an emergency dispatcher. For the rest of the time, they were trapped in the science room they would remain on the phone with 911. Student Melanie Poleschook listened to Miller give the dispatcher directions to the classroom from all the school's entrances.

+ + +

12:11 PM – OUTSIDE COLUMBINE

Rescuers evacuated A/C repairman Chris Clark from Columbine's roof.

+ + +

12:12 PM

Rescue Squad 13 radioed they were heading to the Swedish Medical Center with Sean Graves.

"It's a very bad situation," a reporter at the Yukon and Caley triage area solemnly told viewers. He went on to say that four or five students were being treated and some were bleeding extensively. The victims' identities were still unknown.

+ + +

12:14 PM

The Jefferson County, Denver, and Arapahoe County bomb squads arrived on scene and staged in the parking lot of Clement Park. Bomb technicians from Littleton Fire, the Bureau of Alcohol, Tobacco, and Firearms (ATF), and the Federal Bureau of Investigation (FBI) joined them. The initial response included 16 bomb techs. Some went to the suspects' homes. Some evaluated the divisionary explosives in the back field. Others neutralized explosives inside the school and provided safety information to other responders.

—

Lieutenant Manwaring's understanding of the layout of Columbine predated the 1995 renovations, which changed the floorplan. Mistakenly believing the cafeteria was still on the east side, he assigned Deputy Allen Simmons to take five SWAT officers in through the school's east entrance. Unaware that the shooters were already dead, the rest of the SWAT provided cover fire for Simmons' group.

Kleinschmidt drove the firetruck as close to the school as possible to provide shelter for Simmons' team. As the SWAT neared the east entrance, they saw a pair of hands press against an office window and then disappear. The team contacted dispatch to tell them there was a possible hostage situation.

Jefferson County crime lab dispatched a mobile crime laboratory unit to the scene.

+ + +

12:15 PM

A news helicopter landed in Clement Park to pick up JCSO Sergeant Phil Domenico so he could do aerial surveillance. He stayed in the helicopter for the next several hours watching Columbine's roof and the surrounding area.

Sergeant Hy at the Pierce Street command post reported a possible shooter and hostages at the main entrance. Moments later, a lone student emerged from that entrance with his hands on his head. He ran to the firetruck. Officers patted him down and checked him for injuries and then put him in the back of the emergency vehicle's cab. They couldn't evacuate him since they had no transport or cover other than the firetruck. The boy told officials he was the only one in the office area when he left.

With Simmons' team inside and the potential hostage situation resolved, Manwaring led the rest of the SWAT around the building behind the firetruck. Their goal was the west entrance where they knew there were "bodies down" and active gunfire. The grounds were soaked from recent rains, which made it difficult to drive the heavy vehicle at a walking pace.

Meanwhile, bomb technician Sergeant Euchler heard on the radio that the ACSO bomb squad was sent to the area south of Wadsworth, between Chatfield and Ken Caryl. He headed that way.

—

The Jefferson County Victim Services Unit assigned personnel to the Columbine Public Library to provide aid to the students and parents who were gathering there. Media outlets around the world flooded the city with calls as news quickly spread. Internet forums blew up with questions no one had the

138

answers to. The first "fake news" reports begin to circulate online: It was a military operation. It was the gay Alamo. Bikers were responsible. News outlets saw the posts, took them as facts, and reported them as such.

+ + +

12:17 PM

Deputy Byerly reported to dispatch that a male in a white shirt and black pants was walking outside the school's west side. Officials contacted the armed man at gunpoint. Larry Scott Petty Jr. had heard about the shooting on TV and ran through Clement Park to the school. He was carrying a .22 caliber airsoft/BB rifle and had a knife strapped to his leg. He was taken into custody by Agent Randy McNitt.

Petty, who had a minor criminal history of larceny, criminal trespass, and false reporting, told deputies he was there because he wanted to help the police. He was tested on-scene for gunshot residue by the FBI (negative result) and then interviewed. The deputies determined he was not involved in the shooting. He was released without charges.

+ + +

12:18 PM

Yukon/Caley triage area requested 10 ambulances for 11 patients. Four were in critical condition, four serious, and three stable.

+ + +

12:21 PM

Lance Kirklin was taken from triage to Denver Health Medical Center. He was accompanied by Detective John Healy, who assisted the paramedic by providing Lance airbag ventilation to assist his breathing. The injured teen was in a semi-conscious state, unable to communicate. Head and neck surgeon Steven Batuello performed the first life-saving surgery on him. Lance would have to undergo approximately 34 more surgeries in the following months.

+ + +

12:22 PM

An Air Life helicopter landed in Clement Park.

A student who escaped the school was interviewed on scene by a news reporter. The survivor said the shooters were part of the "TCM" and were getting revenge.

+ + +

12:25 PM

Mark Taylor was taken to University Hospital.

"I'm looking at a dead man," the surgeon said when he examined the critically injured teen. Mark wasn't expected to survive, but miraculously, he did.

—

Jefferson County officials were advised by dispatch to tell parents of Columbine students to go to Leawood Elementary School for information about their missing children. JeffCo counselors were also sent to the school to provide support to stressed families.

Meanwhile, Sergeant Euchler was still trying to find his bomb squad. They had cleared from the Wadsworth location before he could reach them. He contacted dispatch to find out where to go and was told by Investigator Singleton to head to Coal Mine Road and South Pierce Street.

—

LIBRARY

Jeanna woke in agony on the library floor. She struggled to her feet and started toward the exit, checking the computer lab for her sister Kathy on the way. She didn't find her, so she left the building. Outside, she got herself to the squad cars where she collapsed. Roughly 40 other people were hunkered down there. Jeanna had lost a lot of blood and was getting weaker by the second. The other students comforted her and told her she would be okay. She and Valeen were sent west to the athletic shed. Val's middle was bleeding badly. Jeanna was missing a large portion of her shoulder. Bree assisted her, tying a jacket around Jeanna's leg to slow her blood loss and talking about prom to keep her awake. It would be four days before Bree slept again.

Evan and Ryan were taken from behind the shed to the cul-de-sac where the first triage station was. Neither was injured, so they walked to Ryan's house nearby where Evan called his family to let them know he was safe.

Deputy Searle and other officers took cover behind Deputy Taborsky's patrol car. Another police unit pulled up. Deputy Smoker put Mike Johnson, Kacey Ruegsegger, and two other injured students in the vehicle so they could be taken to triage. In a panic, the patrolman accidentally shut the door on Kacey before she was fully inside, adding to her pain. When that cruiser left another officer pulled up to collect Jeanna and the other wounded teens. The squad cars were only taking the injured at the time. There was no room for other survivors.

+ + +

12:26 PM – TRIAGE

Mike Johnson was taken from triage to St. Anthony's Hospital. Dr. Winston Tripp treated him for six gunshot wounds, one of which paralyzed his leg.

The media announced there were eight victims and two shooters.

+ + +

12:27 PM

Jeanna Park was transported to Denver Health Medical Center. Kacey Ruegsegger was taken to St. Anthony's Hospital where Dr. Dury reported her injuries to the police. The bone that was destroyed by shotgun fire doctors replaced with a cadaver bone.

+ + +

12:28 PM – OFF CAMPUS

With the help of a local news station, Jefferson County School District announced a parent hotline had been established.

+ + +

12:30 PM – OFF CAMPUS

A SORT (Special Operations Response Team) was dispatched to Leawood Elementary where evacuees were being taken, and parents and the media were beginning to gather. Normally the SORT team managed jail disturbances and crowd control.

—

Chris and Cory headed to Columbine in Chris' car to check on their friends. They couldn't reach the school, so they stopped by a nearby IHOP they often hung out at. They didn't find their friends there. While they were out Chris received several calls on his pager. The two teens went back to the Friesen residence where he tried to return calls to everyone. One was from his girlfriend Nicole. When Chris phoned her, she said she was at the IHOP. He and Cory drove back to the restaurant, this time in Cory's truck because Chris' car was starting to overheat. By the time they got there, she'd already left. They found her at her house.

"Thank God you're safe!" Chris said as he ran up to her.

He told her he was going to call the police to tell them who he thought was behind the attack. He and Cory drove back to the Friesen residence so they could make phone calls and wait for information about Cory's dad Kent.

Chris' mother worked for the Cherry Hills Police Department. When she paged him, Chris called her back and told her what was going on. She had him speak to a Cherry Hills detective who said he would pass the information to the proper authorities. After he got off the phone, Chris tried the Jefferson County Sheriff's Office again and was able to get through to Investigator Tom Acierno. He told Acierno who he thought the suspects might be. The investigator told him to stay at the Friesen house so the police could come and speak with him.

+ + +

12:31 PM – OUTSIDE COLUMBINE

Valeen Schnurr was taken from triage to the Swedish Medical Center where she faced the first of multiple surgeries to remove 34 pellets and shrapnel from her body. Four bullets would remain in her permanently.

—

Lieutenant Manwaring's SWAT team reached the school's north side.

+ + +

12:36 PM – OUTSIDE COLUMBINE

Manwaring's team got to the school's west upper level and saw two people down outside the destroyed entrance. One, Richard Castaldo, painfully waved an arm for help.

The team reported the situation and, using the firetruck to shield them, they moved in. They wanted to get as close to the victims as possible before attempting a rescue. The wet turf made it impossible to get right next to them as the truck got mired. Its tires spun and sprayed mud. They had to leave it at the sidewalk and brave the last few feet without cover.

Ducking down, Captain Vincent DiManna and Lieutenant Pat Phelan hurried to rescue the victims. Sergeant O'Shea, Officer Bloodworth, and two other officers provided cover fire. Deputy Taborsky also covered them from behind his patrol car nearby. DiManna carried a riot shield while O'Shea fired four suppression shots, unaware the gunmen were already dead. Some of their shots ricocheted back at them, bouncing off the exterior walls of the school and making them think they were under fire.

Phelan grabbed Richard and dragged him by his ankles to the end of the firetruck furthest from the school. The team lifted him up and put him on the bumper. The boy was unconscious and breathing shallowly. The rescuers could see he had bullet wounds in his chest.

+ + +

12:38 PM

Fearing attack from the shattered west entrance, Manwaring's team waited before attempting to rescue Rachel Scott. The only man with a riot shield went first while the others, joined by an armed officer already on the scene, provided cover. The rescuing official took Rachel by the arm and leg and dragged her back behind the firetruck. He didn't get very far before he realized she was dead. He dropped her.

+ + +

12:39 PM – OFF CAMPUS

JCSO's Command 500 bus arrived and set up on Pierce Street. The vehicle was equipped with a mobile dispatch center. It made it easier for Lieutenant Walcher and the command post team to coordinate 47 different agencies. Sergeant Hy assisted dispatchers with managing the information flow from the scene to headquarters.

+ + +

12:40 PM

Dan Steepleton was transported to Littleton Hospital.

SWAT discovered the gas leak in the science room. Public Service Company was contacted and brought to the scene to shut off the main valve as soon as the area was deemed safe.

Sergeant Euchler arrived at Coal Mine and Pierce, but the ACSO bomb squad was nowhere to be found. Checking in, he learned they were staged at Leawood Elementary. He headed down South Pierce to a checkpoint at West Weaver Avenue where he was directed to the Columbine's south side. When he arrived, he saw officers with long guns, shotguns, and handguns out, all behind cover. Euchler pulled over and flagged down a JCSO sergeant to ask him how to get to the bomb squad staging area. The sergeant told him the squad was at Leawood Elementary down the next street, West Fair Drive.

"Gun it and make a right," he told Euchler.

+ + +

12:41 PM –COLUMBINE

Students trapped in the school used their cell phones to contact their families and to call the police. When they got busy signals from 911, some phoned local television stations instead and were put on the news live.

One news station mistakenly aired a message urging students who escaped to call the Jefferson County Sheriff's Office to report their safety. Incoming calls flooded the lines, jamming them until JSCO contacted the station and got them to run another broadcast that told people to contact the hotline instead.

Jefferson County SWAT team commanded by Sergeant Barry Williams arrived at the command post on Pierce.

145

+ + +

12:43 PM – INSIDE COLUMBINE

Deputy Allen Simmons' SWAT team cleared classrooms in Columbine's east side. With many rooms to search, he split his six-man team in two then radioed a request for additional SWAT. The school was in lockdown, so each room had to be broken into and searched for victims and suspects before they could move on. The noise from the fire alarms was so loud, they had to communicate by hand signals. They couldn't hear any sounds of movement, so they had to assume a gunman could be anywhere. JeffCo communication center instructed officials to treat all students as suspects since the shooters could have changed clothes and might be trying to leave with the rescued students.

+ + +

12:44 PM – TRIAGE

Makai Hall was transported to Littleton Hospital.

—

INSIDE COLUMBINE

Students with Coach Sanders made telephone contact with an EMT dispatcher, who reported it to the authorities.

+ + +

12:45 PM – OFF CAMPUS

At least 150 mental health workers and victim advocates went to meet with parents whose children had not yet been found.

Lists of student names were posted with information about whether they were at Leawood Elementary or Columbine Public Library. But the lists were incomplete, causing more panic and frustration for parents. As an added complication, many students fled to neighboring homes and locations and never set foot in either the library or the elementary school. Officials had no idea where those kids were, or what condition they were in. Eventually, lists of students in hospitals would be posted.

—

OUTSIDE COLUMBINE

Deputy Taborsky pulled his patrol car up to the firetruck outside Columbine's west entrance. He had already transported other wounded survivors from the area to triage and knew where to go. Two SWAT team members moved the critically injured Richard into his patrol car. Rachel was dead, so they left her on the grass. They made a try for Danny next, unaware that the boy at bottom of the stairs was dead too.

+ + +

12:50 PM – TRIAGE

Nicole Nowlen was transported to Lutheran Medical Center where she was dubbed a "miracle girl" because she survived a close-range shotgun blast. She'd been hit with nine buckshot pellets, three of which went through her. Surgeons were only able to remove one remaining pellet. She would be sent home the next day with five still in her midsection. It was the second time in her life Nicole defied the odds. She was born 13 weeks premature, weighing only 2 pounds 4 ounces.

—

OUTSIDE COLUMBINE

Sergeant O'Shea and the SWAT team closed in on Danny's body at the base of the outdoor stairs. O'Shea provided cover fire while other officers checked on the victim. Finding him dead, they returned to the firetruck without him. They passed the news to Taborsky who sped Richard away to the triage point.

—

Sergeant Williams commandeered a front-end loader from a nearby construction site for cover to move into position near Columbine's west side. Two team members were deployed to gain "high ground" on rooftops of houses on Polk Avenue, the first street south of the school. They would have a clear view of the south parking lot, library, and cafeteria from there. The rest of the team went to the school's northwest corner, shielded by the front-end loader. When they got there, Manwaring's team informed Williams' team that students had been shot, numerous bombs had detonated, and the number of suspects was unknown. Williams' team was also informed that Simmons had taken a team in through the east.

—

Sergeant Euchler was still trying to find the bomb squad. He got to West Fair Drive and Marshall Court where he contacted two Denver police officers. He asked them where Leawood Elementary was, but neither of them knew. Euchler found it in his map book and headed that way. When he arrived at Leawood Drive and Jay Court, he found the street full of cars. He spoke to a uniformed motorcycle officer who was directing traffic. The officer recommended he turn around and stage at the end of Leawood Drive. Euchler found a parking spot in the sea of cars and went looking for his team. He found the ACSO bomb squad truck. When he arrived, he was told to bring his car into the parking lot south of Clement Park.

+++

12:51 PM

The media reported several local schools were in lockdown. "No one goes in, no one goes out."

—

When they rescued Richard, Manwaring's team saw an undetonated bomb next to the west entrance doors. The device was constructed from a one-gallon propane tank with nails and buckshot duct taped to it. Manwaring decided to use the firetruck to ram the already-damaged doors to provide access for his team.

"If the bomb goes off," thought Manwaring. "Maybe the firetruck can take the brunt of the bomb blast since it's carrying about 1,000 gallons of water."

However, due to the recent spring rains, the emergency vehicle got stuck in the mud. The more Kleinschmidt tried, the deeper the firetruck sank.

+ + +

12:52 PM

Parents were told they could pick up uninjured students at Leawood Elementary School.

+ + +

12:57 PM

Austin contacted his family from behind a police car. He was transported to triage shortly afterward where he received first aid in preparation for transport to the hospital. When his father arrived, the man was so frantic he vaulted over a fence to get to his son. Shot in the hand and knee, Austin collapsed in his father's arms as shock gave way to horror.

"They killed Corey!" he told his dad. Then he broke down sobbing.

—

TRIAGE

Austin Eubanks and Jennifer Doyle were transported to Littleton Hospital.

+ + +

1:00 PM – COLUMBINE

More students were freed from downstairs areas where the shooters hadn't been. The SWAT team was getting conflicting reports about where the gunmen were. They checked the auditorium, where they forced open locked storage room doors. Terrified people were hiding everywhere, and no one was going to answer a knock.

+ + +

1:03 PM — TRIAGE

Paramedics had Nick on a gurney and were wheeling him to a waiting ambulance. The senior was distraught, grabbing at his head.

"Excuse me," he said insistently. "Where's my brother?"

The female paramedic to his left tried to reassure him. "Your— your brother will be okay."

That wasn't good enough. Nick sat up like he was thinking about hopping off the gurney, demanding: "Where is my brother?"

"No! Calm down!" The paramedic pushed him back down.

The other paramedic, a male, moved her hand off the teen then addressed Nick.

"We don't know where your brother is but they're gonna find him."

150

"He's my twin, man!" Nick said. "My twin!"

"I know," the paramedic replied. "They're going to find him."

They loaded him into the ambulance despite his protests and took him to Littleton Hospital.

+ + +

1:04 PM

Richard Castaldo was taken to the Swedish Medical Center.

+ + +

1:05 PM – OFF CAMPUS

Arapahoe County Sheriff's Office sent investigators to the Swedish Medical Center.

+ + +

1:09 PM – OUTSIDE COLUMBINE

The SWAT outside needed to get to the library, one of the "hot zones". Because there was a live bomb at the west entrance, they decided the best point of entry was through the cafeteria beneath the library. The cafeteria was another "hot zone". A window in the staff lounge provided access. One by one they went in, greeted by the deafening sound and strobing lights of the fire alarm. Three inches of water had seeped under the closed door from the cafeteria. They secured the lounge and opened the door.

The sight was surreal. The common area was destroyed. Smoke made the air hazy, pressed downward by the sprinkler system. Water stood nearly four inches deep. The sprinklers continued to rain down on the scorched room. Acoustic tiles and exposed wire dangled from the blackened ceiling. There were melted and toppled chairs scattered about. Hundreds of abandoned backpacks were scattered on the floor. Shoes and paper floated in the water.

Williams' team split up. Part of the group went to the auditorium while the other half stayed at the cafeteria entrance to secure it and cover those going into the warzone. They wouldn't enter the flooded room for another 36 minutes. They heard hissing and spraying from the cafeteria, and believed they smelled natural gas. Williams was concerned a gas line had burst. So, they circled around to the kitchen.

—

TRIAGE

Lindsay and Rebecca weren't injured, so they walked to the triage site. Lindsay was looking for her younger brother Chase. He wasn't there, but Lindsay kept Mark Kintgen company while he was waiting for paramedics to treat his injuries. Once they got him stabilized, they transported him to Denver Health Medical Center. Rebecca's mother picked her up. Lindsay eventually got a ride to Leawood Elementary School where her youth minister from Lakewood Church of Christ gave her a ride home. Her brother was found safe, having fled his Geometry class when the shooting started.

+ + +

1:11 PM

Brian Anderson was sent to Lutheran Hospital. Triage at Yukon and Caley reported that all the injured there were transported.

+ + +

1:18 PM – INSIDE COLUMBINE

Deputy Simmons' half of the SWAT team evacuated 30 people from classrooms in the upper-level south hall. The survivors

152

were sent down to the teachers' lounge and out the broken window.

+ + +

1:22 PM – OUTSIDE COLUMBINE

Arapahoe County SWAT arrived on the scene.

+ + +

1:26 PM – INSIDE COLUMBINE

Sergeant Williams' SWAT team found students hiding in kitchen storage rooms, terrified and up to their ankles in water. They were slow to respond to SWAT commands to evacuate. The officials wore black uniforms and carried weapons like the shooters had. Roughly 30 students were evacuated, including Matthew Depew and Emily Wyant's twin sister Lindsay. Custodians Gallentine and Curtis were freed from the walk-in coolers.

The SWAT team sent them to the staff lounge in a single-file line. From there they were sent out the window. Officials thought the shooters might try to escape by changing their clothes to blend in, so they checked everyone who left the building for weapons as well as injuries. The scene was one of the first to get widespread airplay on national news. As a baffled nation looked on, students streamed out the broken window in the lounge only to be forced away with their hands on their heads by men in black fatigues armed with automatic weapons. It looked as though they were being taken prisoner by terrorists.

No one knew what was happening, but everyone who saw the shocking footage knew they were seeing something big.

—

Once out of the school, freed students were ordered to run single file up the outside stairs past Danny's body, then past the destroyed west entrance where they had to jump over

153

Rachel's body. After seeing several students hop over her body, two deputies dragged the dead girl by her arms across the sidewalk and behind the fire engine. They left Danny where he was.

+ + +

1:30 PM

Williams' team moved from the cafeteria to the school's second level. Close to where they were, the sign in the window: "1 BLEEDING TO DEATH" was still up. The SWAT team was told about the sign and that the room had a bloody rag tied to the handle. But seeing pipe bomb fragments, the team proceeded cautiously.

+ + +

HARRIS RESIDENCE

ASCO Sergeants Richard Euchler and Scott Linne were sent to South Reed Street, the home of Eric Harris. A strong odor of something like gasoline had been detected inside the house and in the garage.

+ + +

1:35 – OFF CAMPUS

Captain Leuthauser was assigned to Leawood Elementary, the station for students rescued from Columbine High School. The Columbine Public Library was chosen as the gathering point for parents. Sergeant D. Jones was assigned to search Columbine's grounds for bombs, supervising plain-clothes detectives. DEA agents arrived to assist. Jones was joined by Agents Mike Pope, Todd Gregory, and others. A bomb dog was ordered to the scene.

+ + +

1:40 PM – TRIAGE

Makai Hall was airlifted by Air Life from Littleton Hospital to St. Anthony's Hospital. Dr. Charles Rowland operated on him. He removed one projectile from Makai's leg but left another as it was imbedded in the leg bone and removing it wasn't medically necessary.

Students rescued from the school who weren't in desperate need of medical attention were routed to detectives to be interviewed and debriefed.

+++

1:44 PM – OUTSIDE COLUMBINE

Three individuals dressed in black were detained by authorities in the field behind Columbine. Their clothing seemed to fit the descriptions of the shooters. News cameras captured the developing situation and aired it live, causing public speculation about their involvement.

The group identified themselves as the "Splatter Punks" – Matt Nalty/Christianson, Matt Akard, and James "Jim" Brunetti. None were Columbine students. They said they showed up out of curiosity after hearing about the shootings from Brunetti's sister, who was watching the news. The three were cleared and released the same day. They were reinterviewed on April 24 and found to have no association with the shooters or the Trench Coat Mafia.

+++

1:45 PM – INSIDE COLUMBINE

Sergeant Williams' SWAT team entered the flooded cafeteria. They moved carefully, single file, with a rolling bullet-proof riot shield in front of them. Once they cleared half the room, a second team followed and secured the stairwell.

—

155

OUTSIDE COLUMBINE

A Denver Mobile Command post arrived at the scene. The Salvation Army arrived to set up food service for first responders. They were directed to Leawood and Pierce. Commanders established a secondary overflow site for students and parents at Calvary Church located at Pierce and Ottawa.

Meanwhile, Jefferson County sniper Dennis Beery was stationed on a house roof south of Columbine saw the "1 BLEEDING TO DEATH" sign and radioed it in. Continuing phone calls from teachers Al Cram, Kent Freisen, and Theresa Miller kept Command up to date about Sanders' worsening condition. Dispatchers kept telling them help would be there "in 20 minutes". SWAT was told the room he was in had a rag tied to the handle so they could find it easily.

—

HARRIS RESIDENCE

Sergeant Euchler and Sergeant Linne arrived at the Harris home. Sheridan Lieutenant John Iantorno was already on the scene with other officers, along with Littleton Fire 12. Iantorno confirmed there was a strong odor of gasoline and told the sergeants the house had not been cleared.

Euchler contacted the fire department to have them shut off power and natural gas to the property. He and Linne approached the home. Even from outside they could smell gasoline. They checked the upper level with an AIM 3250 gas meter. While investigating, they heard a noise in the basement and requested backup. Iantorno and another officer joined them. The group checked it out but found the basement empty. They decided it must have been wind.

Euchler and Linne located possible explosive devices in Eric's room as well as bomb-making components. Then they checked the garage. Euchler ordered everyone out when the AIM meter alerted an explosive atmosphere. They had to fall back and request additional assistance before they could proceed.

—

Police investigation of their home forced the Harrises to relocate. Their attorney contacted Private Investigator H. Ellis Armistead to protect them from the press and help if they needed any investigation done on their behalf. Armistead, who assisted Oklahoma City bomber Timothy McVeigh during his appeals process, booked a room at the Warwick Hotel for Wayne and Kathy Harris under his name. Once they were checked in, he went to visit them. Entering the room, he found Kathy curled up in a fetal position on the bed sobbing. Wayne was seated in a chair with his head in his hands.

Wayne rose and shook hands with Armistead. Harris was visibly angry at his son and worried about the victims and their families. About Eric he said: "Just flush him!"

Despite the scathing remark, Armistead would come to know the Harrises quite well over the next few months as two of the nicest people he'd met.

+ + +

2:00 PM – OUTSIDE COLUMBINE

Lieutenant Kriefer arrived with bomb dogs and was assigned to coordinate with Sergeant Jones. Law enforcement noticed media arriving at the staging area.

+ + +

2:08 PM – INSIDE COLUMBINE

Students were evacuated from the Technology Lab on the first floor.

—

OFF CAMPUS

JCSO police arrived at the Friesen residence where they had Chris empty his pockets before placing him in handcuffs. They transported him to Clement Park and put him in a van where he was questioned by officials. Following the questioning they took him to the Sheriff's Office.

+ + +

2:10 PM – HARRIS RESIDENCE

JCSO Deputy Glen Grove arrived at the Harris home, joining Sergeants Linne and Euchler and other officers. Using bunker gear and air packs, they entered the garage. They found two large red and black jugs of AMF lane conditioner and a bottle of SoftSoap in a plastic crate. Determining the garage door was safe to open, they ventilated the area to dispel the explosive atmosphere.

+ + +

2:11 PM – OUTSIDE COLUMBINE

Officer Wayne Depew provided information about the possible location of the suspects.

+ + +

2:15 PM

SWAT positioned on a roof across the street from the school reported seeing the sign in the upstairs window: "1 BLEEDING TO DEATH".

The Eplings still hadn't heard from their son Nathan. Worried, they asked Kristi to find him. She went to the Columbine Public Library to look for him. She didn't find him there, but he was eventually located safe and uninjured.

+ + +

2:17 PM – INSIDE COLUMBINE

Williams split his team up so they could clear the computer and business classrooms. They freed two more people.

+ + +

2:19 PM – OFF CAMPUS

Parents of Columbine students were sent to Leawood Elementary to wait for buses to drop off evacuated kids. Bus after bus came and went. Some families were reunited while others had to wait and hope the next bus would bring their missing child.

+ + +

2:24 PM - TRIAGE

Adam Kyler was transported to Littleton Hospital.

—

INSIDE COLUMBINE

The SWAT team forced open the locked office closet in the Music room. Among the choir robes they found roughly 60 students hiding. The teens were so terrified, they refused to respond to officials and wouldn't leave the closet. Like the kitchen survivors, many had seen the black combat fatigues and boots the shooters wore. The SWAT wore the same type of clothing. The traumatized kids thought they were the people who had been shooting up the school.

+ + +

2:25 PM – OUTSIDE COLUMBINE

Lieutenant Ryan advised command of the removal of a DOA student. Metro SWAT was assigned to assist with removal.

+ + +

2:26 PM – LIBRARY

Pat Ireland had come to and blacked out several times over the past two and half hours as he slowly dragged himself across the floor. He didn't see anyone else moving. He lost consciousness again. When he woke, he decided to try for the window to the west. It was closer than the exit. He was afraid the shooters would come back at any moment. As he continued his agonized crawl, Pat noticed his right shoe was missing. He had no idea when or where he lost it.

He had to shove chairs out of his way to get to the window. As he did, he passed a blond kid lying under the south computer table who wasn't moving. A blue chair pushed up against the wall gave Pat a way to reach the window ledge. He swept broken glass from the sill with his functioning arm, his movements weak from blood loss. Though he wasn't feeling any pain at the time from his life-threatening wounds the effort made him black out again.

From the Channel 7 helicopter Sergeant Phil Domenico spotted the boy trying to climb out a broken window on the second floor. Pat had regained consciousness and in a desperate bid to save his own life hauled himself up onto the windowsill.

+ + +

2:29 PM – HARRIS RESIDENCE

Jefferson County deputies and bomb technicians responded to the Harris residence to investigate.

+ + +

2:30 PM – INSIDE COLUMBINE

Sergeant Williams' SWAT team cleared the cafeteria stairs. Upstairs, they saw Simmons' team clearing rooms to the east. There was a rag tied to the handle of one classroom door. Painted alongside the door were the words: "SCIENCE ROOMS".

The stairs opened to an intersection between two hallways. One led west to the library. Straight ahead and east were the science and foreign language halls. There was broken glass everywhere. The carpet was burnt where a pipe bomb had exploded. A large puddle of blood stained the floor and splashed across a nearby window. A trail of blood led from the puddle to one of the science rooms. There was live ammunition and spent casings scattered on the floor. It was a nightmare.

—

OFF CAMPUS

Casualties began to arrive at two local hospitals. Five people suffering from serious gunshot wounds were taken to the Swedish Medical Centre in Denver.

—

INSIDE COLUMBINE – LIBRARY

Lisa lay on the floor bleeding. She kept track of time by listening to the class period bells. Just before the 2:30 bell she tried to get up, but she got light-headed. Her wrist was broken, and she couldn't move her arms. She heard the bell go off. It didn't stop this time. It just kept on ringing. With great effort she crawled out from under the table and made it halfway to the next one before she passed out.

+ + +

2:33 PM – OFF CAMPUS

During a scheduled news conference about the American economy, President Bill Clinton addressed the Columbine shooting.

"Ladies and gentlemen," he said, his genial face uncharacteristically grim. "Let me begin by saying… we all know there has been a terrible shooting at a high school in Littleton, Colorado. Because the situation, as I left to come out

161

here, apparently is ongoing, I think it would be inappropriate for me to say anything other than I hope the American people will be praying for the students, the parents, and the teachers and we'll wait for events to unfold and then there'll be more to say."

+ + +

2:38 PM – OUTSIDE COLUMBINE

SWAT moved to rescue Patrick. Slipping in and out of consciousness, using his good leg he rolled out onto the ledge where he dangled with nothing to land on below but concrete. He heard someone screaming but he couldn't understand what they were saying. Then he heard someone shout "stay". He was confused; he couldn't see who was yelling at him. With news cameras capturing everything, the SWAT moved in under the cover of an armored unit to get to Pat before he fell. He stayed where he was until he heard someone call to him again.

"It's okay to jump!"

The critically injured boy leaned forward and fell out of the window, into the arms of rescuers.

—

In SCI-3, students with Coach Sanders gave up waiting for help and snapped the legs off a table to make a gurney. They were going to drag him out themselves.

+ + +

2:39 PM

Patrick Ireland, "the boy in the window", was transported to St. Anthony Central Hospital. A few minutes after 3 p.m. he arrives to undergo the first of 35 surgeries. With critical gunshot wounds to the head, arm, and foot, he was unable to move his right side and was suffering from slow mentation. An hour into surgery doctors discover one bullet entered his skull while another diverted around to the back of his head.

162

+ + +

2:40 PM – INSIDE COLUMBINE

40 students were evacuated from the choir room.

—

HARRIS RESIDENCE

With the air so toxic and volatile, Littleton Fire shut off gas and electricity to the Harris home.

+ + +

2:42 PM – INSIDE COLUMBINE

Sergeant Williams' SWAT team finally made it to SCI-3 where students were hiding behind a barricade of tables flipped on their sides. When they entered, teacher Al Cram tried to tell them about Sanders, but they saw him holding a fire extinguisher and pointed their guns at him. They ordered him to lay face down. One put a gun to his head while others frisked him. They asked him if he had a master key to the doors, so he gave them his keyring which also had his house keys and car key, and a brass fob that said: "The Brass Ass". They split him away from the students. Though he wanted to ensure that they got out of the school safely, he wasn't allowed to stay with them.

Kevin Starkey and Aaron Hancey were still with Sanders, who lay in a large puddle of blood. SWAT radioed for medical assistance to be sent in for the coach. The students had finished their makeshift gurney to move Sanders with, but the SWAT team wouldn't let them use it. They made the students and teachers put their hands on their head and form a line. Aaron and Kevin were reluctant to leave Sanders, but they had no choice. One SWAT member led the survivors out. Another officer stayed with Sanders, applying pressure to his wounds and talking to him until the other officer returned.

Outside the east entrance, two Littleton paramedics were geared up with a gurney, waiting for the signal to enter the school. But the science section wasn't cleared. It was considered too dangerous to send them through that entrance. Williams asked for a paramedic to come from the west side as the route through the cafeteria was clear and protected by Denver SWAT.

+ + +

2:47 PM

The SWAT team rescued approximately 60 people from the science area. They frisked the kids and faculty two to three times, some as many as five times, before sending them downstairs. The whole world watched in horror as kids were herded out at gunpoint through the broken window in the teachers' lounge, their hands on their heads.

+ + +

3:00 PM – OUTSIDE COLUMBINE

Mary Baribeau, Nick Foss, Tim Kastle, and Josh Lapp were interviewed at the scene by Channel 7 News.

—

The two SWAT members with Sanders realized help wasn't coming or couldn't get in. They needed to evacuate him themselves or at least get him closer to an exit route. They decided to take him downstairs and out through the faculty lounge. Putting Sanders in a rolling chair to make it easier to move him, they pushed him through the northern storage room. That's when Denver paramedic Troy Laman arrived. He checked the injured man and found no pulse. Despite the valiant efforts of Columbine's students and faculty, Sanders died from blood loss three hours after he was shot. A student who had been with him said Sanders' last words were: "Tell my family I love them."

+ + +

3:15 PM – INSIDE COLUMBINE

The men with Coach Sanders rejoined their SWAT team to continue searching the science wing. They found 50-60 more students and two staff members hiding in the darkened rooms. SWAT evacuated and sent them out of the now-secure east side.

+++

3:20 – OUTSIDE COLUMBINE

An armored carrier unit arrived on scene. Bomb squads discovered additional explosives. The sheriff's office orders people in the neighborhood south of Columbine to evacuate until the area is declared safe.

—

INSIDE COLUMBINE

When the science area was clear, the SWAT team moved to the hall where the library was—the last room left to be checked. They reported bullet holes in windows, broken glass, bomb fragments and shrapnel on the floor, and a pipe bomb embedded in the wall outside the library. The glass trophy cases in the hall were broken and looking into the room through the shattered hall windows the SWAT could see bodies on the floor.

+++

3:22 PM - LIBRARY

Lisa heard yelling from the hall, different than that of the shooters. It sounded like the police, and they were in a hurry. Four members of Williams' SWAT team had reached the library. The injured girl called out for help. The four officers had to step over bodies and bombs to reach her. They reassured her and called for paramedics. One officer stayed with Lisa while the others picked their way to each of the other victims. Eventually she learned she was the only one left alive in the library.

165

+++

3:25 PM – HARRIS RESIDENCE

Investigators found live bombs and gasoline in the home, particularly in Eric's basement room. Neighboring houses were evacuated.

+++

3:26 PM – INSIDE COLUMBINE

SWAT command met at the east entrance to discuss follow-up sweeps of the school and the replenishment of the teams with fresh members from other agencies. Simmons' team finished clearing the gymnasium and weight room. From there they entered the library hall. Williams' team was still clearing that room.

+++

3:27 PM - LIBRARY

Teacher Peggy Dodd heard voices and footsteps in the library. She peeked out the window in the magazine room door and seeing helmeted SWAT officers she came out with her hands up. One told her to walk behind him and to look only at the back of his helmet. She did as he instructed, something she would be grateful for later when she learned about the bloodbath she had passed. Shaking uncontrollably, she was evacuated, put into an armored vehicle, and interviewed by officials.

+++

3:30 PM

Carole Weld and Lois Kean came out of hiding and went to the library kitchen.

"Patti?" Kean said. "Are you still in there?"

Both women called for her to come out. Then Weld continued to the A/V room where she was spotted by a SWAT member in the hall outside the library.

"Are you staff?" the man asked.

Weld said they were.

"How many persons are there?"

"Three," said Weld.

She was including Patti Nielson, who was still hiding in the kitchen. Over three hours after her desperate call to 911, risking her life to provide details of the assault in progress, no police came to the rescue. She was left to climb out on her own and join the small group of teachers who were leaving the library. SWAT said the suspects hadn't been apprehended yet and the building was full of bombs. The leader told them to put their hands on their heads and keep them there. Kent Friesen and Al Cram came out of the science area and joined them. They were taken downstairs, through the cafeteria, and out the west doors. Weld had to step over Danny Rohrbough's body.

—

Upstairs, the SWAT team found the shooters' bodies heaped near each other in the southwest portion of the library. Eric was slumped against a bookshelf, his sawed-off shotgun between his legs. Dylan was lying on the floor with the TEC-DC9 in his left hand. His shotgun was near his foot. The rifle was on the floor between them. Both were armed with several weapons. There were numerous explosives scattered on the floor. Blood darkened the carpet beneath and around them.

Williams reported the grim findings to Command: 12 DOA, 2 self-inflicted. The males with self-inflicted gunshot wounds matched the descriptions of the suspects. Because of the number of explosives in the library, the SWAT team ordered everyone out and called for the bomb squad. And though the bodies of the shooters had been found, there were reports of possible additional gunmen. Officers were unsure if other shooters were hiding inside the school or escaped.

—

OUTSIDE COLUMBINE

The bomb squad was called in to sweep Columbine High.

+ + +

3:36 PM – INSIDE COLUMBINE

SWAT team initial responders were replaced by a fresh team.

+ + +

3:37 PM – LIBRARY

Paramedic Laman went to the library. He was warned by SWAT not to move anyone because the bodies might be booby-trapped. He carefully touched several people, checking for signs of life, before finding Lisa. He asked her if she was hurt, then rolled her onto her injured shoulder, inadvertently causing her excruciating pain. After strapping her to a backboard, he removed her shoes and took off her Eeyore watch, tossing it into one of them.

"We have to get her out of here in a hurry," a SWAT officer said.

The severely injured girl was immediately taken to the Denver Health Medical Center. She was the last surviving victim to be removed from the school.

+ + +

3:40 PM – TRIAGE

Patti Nielson was transported to Littleton Hospital.

+ + +

3:55 PM – OUTSIDE COLUMBINE

Lakewood SWAT found two cars which they reported as possibly being boobytrapped. The cars belonged to Eric Harris and Dylan Klebold.

+ + +

AROUND 4:00 PM

Sheriff John Stone and Public Information Officer Steve Davis held a news brief and made a tentative initial estimate of 25 dead students and teachers—10 more than the actual body count.

—

HARRIS RESIDENCE

Bomb technicians removed an explosive device from the home.

+ + +

4:04 PM

The Fire Captain entered Columbine to turn off the fire alarms and sprinkler system.

+ + +

4:05 – LEAWOOD ELEMENTARY

An anxious parent suffered heart trouble while waiting for news about their child. Paramedics were dispatched to take them to Littleton Hospital. A reporter at the school had to stop her live broadcast, too overcome with emotion to continue.

+ + +

4:10 PM – OUTSIDE COLUMBINE

ASCO Sergeant Richard Euchler was assigned to work with Littleton Fire/ACSO Posse Deputy Rick Young to mark and photograph explosive devices at Columbine's west side.

+ + +

4:34 PM

Emergency room physician Dr. Christopher Colwell and paramedic Robert Montoya were called in from the Denver Health Medical Center to search for signs of life. Outside, Dr. Colwell pronounced Rachel Scott and Danny Rohrbough dead.

+ + +

4:45 PM

The SWAT teams finished combing all 250,000 square feet of Columbine High School. Dr. Colwell entered the blood-soaked library where he pronounced 12 more students dead. SWAT escorted him to the science area next where he pronounced Dave Sanders dead. He picked 4:45 p.m. as the official time of death.

+ + +

5:00 PM – OFF CAMPUS

Brooks and his friend Stephen Partridge, a CHS junior, were sitting on the Browns' front porch processing the situation. Brooks' brother Aaron had been on the phone all afternoon and came running out to give them an update.

"Rachel Scott's dead."

He didn't know Steve had dated her for nearly a year. On hearing the news of her death, the teen fell silent. Then he collapsed.

+ + +

170

6:00 PM – COLUMBINE

Sergeant Euchler and Deputy Young were pulled off their assignment when the bomb squad discovered that the black BMW, later identified as Dylan's car, contained a pipe bomb attached to a 20-pound propane tank and a clock.

The sheriff declared the whole school a crime scene and cordoned it off with the dead still inside. The bodies couldn't be removed until a full investigation was done. Euchler and Young were sent to the school library to photograph and mark evidence while ACSO Sergeant Scott Linne and JCSO Investigator Michael Guerra donned bomb suits and started clearing the room of explosive devices flagged by techs in an earlier walk through.

Linne went to one of the suspects' bodies, a male dressed in a black T-shirt and removed 8 explosive devices from his left side pants pocket. The first was a pipe bomb wrapped in gray duct tape with a fuse surrounded by matches. Linne taped the matches to ensure they wouldn't accidentally strike something. He also removed several CO_2 cartridge bombs. He and Guerra searched both bodies for booby traps and explosives.

—

OFF CAMPUS

The Columbine Public Library closed for the day. Victim services were moved to Leawood Elementary. Officials knew there were fatalities but still didn't know how many, or who they were. They asked parents still at the elementary school who hadn't found their children to fill out forms to identify their missing loved ones: Name, age, what they were wearing, and if they had any distinguishing marks. Victim advocates ended up with sixteen filled-out forms, though there were twelve dead students and one dead teacher. Four of the missing kids would return home the following day.

At least two advocates were assigned to each family that was missing a child and to anyone whose family member was injured. The advocates stayed with them as long as they were needed, then remained accessible twenty-four hours a day. They left Leawood at 2 a.m. but many would be back by 4 a.m. to offer comfort to the families who remained. Like them, the counselors couldn't make themselves stay home at such an emotional time.

+ + +

10:00 PM – OFF CAMPUS

All students evacuated safely from Columbine were reunited with their families. At Leawood Elementary, Principal Frank DeAngelis saw how many families were left waiting and knew some would soon be getting heartbreaking news.

+ + +

10:40 PM – OUTSIDE COLUMBINE

Sergeant Euchler and ACSO Investigator Dan Davis collected several pipe bombs from Dylan's BMW. They put the first six into a containment vessel but the fusing mechanism of the seventh ignited as Euchler put it in.

"Get down! Get down!" he yelled.

Davis helped him down from the bomb trailer and they both dove to the ground as the explosive detonated. The blast threw out fifteen other devices. Two exploded when they landed. No one was injured.

+ + +

10:45 PM

The time bomb on Dylan's car went off when an official tried to defuse it. It damaged the BMW without injuring anyone.

Chris Morris was scheduled to work at Blackjack Pizza that night, but he didn't show up or call off. (As of April 22,

172

1999, the manager still hadn't heard from him.) He was detained by officers earlier but was released the same day. He eventually would help law enforcement build a case against Philip Duran, who helped provide guns to the shooters.

—

Roughly 1,000 law enforcement and rescue personnel were on the scene. By the day's end they rescued roughly 1,400 students and 100 faculty members.

That same day, KMFDM's album "Adios" was released.

+++

April 21, 1999

The day after the shootings, forensics teams investigated the school and identified the dead. Thousands of people visited the parking lot and nearby Clement Park where they left flowers and memorials for those who died.

It was sunny that afternoon, but when the shooters' bodies were removed from the school, an unseasonal snow began to fall.

+

In 1998, the Jefferson County Sheriff's Victims Services unit assisted 2,000 individuals. First responders assisted more people on April 20, 1999, than they did in all of 1998.

SECTION II
TIMELINE / WHEN

Section II – Timeline

1912 —Leo Yassenoff, Jewish-Russian immigrant's son and Dylan Klebold's great-grandfather, settles in Columbus, OH.

1947 —Thomas Klebold born.

1949 — Susan Yassenoff born.

1951 — October 22: William David "Dave" Sanders born.

1960 — Byron Klebold born. Kevin Harris born.

1970 — April 17: Wayne Harris and Katherine Poole marry.

1971 — Leo Yassenoff dies, leaving a considerable portion of his assets to the Jewish Center. Thomas Klebold and Susan Yassenoff marry.

1973 — Fall: Columbine opens.

1974 — William "Dave" Sanders starts teaching at Columbine.

1980 — August 4: Isaiah Eamon Shoels born.

1981 — January 17: Lauren Dawn Townsend born.

April 9, 1981: Eric David Harris born.

August 5, 1981: Rachel Joy Scott born.

September 11, 1981: Dylan Bennet Klebold born.

November 6, 1981: Cassie Renee Bernall born.

1982 — March 3: Corey Tyler DePooter born.

May 5, 1982: Kyle Albert Velasquez born.

September 1: John Robert Tomlin born.

1983 — January 6: Kelly Ann Fleming born.

February 19, 1983: Matthew Joseph Kechter born.

June 23, 1983: Daniel Conner Mauser born.

October 2, 1983: Modernized Jewish Community Center of Greater Columbus named after Leo Yassenoff during dedication ceremony.

1984 — March 2: Daniel Lee Rohrbough born.

August 28, 1984: Steven Robert Curnow born.

1986 — Fall: Chatfield High School opens.

1986-1991 — Dylan Klebold and Rachel Scott meet in kindergarten. Klebold meets Brooks Brown in 1st grade. The boys become best friends and are in Cub Scouts together. Klebold attends Normandy Elementary School in 1st and 2nd grade. He transfers to Governor's Ranch Elementary where he's placed in the CHIPS (Challenging High Intellectual Potential Students) program. Brown later says Klebold was unhappy in the program as it cut him off from his friends. Other kids at his new school don't like the "gifted" students.

1991 — Apogee Software releases *Duke Nukem*.

1992 — August 9: Midway Games releases *Mortal Kombat* game.

1993 — Apogee Software releases *Duke Nukem II*.

July 1993: Wayne Harris is forced to retire from the air force due to military cutbacks after He holds 11 different positions in 6 different states, including Ohio and Michigan. Plattsburgh, NY is the Harrises' last place of residence before moving to Colorado.

December 10, 1993: id Software releases the first *DOOM* game.

1993-1995 — Brooks Brown, Eric Harris, Dylan Klebold, Nathan "Nate" Dykeman, and Daniel Mauser attend Ken Caryl Middle School. Harris and Klebold meet in 7th grade.

1994 — January 26: *DEU* (*DOOM Editing Utility*) released so players can create custom levels. The first user-made WAD (Where's All the Data?) files emerge.

August 26, 1994: Film *Natural Born Killers* opens in theaters.

September 30, 1994: id Software releases *DOOM II: Hell on Earth* game.

176

December 1994: Eric Harris has surgery to correct a congenital birth defect, *pectus excavatum* (funnel breast), where the sternum is sunken in. Surgery involves placing a temporary steel rod to brace his chest while it aligns.

1995 — April 19: Oklahoma City Bombing, committed by Timothy McVeigh and Terry Nichols, wounds 680 people and kills 168. The tragic aftermath is televised for weeks and is on every magazine cover and newspaper front page.

April 30, 1995: id Software releases *Ultimate Doom* game.

Summer, 1995: Columbine High School gets a $15 million-dollar makeover. The cafeteria is brand new, as is the student (front) entrance.

June 1995: Eric undergoes a second surgery on his chest to remove the temporary strut.

August 1995: Eric Harris and Dylan Klebold start attending Columbine High School along with Brooks Brown and Nate Dykeman. Dykeman meets Harris in Spanish class, then meets Klebold at Harris' house. Brown rides the same bus as Harris.

September 26, 1995: *Natural Born Killers* film releases on VHS.

1996 — 3D Realms (formerly Apogee Software) releases *Duke Nukem 3D*.

Helen Fuller, sister of Jefferson County District Attorney David Thomas' wife Shirley, is shot five times by her husband Arthur. The murder follows a violent argument in the family's Wisconsin basement. Arthur dismembers her and leaves her in a state park. He is arrested and sentenced to life in prison. The Thomases adopt their orphaned 4-year-old daughter Maggie.

March - September: The Harrises purchase a $180,000 house on Pierce Street, south of Columbine High, minutes away from where Brooks Brown lives. Eric Harris is highly active on the internet, posting as many as 11 Doom WADs he creates.

Spring 1996: Kevin Harris, Eric's older brother, graduates from Columbine.

May 31, 1996: id Software releases *Final Doom* game.

June 22, 1996: id Software releases *Quake* game.

October 10, 1996: Midway Games releases the *Mortal Kombat Trilogy* game. It's the first *Mortal Kombat* home release.

December 25, 1996: JonBenét Ramsey murdered in Boulder, Colorado. The child pageant star's death is the focus of every media outlet. The *Los Angeles Times* later describes media behavior as "one of the foulest chapters in contemporary U.S. journalism".

December 26, 1996: Master levels for *Doom II* expansion are released.

Late in the year: Brooks Brown and Trevor Dolac have been doing ride share, splitting the week so one drives then they switch off. Harris has been bumming rides. Brown is chronically late, and this results in a big fight between him and Harris. Brown tells Harris he won't be giving him rides.

1997 —Cassie Bernall becomes a born-again Christian.

Sometime this year, Chris Morris introduces Harris to Robert "Bob" Kirgis, owner of the Blackjack Pizza where Morris works. Kirgis hires Harris as a cook ($6.50/hr) 6 months after hiring Morris.

Columbine student Scott Fuselier and friends make a "Get Smart" parody video for a school project featuring them in trench coats shooting at each other in and around the school. It ends with four teens walking away from the school as it blows up.

February 7, 1997: Harris posts on his Rebel Clan webpage about pranks he and his "*Quake* clan" have been doing. He says they aren't a gaming clan at all but a gang who plan and execute "missions" against anyone who pisses them off. He posts a *Duke Nukem 3D* map (CORRIDOR.MAP) of the area where they conduct their "missions" so others can see the team's "accomplishments". Under MISSION LOGS Harris posts descriptions of 6 different "missions":

1. The first "mission" Harris says was retaliation against people who shot at Klebold's bike. The "clan" set off loud fireworks at 1:00 a.m. in a tunnel near the person's house. He says they'll do it again, only louder, and hit other houses. He also says they get drunk after each "mission" and lists Aftershock, Irish cream, tequila, vodka, whiskey,

178

rum, and Everclear as their drinks of choice. He gleefully says he'll have his driver's license soon and they'll be able to drive anywhere they want to.

2. This "mission" took place at Nick Baumgart's house. Baumgart, who Harris calls a "complete and utter fag", was in Cub Scouts with Klebold. They were in the same class from 3rd to 5th grade, and in 7th and 8th grades. When Harris befriended Klebold, Baumgart stopped hanging out with him. The "clan" got to his house around 12:15 a.m. and toilet papered the tree. They Super Glued the doors and mailbox and left broken eggs in the bushes and on the doorstep.

3. Another revenge "mission" on the people Harris claims shot Klebold's bike. They hit random houses too. They sneaked out at 1:55 a.m. to set off explosives, then went to Brooks Brown's house and poured model putty on his car. Harris posts Brown's address and phone number, telling others to prank him. They prank another kid's home and moved large rocks onto random driveway, then tagged a fence. Afterward they went back to his house to get drunk while watching *Bordello of Blood*.

4."REB", "KiBBz*", and "VoDkA" sneaked out to set off fireworks in a field and almost got caught. They returned home around 4:30 a.m. The "mission" is liquor-free because Brooks Brown told Harris' parents that he had alcohol in his room after he broke Brown's windshield. Harris claims in this log it was a little nick from a snowball but according to Brown's book *No Easy Answers: The Truth Behind Death at Columbine*, Harris threw a large chunk of ice. (see Feb. 27 below).

5. This "mission" started at KiBBz's house and took place in his neighborhood, "one of the best" they did. They went to a soccer field and set off some bottle rockets, thunder bombs, and Black Cats— things that made noise but no visuals. KiBBz and VoDkA signaled from the other side of the street and REB set them off. One he detonated with a "cigarette fuse". They celebrated by drinking Aftershock liquor.

---

* Zach Heckler's username. Comes from "Kibble", a nickname earned at because he brought snacks to school.

6. Harris says his dad was the only parent home at the time of this "mission", so it was easy to sneak out despite the backyard rocks making noise and the neighbor's dog barking. They set off fireworks at Brooks Brown's home then he, Klebold, and Heckler headed to a construction site where they stole fence signs.

February 27, 1997: Harris is throwing snowballs at people while waiting for the school bus. Seeing Trevor Dolac and Brooks Brown drive by in separate cars, he throws a chunk of ice from the gutter at Dolac's car, denting it. He throws another chunk at Brown, putting a spiderweb crack in the windshield. Brown went straight to Harris' parents about it and the "missions" Harris has been doing. When Kathy Harris doesn't seem to believe him, he tells her to search Eric's room for hard liquor and spray paint hidden there. Brown and Dolac get Judy Brown involved. She tries to tell Harris' parents about the problems. Kathy seems to want to listen, but Wayne refuses, saying Eric told him he feared Brooks.

February 28, 1997: In a 60-page Steno notebook marked "ERIC" on the front, Wayne Harris makes a record of Brooks Brown's parents contacting his family about damage to Judy's car. There's a crack in the windshield. This follows an incident where he grabbed hold of her car door handle, enraged, and wouldn't stop trying to get into the car until she drove away. He flew into that rage because the Browns had his backpack in their car and said they could have it back when they talked to his parents.

March 3, 1997: Wayne Harris records information in his diary about a meeting with Dean Place at Columbine with Eric and Brooks Brown. He makes notes about damage to Brooks' car, "plotting against friends' houses", and concerns about how Eric is getting alcohol. Wayne also notes how Nick Baumgart's house was egged and TP'd.

March 4, 1997: Wayne Harris writes in his notebook that Eric denied knowledge of any alcohol and doesn't know what Mr. Place is talking about. Which is a lie: Eric had alcohol in his room and car even then.

March 31, 1997: Klebold writes "El Thoughtzo's" entry in his journal. He puts his name at the top of his pages, using the handle "VoDkA". He writes this entry while "half drunk w. a screwdriver", reflecting on how different he feels. He also mentions the Nine Inch Nails song "Piggy" and the movie *Lost Highway* (which has a soundtrack created partly by Trent Reznor of NIN).

April 15, 1997: Klebold writes "Da ThoughtZ Jeah" journal entry about hating his life and wanting to die. He talks about how he deliberately cut himself that night. Complains about girls and rambles about existence.

April 18, 1997: Wayne Harris contacts Bonnie Baumgart about the TP/egg incident. Tells him about her door being glued at the same time. Said she hadn't contacted the police because there was no true damage.

April 19, 1997: JeffCo Deputy A.D. Walsh contacts Wayne Harris about the accusations against Eric. In his diary, Wayne expresses feeling "victimized too", that Brooks Brown was "out to get Eric". Wayne writes that he doesn't want Eric to be accused "every time something supposedly happens" when "Eric not at fault" and that Brooks is manipulative and a con artist.

April 21, 1997: Harris writes a two-page hate-filled rant focused on education and how people need to learn to think for themselves or they'll die. He calls the world worthless and expresses plans to leave it.

April 27, 1997: Wayne Harris makes a follow-up call to the Browns to see if there have been any further problems with Eric. According to Dean Place, the boys are leaving each other alone at school per their agreement. Again, Wayne makes notes about "we feel victimized too" and "manipulative con artist".

May 7, 1997: Klebold writes "Thoutz" entry. Complains about being an outcast and conspired against by "everyone", and how he's smarter than the average person. This is followed by an undated entry where he calls other people "zombies".

Summer 1997: Zach Heckler is hired by Blackjack Pizza. Bob Kirgis says he "drove like crap" and quit after two months. Later that year, Kirgis hires Klebold as a line cook. He also hires Nate Dykeman and Brian Sargent.

July 23, 1997: Klebold writes "VoDkA's Thoughts - The [name redacted] Situation". He says his best friend getting a girlfriend is the same as him being dead. He complains about how sad and lonely he is since this friend spends all his time with her and has abandoned him. He talks about how this friend did everything with him, from smoking cigars to sabotaging houses.

Sometime between July 23 and September 5, Klebold suddenly finds "true love", a secret crush. He doesn't say who she is. The first entry he mentions her in is titled "My 1st Love???".

August 7, 1997: An unidentified citizen calls the Jefferson County Sheriff's Office to complain about Eric Harris' violent website. The tip is investigated by Deputy Michael Burgess, who forwards the report and printouts of the website to the investigator in charge of computer-related crime, John Hicks.

Late August 1997: Kelly Fleming and family move to Littleton.

September 1997: 18-year-old Columbine senior and honors student Robert Craig shoots and kills his stepfather Stephen Sharpe, then kills himself. Robert's mother Joanne was married to Stephen for 11 years. Her son and husband had a close relationship and didn't fight. She said she missed warning signs her son was depressed. She tells the *Denver Post* she believes Robert did it to punish her and Stephen for not noticing how much he was suffering.

September 5, 1997: Klebold writes "My thoughts" entry describing how his best friend "ditched" him to spend time with his girlfriend. He complains that the girl he was interested in doesn't care about him. Says someone he knows can get him a gun to use on a "poor S.O.B.". He says he's tried to change (stop watching porn, picking on people) but it doesn't matter because everyone hates him. An undated entry follows: Sad poetry and what looks like a suicide note in the margin.

October 2, 1997: Harris, Klebold, and Heckler are suspended by new Dean Peter Horvath for hacking Columbine's computers to steal locker combinations and breaking into lockers. Heckler left student Kevin Starkey a threatening note that told him to stay away from Heckler's girlfriend, Devon Adams, whom Starkey also once dated. Heckler is given 5 days detention. Harris and Klebold are given 3 days. It's Horvath's first disciplinary action at CHS. Horvath meets with each boy's parents, all of whom say the punishment is too harsh.

Side note: Eric refers to Starkey as "Scoop" on his "shit list", a nickname Heckler gave him that Harris and Klebold latched onto. Starkey worked at the Cooper 7 theater next door to Blackjack Pizza. He ordered pizza from both Dylan and Eric and thought they seemed nice. Heckler didn't like him, though, and harassed him until Starkey's cousin told him to stop. A short time later, someone shot and broke a picture window at Starkey's home.

October 14, 1997: Klebold writes "Thoughtz" entry about how he's "been to the zombie bliss side" and hates it as much if not more than the "awareness" state he believes less-intelligent people aren't capable of. He says he wants to die and complains the "zombies" get ahead while he, who is smart and worthy and just wants love, is miserable. He injects random cusswords and talk of suicide, ending with "Fuck me Die me".

November 3, 1997: Klebold writes "ThoughtZ" journal entry about drifting farther away from reality. Says he gets more depressed every day. Mocks his own god complex. Complains he has no ambition because everyone and everything is against him. References Nine Inch Nails music and makes a list of girls he might love. He seems to be in love with the idea of being in love.

December 9, 1997: id Software releases *Quake II* game.

December 10, 1997: Harris writes a school essay: *Guns in School*. To deter shootings, he suggests metal detectors and police. He says some sprees can be prevented, some can't.

1998 — Early in the year Harris and Klebold sneak out to do more "missions". They stop by Brooks Brown's house at about 3 a.m. and knock on his bedroom window. He lets them in. Zach Heckler and Chris Morris are already there.

Spring 1998: Klebold is caught scratching something into a freshman's locker. He becomes very agitated while waiting in Dean Horvath's office for his father to arrive. Horvath tries to calm him down, but Klebold cusses at him. He says he's very upset with the school system and the way Columbine handled people, including people who picked on him and others. Horvath gets the impression that while Dylan's a "pretty angry kid", and that he's also upset with his dad for "stuff at home". When Tom arrives, he disagrees with the disciplinary action taken against Dylan for scratching the locker.

Harris writes a list of names in a journal and titles it "Class of 98 - Top of the "you should have died" list". The list includes jocks and girls who didn't want to date him. Several boys in gym class, mostly friends of Rocky Hoffschneider, regularly tease Harris about being bad in sports. His skinny body and large head draw taunts. These teens are on Harris' "should have died" list and later tell investigators they didn't tease him outside of gym class.

Joe Stair horses around, acting like he's "humping" Eric Dutro from behind to bother the jocks, who yell at him "knock it off, faggot". Stair yells back that he'll blow up the school because he doesn't like anyone there. The jocks report them to peer counselor Lindsey Woyziak, who talks to Stair and Dutro.

January 2, 1998: In his journal, Klebold lists all the people he loved or at least liked. Laments again about his friend having a girlfriend and wonders if he, Dylan, will ever find love.

January 30, 1998: Klebold and Harris arrested by Jefferson County Deputy Tim Walsh and Phil Lebeda for breaking into an electrician's white van and stealing $250 worth of equipment. Wayne Harris records an entry in his diary dated 1/29/98: 1st degree criminal trespass. Class V felony. 1-3 years. Says that his son admitted guilt and is willing to do community service and "counciling" [sic]. As low-risk first-time offenders, the teens are assigned to juvenile diversion, including anger therapy for Eric and the stipulation that neither can own a gun.

February 2, 1998: The Harrises pick Dr. Kevin Albert from a list of therapists to take Eric to.

Klebold writes entry "Existence & UnderstanD" about being in love with a girl who loves him back and nothing else matters. He writes "Its so good to love" and "I love her & she loves me" but then talks about plans to commit suicide or "get with [name redacted] & it will be NBK for us". It's the first time he references the film *Natural Born Killers* in his writing. He says he was caught for "drinking, smoking, vandalism, pipe bombs". Says if the girl he loves doesn't love him back, he'll slit his wrist and blow up a pipe bomb (Atlanta) strapped to his neck. He declares his parents "zombies" and calls himself and his friend [name redacted] gods. He expresses a desire to punish all "zombies" for their "arrogance, hate, fear, abandonment, & distrust".

Later undated entries talk about love and how he loves a girl. He doesn't describe her or what he likes about her. He just says he needs love; she is his soulmate, and she'll make him happy. A love letter follows which he never delivered. He professes love but leads with a barrage of self-deprecation implying that, while he "needs" her, she's

184

likely unattainable. Hints at plans to kill himself and tells her not to feel guilty when he's gone. He signs it with "goodbye & I love(d) you".

February 13, 1998: Eric Harris writes in his father's notebook that Bob Miller in evidence has his stuff and needs a release note from Detective Healy to let him have it. Wayne notes while talking to a lawyer that it was a "bad choice to tell all that evening" and to "be careful what we said". He also notes diversion could be between 6 months to 1 year, plus counseling, community service and paying restitution to the victim.

February 15, 1998: Using a search warrant, Jefferson County sheriff's deputies find and defuse a pipe bomb in a field at Garrison and Field Streets., just a few blocks from the Harris house.

February 16, 1998: Eric Harris has his first appointment with Dr. Kevin Albert at 3:00 p.m.

March 3, 1998: Wayne Harris speaks with Diversion Counselor Andrea Sanchez about Eric's court date and intended plea.

March 17, 1998: Brooks Brown gives his parents a scrap of paper he and his brother wrote web addresses on. Brown tells his mother "someone" said he needed to see them but can't say who because the person is afraid of Eric Harris. Later, Brooks admits it was Dylan Klebold who told him.

March 18, 1998: After discovering the hateful rant Harris wrote targeting their son, Randy and Judy Brown contact the police. The Browns give the web addresses and 10 printed pages of the website to Deputy Mark Miller to investigate. The report is designated to be forwarded to Deputy Neil Gardner, but he later claims he never saw it.

March 19, 1998: Harrises have an appointment with diversion counselor Andrea Sanchez for an interview. They are told diversion will offer limited liability and anything Eric tells his therapist cannot be used in court. Eric fills out a mental health self-evaluation forms which say he's experiencing homicidal thoughts, mood swings, anger, anxiety, depression, and loneliness. He describes himself as confused and suicidal. The form his mother fills out at the same time suggests she doesn't see half the things Eric reports.

March 24, 1998: Jonesboro massacre at Westside Middle School makes national news.

March 25, 1998: Harris has a follow-up appointment with Dr. Kevin Albert at 2:00 p.m. and soccer practice. He also has community service.

March 26, 1998: The Brown case is closed without being assigned to an investigator. That same day, the Browns follow up on the report, but the detective they speak to can't find it.

March 31, 1998: Investigator Mike Guerra, Detective Glenn Grove, and Deputy John Hicks meet with Randy and Judy Brown at JeffCo Sheriff's Office. The Browns are not aware their case has already been closed.

Guerra is looking into case #3365, a report of an unexploded pipe bomb found 2-3 miles from the Harris home. He suspects it might be tied to the bombs Harris' websites say he made. The investigator works on the case for 3-4 days and finds Eric's "shit list" of people he wants to die. Guerra writes an affidavit for a search warrant for the Harris house, but the District Attorney says there's no probable cause. Lieutenant John Kiekbusch says there isn't enough information to proceed with the case. The warrant isn't filed. Technically, no search warrant is needed because Harris is already on probation. The Browns' complaint should have called for investigation even without finding a bomb.

Late March to early April: Dr. Kevin Albert prescribes Zoloft to Eric Harris to help him with his anger management and depression.

April 2, 1998: JSCO claims a criminal background check on Eric Harris turns up nothing in their computers.

April 7, 1998: Wayne Harris makes note of Eric's diversion requirements: Individual counseling (doing), anger management (1 time), MADD victims panel (1 time 2 hours), letter of apology to victims, Juv. Justice class (1 time, 5 hours + parent, Saturdays), and 45 hours community service.

April 10, 1998: Harris writes 2-page rant saying he hates the world, that only he and "V" have "self-awareness", they know what everyone is thinking, and everything is corrupted. He says he will die soon and "so will you and everyone else". He rages about how no one is original, everyone is a follower, and spelling is stupid. He ramps up to incoherent rambling about "natural selection". His handwriting gets more erratic as he gets enraged over nothing.

April 11, 1998: Judy Brown contacts JeffCo about a threatening email her son Brooks receives. Unfortunately, the email was deleted. A deputy makes a "suspicious incident" note to forward to Investigator Hicks.

April 12, 1998: Harris writes another journal entry raving about natural selection. He says he feels like God and wishes he could have everyone "officially" be lower than him because he knows he's "higher than almost anyone" in terms of "universal intelligence". Rants about how someone who leaves their van parked out in plain sight deserves to be robbed. Again, the writing dissolves into incoherent, enraged rambling, lists of hateful words to describe how he wants everyone to die.

April 15, 1998: Dr. Albert advises Harris family physician Dr. Jon Cram that "Eric's depression leads to negative thinking and he cannot stop this process—his thinking is a bit obsessional." Due to his obsession with suicide and homicide, Dr. Cram switches Harris from Zoloft to Luvox (Fluvoxamine Maleate).

April 21, 1998: Harrises attend diversion orientation with Sanchez. This is the last entry in Wayne's "ERIC" diary.

That same day, Eric pens another hate-filled rant that starts off philosophically about why we go to school but quickly devolves into a curse-word laced, angry ramble accusing humankind of daring to think that they are even the same species as him. The rant gets more emphatic, the handwriting more erratic as he goes. He ends it saying he will "kill whoever I deem unfit for anything at all".

April 26, 1998: Harris posts NBK.doc online about how great it would be if God removed vaccines and warning labels and let natural selection take its course. He glorifies WWII, talks about *Doom* WADs he created, and how he'd like to see "all you fuckheads die". He rants about how in April he and Klebold are going to take revenge and kick natural selection up a few notches. Harris says he wants to go into Brooks Brown's house, torture and kill everyone there, then burn the house down. Afterward, he and Klebold (whom he refers to as "V") will go to Columbine during "A" lunch, get geared up with sunglasses and bags of guns. They'll play music to get pumped up and start throwing "crickets"—the CO_2 bombs they made. Klebold will shoot

187

while Harris throws firebombs. Then he'll shoot while Klebold throws crickets, after which they would go upstairs and pick off people in the classrooms. He wants to hijack an awesome car afterward and drive to a neighborhood of their choice to throw Molotov cocktails. He says if they figure out time bombs, he'll have hundreds of them rigged all over Denver. He imagines it being like the L.A. riots or the Oklahoma City bombing. He wants to kill police, murder and damage as much as they can. If they're unable to get away, the plan is to commit suicide in a way that will take out the most people possible. If they do get away, he says they'll steal a plane and crash it in New York City. He also says not to blame anyone but him and Dylan. "Don't blame the school. Don't change any policies just because of us."

May 1998: Harris serves 10 hours of community service each week.

May 6, 1998: Harris hand-writes a 3-page journal entry about how the human race sucks and isn't worth fighting for. The penmanship is steadier, but the content collapses into an aimless, angry rant ending with "fuck you all".

May 9, 1998: Harris gets his yearbook. Writes a journal entry about how it confirms the human race isn't worth fighting for, only killing. He accuses everyone in it of being the same and says he doesn't want to be like them.

May 20, 1998: Kip Kinkel shoots his parents and 27 of his schoolmates at Thurston High School in Springfield, Oregon.

That day, Harris writes another entry, starting with: "Alright you pathetic fools, listen up". He goes on a rant that includes racism, gay-bashing, and how the human race ostracizes things that are different, even if they're better than they are. Rants about how women will "always be under men". Midway through, his handwriting shifts drastically twice. He ends by telling people to "deal with it or commit suicide".

Late spring 1998: Klebold writes a lengthy letter in Harris' yearbook summing up their junior year. He describes "laffin' at fags" and how "fag jocks" should "DIEEE". Looking forward to the next year, he refers to "the holy April morning of NBK ". He also says they can't beat each other at bowling because it's "as equal as a nigger to a spade".

188

June 8, 1998: Klebold writes another journal entry proclaiming his love for the girl he can't bring himself to call. Drawings of hearts and poetry follow.

June 12, 1998: Harris hand-writes a journal praising the Nazis and in huge bold letters "KILL MANKIND". The entry gets angrier the longer he goes. Midway his handwriting shifts drastically from cursive to print and becomes mostly cursing and threats, with lots of extra punctuation.

June 13, 1998: Harris writes an entry about a Discovery Channel documentary regarding satellites, radar, and aircraft, things in the military that make him think humans are advanced and America is awesome. Reconsiders whether he wants all people dead or just the "civilized, developed" places. He contemplates leaving some tribes of natives in the forests.

July 1998: Sasha Jacobs meets Harris and Klebold through their mutual friend Chad Laughlin. She goes out with them a couple of times. They make her uncomfortable, so she stops hanging out with them. In July she receives intimidating phone calls from someone threatening to kill her who says: "a bomb is coming". She suspects Harris is the caller. She also receives an email from him saying he's trying to "tie up loose ends" and she's one.

July 4, 1998: Columbine student Peter Maher and his friends have an altercation with Harris, Klebold, and a few of their friends at a convenience store. Maher sees one of the boys in a trench coat with a "big pistol-grip shotgun in the air". The two groups cross paths again later that day at a fireworks booth and another conflict begins. One of the "trench coat boys" pulls a knife. Another says they have a shotgun. Maher and his friends talk the situation down and get away from the group.

July 10, 1998: Harris reports to a diversion counselor every two weeks. He tells the counselor this week his Luvox prescription has been increased to 100mg.

July 19, 1998: Randy Brown reports that his garage window is broken by paintball fire and that he suspects Eric Harris. The officer on the call writes that there are no suspects and no leads.

July 29, 1998: Harris hand-writes a journal entry about how people die and get judged all the time. He says humans have freedom of choice, so he thinks he'll choose to kill and damage as much as he can. He acknowledges he could get killed, but that's the consequence of his actions. He says it's his choice, not one made by his friends, family, music, games, or the media.

Fall 1998: Klebold is assigned locker #837 at Columbine. Harris is assigned locker #624.

Klebold tackles girls during touch football, shoving them to the ground. When sophomore Tara Zobjeck tells him to knock it off, he calls her a bitch. He starts bothering her at school, calling her a bitch and yelling at her until her boyfriend intervenes. He tells Klebold he'll kick his ass if he doesn't leave Tara alone. The harassment stops after that.

August 3, 1998: Harris is assigned an essay as part of his Diversion. The subject is "Violence is Preventable" and it's due December 1.

August 10, 1998: Klebold writes two rambling journal entries about fate. In another undated entry, he says he wants to call the girl he likes but doesn't because it's "zombie behavior". He talks about guilt he's feeling for looking at fetish porn which he blames on his "human side". Another entry follows complaining about being stuck in humanity and how NBK with Harris is the way to break free. The next undated entries speculate on life and love.

A later entry is a list of names the FBI redacted before releasing Klebold's journal to the public. Heart-filled drawings and love poems follow it. One is a poem using letters of a girl's name. He writes two more love letters he doesn't send. In one, he gives his locker combination and says he tried to call the girl but she "must have been asleep" A creative writing story between him and three friends including Harris follows. A later entry questions his religion and Judaism. He spews racist remarks and rants about how much smarter than the "zombies" he is. Seems to equate plans for NBK and dying with getting to be with the girl he likes.

Fall 1998: Harris starts wearing all black at school and a duster coat like the Trench Coat Mafia, which Chris was a member of before they disbanded over the summer. Klebold does too. Klebold and Harris make a video for Film class with them "shooting" friends dressed as

190

jocks. They write plans to kill their schoolmates and make maps of the school, noting places where the most people are. Both take German class and use it to berate and get attention from their classmates. Students in their bowling class hear them shout "Seig heil" when they roll a good ball. At least one set of parents and two teachers express concern to the shooters' parents that the boys are exhibiting violent tendencies.

August 24, 1998: Harris writes a list of "25 things that make me different" for a school assignment. He includes his love of the game *Doom*, the bullet hanging from his rearview window, trouble controlling his anger, his diversion record, and his nickname (REB) "as long as there's not too many copycats". In the full essay he says that *Doom* is "so burned into my head any thoughts usually have something to do with the game".

September 2, 1998: Harris writes an essay about "Is murder or breaking the law ever justified?". He starts it with: "Yes, it is."

September 14, 1998: Harris is given an Open Topic essay assignment. He writes it about the *Doom 2* level he's working on, Tier 6.

September 21, 1998: For his creative writing essay about "Good to be bad or bad to be good", Harris writes about when he "got into serious trouble with the law" so his parents took away all the weapons he worked so hard to gather and buy.

October 6, 1998: Klebold writes an essay for Language Arts class: *The Mind and Motives of Charles Manson*.

October 13, 1998: In a school assignment titled "What's 35% of 100?", Harris says people who can't answer questions like that should be shot.

October 22, 1998: Harris tracks the bombs he and Klebold make. Today's batch: 10 regular crickets, 3 Alpha batch, 1 Beta batch.

October 23, 1998: Harris writes a journal entry about how people will ask what they, the gunmen, were thinking. His answer: He wants to destroy as much as possible. To avoid feelings of sympathy or mercy, he plans to force himself to believe everyone is a monster from *Doom*. That way he can kill everyone "except about 5 people". He logs the creation of 6 Beta batch crickets.

Klebold and Nate Dykeman make videos in Film class, one for the Rebel News Network announcements and another to show Dykeman's father where he lives and goes to school.

October 31, 1998: Harris logs the creation of 3 Charlie batch crickets.

November 1998: Nolan Kirklin, Lance Kirklin's half-brother, commits suicide while living in Texas with his mother. Bereaved, Lance's father Mike spirals into alcoholism. Lance gives him a reality check when he leaves him a note that says: "*You have another son who needs you.*"

That same month, Klebold picks on Special Ed student Adam Kyler. He threatens to kill Kyler if he tells anyone, but the boy tells his parents. They get the school involved to put a stop to it. Klebold is also openly disrespectful to his French teacher, Cathrine Lutz. He swears in class, and she often asks him to leave. He is even suspended from the class for a time.

November 1, 1998: Harris writes a journal admitting he's lying to everyone as he gathers weapons and bombs. He also says he's a racist. He writes a bunch of racist terms to prove it. He says he would nuke the world if he could because there are "only about ten people" he wouldn't want to die.

November 8, 1998: In his journal Harris describes going to a girl's house that weekend to hang out. He says the girl's mom bought him and VoDkA a bunch of liquor. They smoked cigars and got drunk and played cards until 5 a.m. He says he stashed some of the leftover alcohol in his car and the "nazi report" is boosting his love of killing. Says his brain is like a sponge, soaking up everything that sounds cool and leaving out all that is worthless. He compares this to how the Nazi movement got started and how he'll be that way too.

November 12, 1998: Harris writes a hostile entry in his journal about the Brady Bill and how it's keeping him from getting a weapon even though only wants it for "*personal protection*". "Its not like I'm some person who would go on a shooting spree.... fuckers."

Despite that claim, he then says he has enough bombs to kill 100 people. He complains he's always hated the way he looks, and he has no self-esteem, which he thinks is where the hate grows from: Hating himself. He says he rips on people who look like him because he wants to rip on himself. He adds if he gets bladed weapons, he'll be able to kill maybe 10 more people but that's not enough. He needs guns.

November 13, 1998: Harris writes an essay "The Nazi Culture" for Jason Webb's English class.

November 17, 1998: Harris writes the "HATE!" rant the news later runs constantly when his journal is released to the public. In it he talks about hating every kind of person and says he loves the Nazis. He references Nine Inch Nails music. He claims "this might still be avoidable" if more people complimented him. Rants about how everyone rips on him that dissolves into a violent rape fantasy. Wraps up with a lengthy, gory fictional description of killing someone. His handwriting is very erratic, shifting between cursive and print, scribbly and neat.

November 19, 1998: For his 2nd hour class Harris writes about getting arrested. He claims to be remorseful, describes his punishment afterward including a year of diversion, 45 hours of community service, and how his parents lost trust in him. He ends it by saying he has to be a "literal angel" until March of '99 and that he believes the night of the arrest was "enough punishment for me".

November 22, 1998: Klebold and Harris take their friend Robyn Anderson to Tanner Gun Show in Adams County where she purchases a double-barrel 12-gauge shotgun, a pump-action 12-gauge shotgun, and a 9mm carbine rifle from Ronald Hartmann and James Royce Washington. They also purchase 250 9mm rounds, 15 12-gauge slugs, 40 shotgun shells, 2 switchblade knives, and 4 10-round clips for the carbine. While Anderson buys the weapons, Klebold and Harris ask all the questions. Under Colorado law at the time, an 18-year-old without a felony record could legally provide minors with rifles and shotguns.

Harris writes a journal entry describing the purchase. He says now that they have guns, it's the "point of no return". He addresses his dad, saying it was a shame he wasn't at the gun show; they could have done some major bonding. But because his dad caught him with whiskey, had to punish him by cutting him out of the loop. He says he's happy to cheat and lie because killing people is what he wants to do with his life.

November 30, 1998: Harris gives Klebold the leftover alcohol from his car.

December 3, 1998: The shooters fire their guns for the first time. Harris writes about how great it felt. He names his shotgun "Arlene", after Arlene Sanders from the *Doom* book series. He says VoDkA's double-barrel shotgun looks great sawed-off to the "proper lengths" and that he, Eric, would have made a great Marine, which would have given him a reason to do good. He complains about how difficult it is to balance working on his arsenal, homework, and keep up the web of lies. He mentions an argument on the 22nd with his dad he should have "won an Oscar for". Says he used quotes from the movie *Aliens* to make it more theatrical. Says he never really liked drinking, which is why he gave the liquor to Klebold. He'd kept it because he liked having it around. He expresses interest in legally acquiring guns by getting someone over 21 to buy them at the next gun show. His handwriting shifts drastically as he writes.

December 17, 1998: Harris writes a happy entry about how he'll never have to take another final. Says he'll be ordering 9-10 more clips for the carbine the next day. He says he needs to figure out the time bombs for the commons and how to get them in "without any Jews finding them". He wonders whether anyone will write a book about him and if there is one, it better be good.

December 18, 1998: Harris logs the creation of 4 more regular cricket bombs.

December 20, 1998: KMFDM announces plans to release their new album *Adios* in April. Harris writes in his journal about how appropriate it is. Referring to the KMFDM song "Godlike" he says: "I ripped the hell outa the system".

December 29, 1998: Harris writes a journal entry about Green Mountain Gun shop calling his house. His dad answered, and the shop told him: "the clips are in". Wayne told them he didn't order ammunition. Eric manages to cover the incident and picks up the 13 clips for his rifle. He expresses relief at being able to save the "project" and writes about getting another gun for Klebold.

1999 — Early in the year: Philip Duran, Harris and Klebold's co-worker at Blackjack Pizza, introduces them to 22-year-old Mark Manes, a computer tech who likes guns. Manes purchased a TEC-DC9 (TEC-9) at a gun show in August for $500 and agrees to sell it to the teens at the same price. They pay $300 at the time. Klebold later gives the rest of the money to Duran to pay Manes.

194

January 3, 1999: Klebold and Harris make 4 more regular cricket bombs.

January 5, 1999: Harris writes in his Day Planner: Get shit.

January 6, 1999: Harris writes: Start shit.

January 17, 1999: Harris writes a first-person short story for class based on the game *Doom*. It includes details about weapons and seeing piles of bodies. The paper earns a C+. The teacher's comment: "Yours is a unique approach and your writing works in a gruesome way — good details and mood setting."

January 20, 1999: Klebold writes a journal entry about a girl he likes. Says he's going to leave it to fate to decide whether they should get together. In the meantime, he's trying to give up fetish porn and masturbation. The next few undated entries are about love and feeling alone and sketches of hearts.

January 25, 1999: Harris writes in his school Day Planner: Get more clocks.

February 1999: Klebold writes an incredibly violent and disturbing essay for his 4th hour Creative Writing class about a gunman shooting and killing preps. The essay likens the man to God. It disturbs his teacher Judith Kelly so much she passes it on to paper to Assistant Principal Peter Horvath and the school counselor Brad Butts and calls a conference with Klebold's parents. They and Dylan dismiss it as fiction.

February 3, 1999: Klebold and Harris are released early from the Diversion Program due to excellent progress. Both are given high recommendation.

February 13, 1999: In his Day Planner, Harris works out hand signals to use during the attack.

Spring 1999: A few weeks before the shooting, Klebold calls teacher Peggy Dodd a bitch for telling him to pay for using the library printer. Rich Long calls him into his office to explain what happened. Klebold opens with: "Well, that bitch…". Long stops him, saying: "You can't talk like that." He tells Klebold he's permanently banned from the school computers. The teen replies: "Well, you know, it doesn't matter."

February 1999: Klebold, Harris, Mark Manes, and Philip Duran test out the TEC-9 and 9mm rifle offroad near Rampart Range.

February 8, 1999: Harris logs the creation of 9 more crickets.

February 20, 1999: Harris and Klebold report student Luke Crowley to Dean Horvath for "parking too close and being mouthy" with them. Horvath passes the info on to Crowley's counselor. Aside from this complaint, the pair never report anyone specific for harassing them.

Harris, Manes, and Duran go target shooting in the mountains.

March 6, 1999: Harris and Klebold borrow a video camera from Angel Pytlinski, a coworker at Blackjack Pizza. Harris says he is excited to be going into the Marine Corps after graduation. Klebold seems to be happy with his plans to attend the University of Arizona. She knew Harris was upset at his dad for accusing him of using LSD. Eric also got upset when Pytlinski learned his email address. He wanted to know if she'd seen anything more than that. She worked with Chris Morris too and later tells investigators he seemed to be the ringleader of the three and they all wore their dusters to work. Other employees say Klebold wore his coat "all the time".

The gunmen take the borrowed video camera and go shooting at Rampart Range in Sedalia, Colorado with Mark Manes and his girlfriend Jessica Miklich. They film themselves firing the TEC-9 and sawed-off shotguns using bowling pins and pine trees for target practice. The 30-year-old shotguns are sawed so short, they cause the teens' hands to bleed when fired repeatedly. The police dub it the "Rampart Range" video when they discover it.

March 7, 1999: Harris tells coworker James Thornby he has 7 propane tanks stockpiled and wants to get 9 more with his $300 paycheck. He wants to have 30 propane bombs by "Hitler's birthday". Harris asks Thornby to buy a gun for him, but he refuses, telling Eric he'd be 18 soon and can buy it himself. Before Harris asked him, he asked Philip Duran to do it, but Duran also said no.

March 14, 1999: First of the "Basement Tapes" recorded in the Harris basement, with the last dated April 20. Klebold and Harris give a chilling account of what they plan to do. They admit innocent people will be hurt but they aren't going to let that stop them. Eric quotes Shakespeare as he drinks Jack Daniels: "Good wombs hath borne bad sons." He and Dylan demonstrate how they can fit their sawed-off shotguns in their coats. They talk about the people they hate and what they'd like to do to them. Eric complains about having to move around a lot and being picked on at school. Dylan also talks about being picked on as far back as daycare, acknowledging "being shy didn't help". They both gloat about how many people they've fooled. They mock gun laws and talk about how famous they'll be.

March 18, 1999: Harris and Klebold make a hateful "Basement Tape" of racist rants. They name more people they want to hurt and talk about how graduation will be filled with tears. They want to send copies of their videos and plans to the news but expect authorities would destroy the information.

March 19, 1999: Klebold and Harris create 3 Delta batch crickets and 2 Echo batch.

March 22, 1999: Harris writes a to-do list that includes figuring out napalm recipe and storage, timing the pattern of people in the commons, getting more ammo, practicing in-car gear-up, preparing explosions for distractions, the commons, cars, and grenades. He includes "get laid" in the list. On that same page are lists of weapons, ammo, and bombs they've gathered.

March 25, 1999: The whole Klebold family drives to Tucson to visit the University of Arizona. They pay a deposit for Klebold's dorm room. His family later says he genuinely seemed to be looking forward to college life.

March 29, 1999: Harris logs creation of 5 Delta batch crickets and 2 Foxtrot batch.

March 31, 1999: The film *The Matrix* opens in theaters.

April 1999: Sometime in the first or second week of April, Morris is hanging out with Harris and Klebold at Dylan's house when Harris says something to the effect of "Wouldn't it be funny to kill all the jocks?" and laughs about it. Klebold says in response: "If we're going to do something like that, we're going to have to cut the power to the school and put bombs at the doors."

April 2, 1999: Harris speaks with Staff Sergeant Mark Gonzales about joining the military, saying he thought about college but was interested in the Marine Corps. After sharing personal details with the Staff

Sergeant—post-graduation plans and that he had never done drugs—
Eric is scheduled for an interview.

April 3, 1999: Harris writes a final journal entry about getting the
TEC-DC9 and testing it. He says they have 6 timebombs, 39 crickets,
24 pipe bombs, and napalm that's under construction. (Klebold
references the napalm in his journal as well, saying it's in someone's
fridge.) He talks a lot about NBK – his and Klebold's doomsday. Says
he feels like he's in a movie. Ends with a rant about hating everyone
for leaving him out of all their fun.

April 4, 1999: Harris logs making 14 "super cricket" bombs.

April 5, 1999: Harris drives himself to his Marines test. He wears black
pants, black combat boots, and a black T-shirt with the word
"Rammstein" on the front. He scores Average. At the end of the
interview, he tells the recruiter he wants to think about enlisting and
will discuss it with his parents.

April 8, 1999: Custodian Jay Gallentine arrives at Columbine just
before 5 a.m. and finds all the exterior door locks glued shut. Hearing
voices and footsteps on the roof, he calls the police and replaces the
locks. Someone spelled the word 'seniors' in duct tape across the large
glass skylight. JeffCo Sheriff's Deputy Neil Gardner, a School
Resource Officer assigned to Columbine, reviews security footage
from the student parking lot camera which is only on when school is
not in session. The tape shows two males in dark clothing, with gloves
and masks or hoods.

Harris returns to the military recruiting office to speak to Staff
Sergeant Gonzales again about enlisting. They arrange a home visit
from the Staff Sergeant for April 15th.

April 9, 1999: Harris celebrates his 18th birthday party at the Draft Bar
& Grill. At the party Cory Friesen hears Harris and Klebold talk about
how they wish "the jocks" were dead. He assumes they're joking. Chris
Morris is also there and hears Harris say they could attach bombs to
Columbine's generators to cause an explosion. Not wanting to hear
such things, Morris hangs out with other people.

April 11, 1999: Harris and Klebold make "Reb's Tape"—one of the
Basement Tapes. They discuss their plans and how the event will affect
their parents and people who care about them. They express regret for

the trouble it will cause their families but appear proud of their "two-man war against everyone else".

April 14, 1999: Staff Sergeant Gonzales meets Harris at Blackjack Pizza to confirm his home visit appointment. Angel Pytlinski sees Klebold and Harris. Harris seems depressed and Klebold's mood is "very inconsistent".

April 15, 1999: Klebold writes a poetic, undated journal entry about how in five days his pain will be over. He samples Pink Floyd lyrics and talks about how living was a test, that it's time to die and collect his "reward". He seems to think of love as a thing/person he will get as a prize after death.

Marines Staff Sergeant Mark Gonzales meets Eric and his father Wayne at the Harris home. During a conversation about Eric's future with the military, his mother joins them. Kathy asks if Eric will be eligible if he is taking an antidepressant. She shows the Sergeant one of her son's prescription bottles. He copies the name of the drug, Luvox, and says he'll check and call them.

April 16 or 17, 1999: Staff Sergeant Gonzales leaves a voicemail message at the Harris residence for Eric to call him, but never receives a call back. Gonzales has no further contact with Harris and is unable to inform him he isn't eligible to enlist. The prescription did not disqualify him; he could have requested a medical waiver for it. Harris not reporting his medical condition (*pectus excavatum*) and concealing his psychological history likely contributed to his ineligibility.

April 16-18, 1999: Sean Kennedy, a 12-year-old neighbor who sometimes played roller hockey with Harris, notices two or three months before the shootings that he *"just became a bat. He stayed inside his garage all the time."* Neighbors Debbie Wilde and her husband who live two houses down from the Harrises notice sounds of breaking glass and power saws from the garage. They've seen Klebold's BMW at the Harris house before and later tell the authorities it was there on Saturday the 17th. The teens are making shrapnel for pipe bombs.

Saturday, April 17, 1999: Posters around the school announce the prom date: "4/17/99". Student council senator Kelly Dickson notices someone defaced several posters. The number '17' is crossed out, replaced with a '20'. The words "It's coming" are written beside the date.

Columbine prom night. Twelve kids, including Dylan Klebold and Nate Dykeman, go to prom together in a limousine. Klebold's date is Robyn Anderson. She boasts to a friend shortly before prom: "*I convinced my friend Dylan, who hates dances, jocks, and has never had a date let alone a girlfriend to go with me! I am either really cute or just really persuasive!*"

According to friends, Anderson has a crush on Klebold, but he isn't interested in her romantically. They attend the dance as friends. Klebold is very upbeat. He talks happily about a future attending college in Arizona and plans to stay in touch. Dykeman takes his girlfriend Kristi Epling to prom. To him, Klebold's attitude is normal; everything goes "perfect": Chris Morris takes his girlfriend Nicole Markham. Zach Heckler takes his girlfriend Devon Adams. Rachel Scott goes with Nick Baumgart. Harris doesn't have a date for prom. He asked Sabrina Cooley, but she turned him down as she had a boyfriend. He skips prom and makes plans with Susan DeWitt, whom he met in January. A CHS junior, she works at the hair salon two doors down from Blackjack Pizza. She goes to Harris' house where they watch movies. Harris invites her to the after-prom party, but she declines. He meets his friends at the party. Harris and Klebold leave at around 3:30 a.m.

April 18 or 19, 1999: Klebold writes an undated journal entry saying he'll be dead in 26.5 hours. He relishes the idea there will be suffering and mourning and says everything has a touch of triviality to it in the final hours. The next entry is a Will. He only designates one person in it and their reward for always being there for him is that they get "FUCKT".

The next pages are assault plans, supply lists, and drawings of how the gunmen are going to carry their gear. One of his last journal entries reads: "*Walk in, set bombs at 11:09, for 11:17 Leave, set car bombs. Drive to Clemete [sic] Park. Gear up. Get back by 11:15 Park cars. set car bombs for 11:18 get out, go to outside hill, wait. When first bombs go off, attack. have fun!*" In the "To Do" list of things to buy and do for the assault, including practice in-car gear-ups, is "*Bday shit*".

200

A similar list appears in Harris' day planner in Klebold's writing:

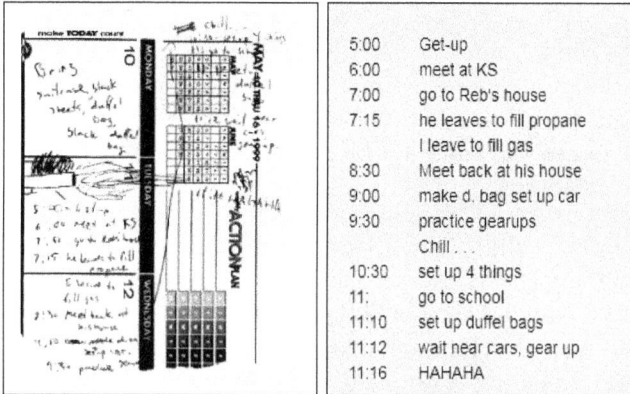

5:00	Get-up
6:00	meet at KS
7:00	go to Reb's house
7:15	he leaves to fill propane
	I leave to fill gas
8:30	Meet back at his house
9:00	make d. bag set up car
9:30	practice gearups
	Chill . . .
10:30	set up 4 things
11:	go to school
11:10	set up duffel bags
11:12	wait near cars, gear up
11:16	HAHAHA

Sunday, April 18, 1999: Zach Heckler calls Klebold for their nightly chat. They often play *Quake* while on speakerphone.

Monday, April 19, 1999: During third hour around 9:30 a.m. Harris and Klebold make a video with friends Eric Jackson and Dustin Gorton—a "looking video assignment" and a "set up video" for the school's morning announcements. In it they drive up to Burger King in Gorton's 1972 Chevrolet Chevelle. Klebold is in the front passenger seat, Gorton is driving, and Harris is in the back. They buy breakfast and drive to Columbine's student parking lot where they eat and end the video. Klebold is supposed to edit the video with Gorton the next morning in class.

Junior Nicholas Romanyshyn, Eric Veik's friend, is in the hall outside the Tech Lab with several other students, filming a video. He sees Harris, who is in the same class, come and sit down on the floor. He notices Harris writing on some white papers. Another student, Ryan Selchert, asks Harris what he's doing. He replies: "I'm just working on finalizing my plans for tomorrow."

Romanyshyn jokes to Mike Vendegnia: *"Yeah, we'll come to school tomorrow and the school won't be here."*

The gunmen skip Creative Writing (2nd to last class of the day) with Brooks Brown and Becca Hines. Brown and Hines go to McDonald's. Klebold and Harris are supposed to meet them after a side trip to Eric's house. They don't return. They skip their last class, Psychology, as well. Kristi Epling sees them in the Columbine parking lot around

201

2:30-2:40 p.m. She finds this unusual because they never stay after school.

Harris asks Mark Manes to buy ammunition for him, though he's old enough to purchase it now. Manes buys 100 rounds for $25 from a local Kmart and gives it to Eric later that night. When he asks Harris if he's going to use the ammo for target shooting that night, Harris tells him: *"No. Tomorrow.".*

A man hanging wallpaper next door hears glass breaking and explosive sounds from the Harris garage. That evening Andrew Beard talks to Klebold on the phone about a fantasy baseball trade. Klebold says he'll think about it and tell him tomorrow. Heckler calls Klebold for their nightly chat. Klebold says he's not in the mood to talk and just wants to go to bed. Heckler thinks it's odd as they are usually on the phone until 12:30-1:00 a.m.

TUESDAY, APRIL 20, 1999: After missing his arranged time to pick up Chris Morris, Harris and Klebold are seen by Andrew Beard outside the bowling alley at around 7:15 a.m. Beard wants to talk to Dylan about the fantasy baseball trade but by 7:30, the teens are already gone. Harris buys two propane tanks at a Conoco gas station at 8:36 a.m. At 9:12 he is seen on CCTV buying another one.

11:19 a.m.: Eric Harris and Dylan Klebold storm Columbine High School, killing Rachel Scott, Daniel Rohrbough, Kyle Velasquez, Steven Curnow, Cassie Bernall, Isaiah Shoels, Matt Kechter, Lauren Townsend, John Tomlin, Kelly Fleming, Daniel Mauser, Corey DePooter and William "Dave" Sanders. They also injure Brian Anderson, Richard Castaldo, Jennifer Doyle, Stephen Austin Eubanks, Nick Foss, Sean Graves, Makai Hall, Anne Marie Hochhalter, Patrick Ireland, Joyce Jankowski, Michael Johnson, Mark Kintgen, Lance Kirklin, Lisa Kreutz, Adam Kyler, Stephanie Munson, Patti Nielson, Nicole Nowlin, Jenna Park, Kacey Ruegsegger, Valeen Schnurr, Dan Steepleton, Mark Taylor and Evan Todd. It is the worst school shooting in American history at the time.

Search warrants issued for the Klebold and Harris houses. Investigator Kate Battan uses Guerra's files on Harris to help draft the warrant for his house.

Sarah Slater talks to Zach Heckler after hearing Klebold was one of the shooters. She also talks to Heckler's sister Jocelyn, who says her brother knew the gunmen were planning the attack, but he never believed they would do it.

Tad Boles calls off from work at Dish Network after the shooting, citing concern for his younger sister. Boles dropped out and got his GED in 1998 and was not at Columbine during the massacre. His employer finds out Boles' sister was home sick that day and that he knew it when he called off.

April 21, 1999: Bomb squads thoroughly search Columbine High for explosives. Thousands of people visit Clement Park, leaving flowers and other memorials for those who died. The park becomes the unofficial gathering place for mourners.

A memorial service is held that morning at Light of the World Catholic Church to honor the victims. Principal Frank DeAngelis gives an emotional speech to the huge crowd, many of whom are Columbine students. DeAngelis promises to stay on as principal until at least 2002, when the current freshmen will be the graduating class. The Colorado Avalanche cancel their first two playoff games. The National Rifle Association (NRA) announces a scaled back program for its convention next week in Denver.

Tad Boles is overheard at work claiming to be best friends with Harris and Klebold, and that his father is in prison for weapons violation. That same day, Alex Marsh, an associate of the Trench Coat Mafia, defends the shooters in a news interview.

8:30 a.m.: The official death toll is released: 15 dead. The bomb squad declares the building safe for officials to enter.

11:30 a.m., April 21, 1999: A sheriff's spokesman tells anxious news crews and their audiences, "The investigation is under way." 13 bodies are still in the school when investigators begin photographing the building.

2:05 p.m.: Two forensics teams investigate the library. Team One covers the east side. Broken glass from the shattered windows falls on Team Two. Growing storm winds blow evidence cards away. The teams focus on ballistics at and in the windows then have the windows boarded up so the rest of the investigation can continue. They document positions of the dead and collect evidence that might be disturbed when the bodies are removed. Team Three investigates the halls.

2:30 p.m.: Jefferson County District Attorney David Thomas and Sheriff John Stone hold a press conference. They suspect others helped plan the shooting. Formal identifications of the dead have not taken place yet. The victims' bodies are removed from the school through the afternoon and late evening. They are taken to the Jefferson County Coroner's Office to be identified and autopsied. The shooters' bodies are removed last. As they are taken out a blizzard begins that lasts through the weekend.

5:00 PM, April 21, 1999: Identities of the dead are becoming publicly known.

AColumbineSite.com comes online. A simple memorial site at first, it soon becomes one of the internet's only reliable sources for updates and information about the tragedy.

April 22, 1999: Officials find an unexploded 20-pound propane bomb in Columbine's kitchen area.

Tad Boles resigns from his job at Dish Network saying he needs "time off". Dish Network suspends him and deactivates his badge.

West Bowles Community Church holds a memorial service honoring the victims of the shooting. Principal Frank DeAngelis is asked to appear. He is greeted by students calling out to him: "We love you, Mr. De!" and "We are Columbine!". He is too overcome to speak, but a counselor tells him later his crying gave students permission to cry as well. Jerry Alber and Rick Dendorfer, parents of Columbine students who survived the shooting, attend the memorial. Rick's daughter Erika is Seth Houy's girlfriend. Houy was in the library during the Columbine shootings. Erika introduces the men to Alex Marsh who tells them: "Yeah, they'd been planning it since December." Then she walks away. Alber gets the impression from her cold, matter-of-fact manner that she knew the shooting was going to happen.

That night, a candlelight vigil is held at St. Frances Cabrini Catholic Church.

April 23, 1999: John Tomlin's funeral is held in his hometown of Waterford, Wisconsin, in Saint Peters Cemetery.

Principal Frank DeAngelis makes his first media appearance on NBC's *Today* show with Katie Couric.

Tad Boles is fired from his job with Echostar Security for making an "unknow offensive statement" regarding the Columbine shooting. That same day, Boles asks Dish Network if he can restart the training program on April 27. They contact their legal team to terminate his employment and keep him off the premises.

Kristi Epling finds some old notes written to her by Eric Harris and mails them to her friend Lindsay Balsam in St. Louis for safekeeping. She also sends a page from her yearbook on which Eric wrote a lengthy message with a note to publish it should anything happen to him. Balsam turns the pages over to investigators. When officials ask Epling about them, she says she mailed them to get them out of her house, that they were painful to look at, but she didn't want to destroy them. By sending them to Lindsay she hoped to retrieve them when her memory of the tragic event wasn't as clear. She denies trying to hide them.

Over 100 investigators meet in the Columbine band room to determine if anyone helped the shooters or had prior knowledge of the attack. Seven teams are formed to interview thousands of CHS students and employees, along with any individuals brought up over the course of the interviews. The teams are:

- **Threats team.** Headed by JeffCo Sheriff's Sergeant JJ Webb. This group handles threats of copycat violence that crop up in the days after the shooting.
- **Internet team.** Follows up on Internet threats and leads.
- **Associates team.** Led by JeffCo Sheriff's Investigator Don Estep and FBI Special Agent Mark Holstlaw.
- **Bureau of Alcohol, Tobacco, and Firearms (ATF)** traces the source of weapons and bombs the shooters used. Headed up by Special Agents Marcus Motte and Matthew Traver.
- **Outside team.** Led by FBI Special Agent Mike Barnett and JCSO Investigators Jack McFadden and Cheryl Zimmerman. They investigate what Dylan and Eric did that morning and interview witnesses who were outside the school during the shooting.
- **Cafeteria team.** Headed by FBI Special Agent Rich Price and Denver Police Department Sergeant Calvin Hemphill.

Interviews witnesses in the cafeteria commons and identifies when the propane bombs were placed.
- **Library team.** Interviews survivors from the library and establishes a second-by-second sequence of events. Led by Arvada Police Detective Russ Boatright, FBI Special Agent John Elvig, and JCSO Investigator Diane Obbema.
- **Computer/Forensics team.** Led by CBI Agent Chuck Davis. Investigates computers and media belonging to the shooters, the Internet sites they created and visited, and sites that sprang up after the shooting.

There are also a **Documentation team** and a **Crime Scene team**.

April 24, 1999: Rachel Scott's 1:30 p.m. funeral at Trinity Christian Center is broadcast by CNN. It is the most-watched event in CNN's history. More than 1,500 people attend. Many friends and family speak at the service, which has Celine Dion's "My Heart Will Go On" on loop to a slideshow of pictures of Rachel. Her coffin is an ivory one that the mourners can write on, much like a yearbook. Her forensics teacher Paula Reed breaks down crying when she signs it. Scott's mother writes: *"Honey, You are everything a mother could ever ask the Lord for in a daughter. I love you so much! – Mom"*.

At the same time, Dylan Klebold's funeral is held. It's a private service with 11 mourners. Reverend Don Marxhausen, who has been the Klebolds' pastor at St Philip Lutheran Church for the past year, presides. Randy Brown, Brooks' father, attends as does Zach Heckler. The service is open coffin. A mound of Beanie Babies hides Klebold's fatal wound. He is cremated after.

There are no services for Eric Harris per power of attorney to H. Ellis Armistead, a private investigator who assists the Harrises. Armistead later works for John and Patsy Ramsey, parents of murder victim JonBenét, and for Oklahoma City bomber Timothy McVeigh during his appeal. In his book *Homegrown: Timothy McVeigh and the Rise of Right-Wing Extremism*, attorney and former CNN legal analyst Jeffrey Toobin says Harris was cremated and kept in an evidence storage locker in Armistead's care. In 2001, Armistead stores McVeigh's cremains next to Harris'.

Principal Frank DeAngelis is allowed back into Columbine for the first time since the shooting, accompanied by FBI Agent Dwayne Fuselier. Fuselier's son Scott made a video for A/V class in 1997 that featured kids shooting each other and Columbine blowing up. Dwayne's younger son Brian was a freshman who was in the cafeteria when the shooting started.

April 25, 1999: Funerals for Kelly Fleming and Daniel Mauser are held together at Saint Frances Cabrini Catholic Church at 5:15 p.m.

An official memorial is held at West Bowles Shopping Center. Vice President Al Gore and his wife Tipper, Governor Bill Owens, Principal Frank DeAngelis, and music artists Amy Grant and Michael W. Smith are there. 70,000 people attend the televised event.

April 26, 1999: Funeral for Lauren Townsend is at 10 a.m. at Foothills Bible Church. William "Dave" Sanders' private funeral is held at 10 a.m. at the Church of Christ adjacent to Chapel Hill Cemetery. Cassie Bernall's funeral is held at West Bowles Community Church at 11 a.m. Daniel Rohrbough's funeral is at Grace Presbyterian Church at 2 p.m.

Officials learn three of the four guns used in the massacre at Columbine were bought by Klebold's friend, Robyn Anderson, shortly after her 18th birthday.

At 12:47 p.m. police are dispatched to the Harris residence on a burglary in progress call. Deputy Paul Magor, Sergeant John Mayns, and Deputy Edward Pearson arrive at around 12:49. All three were on scene at Columbine during the shooting. Nancy D;Amico, one of H. Ellis Armistead's employees, went to the house to fetch some things for the Harrises and heard an intruder. They search the house with a K9 unit but don't find anyone.

April 27, 1999: Kyle Velasquez's funeral held at St. James Presbyterian Church at 10:30 a.m. Because his father Al is a Navy veteran, Kyle is buried at Fort Logan National Cemetery in Denver, Colorado.

Matt Kechter's funeral is at St Frances Cabrini Catholic Church. He is buried at Mount Olivet Cemetery in Wheat Ridge, Colorado.

Later that day, Greg Zanis—known as the "Cross Guy" because he crafts memorial crosses for murder victims—arrives at Clement Park, responding to survivor Brian Anderson's request. Zanis erects 15 crosses on Rebel Hill, 13 for those who were killed and 2 for the shooters. His inclusion of the gunmen is met with harsh criticism, particularly from the victims' families. His rationale is: The parents of

207

the gunmen lost kids too. The families contend memorials to murderers should not be displayed next to those of their victims.

Jen Harmon, cousin of victim Mark Taylor, tells investigators in that the gunmen were trying to "recreate what Robert Craig did" or "follow in his footsteps". Craig, a friend of TCM members Joe Stair and Brian Sargent, killed his stepfather and himself in 1997. According to Harmon, before the murder-suicide Craig told people he was going to kill his stepdad because he was taking his mother's attention away from him.

April 29, 1999: Isaiah Shoels' funeral is held at the Heritage Christian Center. Martin Luther King, Jr. speaks in his honor. Isaiah is buried at Fairmount Cemetery in Denver, Colorado.

Library survivor Lindsay Elmore appears on Denver News Channel 7's special program *Kids in Crisis*.

April 30, 1999: High-ranking officials from Jefferson County and JCSO meet at an Open Space office to decide if they should reveal Investigator Guerra knew of Harris' threatening website two years before the Columbine shootings. In attendance are Sheriff John Stone, Undersheriff John Dunaway, Lieutenant John Kiekbusch, public information officer Steve Davis, District Attorney Dave Thomas, Assistant DA Kathy Sasak, County Attorney Mike Hutfless, his assistants William Tuthill and Lily Oeffler, and Deputy Mike Guerra. They decide to "lose" the Guerra documents for "liability purposes".

JeffCo spokesman Steve Davis and Lieutenant John Kiekbusch speak at a press conference later that day. Davis reads a statement prepared by Lieutenant Jeff Shrader to explain deputy response to the Brown complaint. They say the Browns never met with an investigator (untrue—they met with investigator John Hicks), that they were unable to find anything on the internet about Harris at the time (Guerra accessed Harris' website), that Harris wasn't found in their computer system (Hicks found Harris' burglary record, as did Thomas' assistant), and the Browns didn't want police to contact the Harrises (they didn't want the Harrises to know they were behind the complaint). Kiekbusch reiterates the lies when questioned. Davis says they compared the information about pipe bombs to devices found in the county but there was no match—also untrue. In Guerra's search warrant affidavit, he matched pipe bombs in Harris' web descriptions to a bomb found near the Harris residence. He also connected it to Harris and Klebold's

208

participation in the diversion program. JeffCo releases the Brown complaint to the public, but Guerra's investigative work is not disclosed.

When pressed about lack of follow-up on Harris' websites, Kiekbusch admits they should have called the Browns back, but that Harris' claims were "outlandish fantasy". He says the case remained open and that Deputy Neil Gardner kept an eye on Klebold and Harris, occasionally engaging them in "light conversation". He later says Guerra's records were purged by then—also not true (they still had the documents as of 2001). The sheriff's office has a copy which is withheld from Stone's successors, Russ Cook and Ted Mink.

That same day Brian Rohrbough, father of victim Daniel, tears down 2 of the 15 wooden crosses Greg Zanis made—the ones dedicated to the killers. His father Claude and Danny's stepfather Rich Petrone assist him. Brian says afterward:

> "I don't think any thinking person in this country is going to disagree with me. We never, ever honor a murderer in the same place as the memorial for his victims."

Most onlookers agree with him.

First week of May 1999: Dave Sanders' wedding anniversary should have been celebrated.

May 1, 1999: The NRA holds its national convention in Denver, Colorado, scaled back and downplayed. The 1998 NRA meeting had over 54,000 attendees. In 2000 they had approximately 40,000 attendees. The meeting in 1999 has about 3,000. Roughly 8,000 protesters show up too, including Tom Mauser. This prompts NRA President Charlton Heston to give a defiant speech on the right to bear arms and his position against gun control laws.

May 2, 1999: A student memorial is held at Red Rocks Amphitheater. Public mourning has become a community norm: It's not uncommon to see people crying in public places.

May 3, 1999: Columbine students resume classes at Chatfield High. The school day is divided: Chatfield students use the school in the morning, Columbine students go in the afternoon. Donations from all over pour in: T-shirts, school supplies, blankets, food. The Healing Bear arrives. It was first sent anonymously to the victims of the

Oklahoma City bombing. It is later sent to Area Senior High in Montoursville, PA, after an explosion kills 4 chaperones, 16 students, and 1 teacher during a French Club trip to Paris.

22-year-old Mark Manes surrenders to authorities on felony charges of selling a gun to a minor. He admits to selling the TEC-DC9 to Harris and Klebold.

May 4, 1999: Sheriff John Stone appears on the *Today* show. He claims the Brown family's criticism is a "smokescreen to divert attention" away from Brooks' friendship with the shooters and that he "could possibly be a suspect".

May 5, 1999: *Inside Edition* airs footage from a video Scott Fuselier made for school in 1997 of him and his friends shooting guns at and blowing up Columbine. It is eerily predictive of the 1999 shooting. Scott, who graduated in 1997, is the son of FBI Agent Dwayne Fuselier, a psychologist who is one of three investigators leading the Columbine probe. When reporters asked Brooks Brown about the video, he claimed to be involved in the production but in his book, *No Easy Answers*, says that he said that to take the heat off the investigator. Prior to Columbine, Agent Fuselier was known for being one of the top negotiators in the 1996 Freemen standoff in Montana. He was also at the Branch Davidian standoff in Waco, Texas on April 19, 1993.

May 19, 1999: *Star Wars: Phantom Menace* opens in theaters. Fans of the film who support victim Steve Curnow's wish to be at the opening hold a group attendance in the slain boy's honor.

May 20, 1999: President Bill and first lady Hillary Clinton meet with Columbine victims and families at the Light of the World Catholic Church in Littleton. President Clinton is late to give a graduation speech at Dakota Ridge High School because he felt the people at the church needed him more.

May 21, 1999: Brooks Brown and his mother Judy appear on a special episode of the *Oprah Winfrey Show* (episode 13E99) to tell their side of things.

May 22, 1999: Columbine High School graduation day. Lauren Townsend and Isaiah Shoels should have graduated. The shooters were also supposed to be in the graduating class. Frank DeAngelis presents

Townsend's mother Dawn Anna and stepfather Bruce Beck with a diploma, cap, and gown. Survivors Jeanna Park, Lisa Kreutz, and Valeen Schnurr receive their diplomas though all three are still recovering from injuries. Lisa is in a wheelchair when she receives hers. The gunmen are not mentioned.

May 25, 1999: The Healing Fund, established by Mile High United Way, has received over $2.3 million in donations. The Jefferson Foundation has received $250,000, including $50,000 from Rosie O'Donnell. The amount is so generous it threatens the organization's status as a nonprofit. They ask her to void the check and write a smaller one to the Healing Fund. Other issues with the donation are questions about disbursement as it was marked for "the families of the deceased" which could mean 13 or 15 families. Other donations include $10K from the Colorado Garden Show, $50K from a Denver department store, and over $10K from the CHS Alumni Fund.

May 26, 1999: The SHOUTS center, Students Helping Others Unite Together Socially, opens in the Ascot Theater on West Bowles Avenue. Violent video games are removed from the arcade at Denver International Airport.

May 27, 1999: A $250 million wrongful-death lawsuit is filed by the family of Isaiah Shoels against the parents of both gunmen.

May 28, 1999: The Columbine autopsy reports are sealed by Jefferson County District Court Judge Henry Nieto.

Summer 1999: Rick Townsend, father of victim Lauren, starts the *Never Forgotten Fund* with help from Clear Channel Communication radio to set up scholarships of $5,000 each in the memory of each student who died and in honor of Dave Sanders. The *Columbine Memorial Scholarship Fund* along with *Rocky Mountain News* also grants scholarships to JeffCo students.

June 1999: English teacher Claudia Abbott travels with Columbine students to Conyers, GA to visit victims of the Heritage High shooting on May 20, 1999.

June 1, 1999: Students return to Columbine High to pick up their belongings. Many of them throw away the clothes they wore on April 20th and toss out backpacks without even opening them.

June 2, 1999: Dylan Klebold's parents send letters to the victims' families.

June 3, 1999: Renovations begin on Columbine High so classes can resume in August. Most of the work is done by volunteers.

June 4, 1999: Robyn Anderson admits in court to buying the two shotguns and the rifle used in the Columbine massacre.

June 16, 1999: Authorities announce the surveillance tape from Columbine's cafeteria disproves rumors of a third gunman. Only two shooters appear on the tape: Eric Harris and Dylan Klebold.

June 17, 1999: Prosecutors file charges against Philip Duran, 22 for unlawfully providing a handgun to minors. Duran's younger siblings Julia, a senior, and Simon, a sophomore, were in the school during the shooting.

July 2, 1999: The Healing Fund announces plans to distribute the money it has collected. Ballistics tests confirm "friendly fire" from police officers did not harm anyone at Columbine.

July 14, 1999: Investigators question Brenda Parker, a 24-year-old woman in Broomfield, Colorado. She claimed in internet forums, chatrooms, and instant messenger that she dated Eric Harris, hung out with the gunmen, and helped them plan the shooting. She retracts her claims in a September re-interview.

July 20, 1999: Students and families return to CHS to decorate memorial tiles. Religious symbolism is not allowed or anything that might be considered controversial, violent, or hateful since the tiles will be displayed in the school.

August 16, 1999: Four months after the shootings Columbine High School, newly remodeled, reopens its doors. 2,000 students show up, shielded from media by parents and faculty members who line the sidewalk. Students attend a *Reclaim the School* rally before class where everyone chants: "We are Columbine". The American flag that stood at half-mast since the tragedy is finally raised again. A new school year officially begins.

The football season is dedicated to Matt Kechter. Players wear blue ribbons in his honor. Jersey #70, Matt's number, is retired. Some players get tattoos of the number.

August 18, 1999: Three swastikas are found etched on the walls of Columbine, roughly an inch big. One is scratched into a brick wall and two are found inside a girls' bathroom.

Mark Manes pleads guilty to providing a handgun to a minor and illegal possession of a sawed-off shotgun. He is to be sentenced November 12. He sold the TEC-9 to Dylan Klebold for $500. Introduced to the gunmen by Philip Duran, Klebold paid Manes $300 up front then gave Duran $200 to give to Manes.

August 20, 1999: Richard Castaldo released from Craig Hospital. Partially paralyzed, he is the last survivor to leave the hospital.

August 31, 1999: The Healing Fund accepts its last donations, bringing the grand total received to $4.4 million.

September: Matt Kechter and Daniel Mauser are posthumously accepted into the National Honor Society.

Lance Kirklin, his dad Mike, and uncle Mitch go hunting in the town of Cope to help Lance reclaim his life. He was a hunter before the shooting and finds the experience empowering.

English teacher Jason Webb notices faculty and students are avoiding the temporary library that's housed in a double-wide trailer. With help from donations of fish and equipment, he starts a "fish therapy" project setting up an indoor salt reef inside the library. Soon he has a team of student helpers. Enthusiasm spreads to the faculty who create aquarium-oriented lessons and assignments. The HOPE foundation includes a larger, built-in reef aquarium in their plans for the new library.

September 1, 1999: Security is tightened at schools in Jefferson County after five high schools receive a series of anonymous threatening letters.

Misty Bernall publishes her book, *She Said Yes: The Unlikely Martyrdom of Cassie Bernall*, about how her daughter told the gunmen she was a Christian and was shot for her belief. This claim is later proven untrue by journalist Dave Cullen. Bernall stands by her book as a testament to her daughter's spirit and the plight all the victims were in.

213

September 7, 1999: Investigators conduct a follow-up interview with Brenda Parker about her claims of being involved in the Columbine shooting. Parker admits she made everything up, she has no intention of harming anyone, and she has "no life and spends way too much time on the Internet".

September 10, 1999: Dave Sanders Memorial Softball Field is dedicated before the start of the Columbine Rebel girls' softball season. Winslow Construction, owned by Columbine alumnus Bryant Winslow, helped build the field.

September 16, 1999: Carla Hochhalter, mother of survivor Anne Marie, seeks help at the hospital for her mental state. She was battling depression for at least three years prior to the shooting.

September 22, 1999: Salon.com publishes excerpts from Harris' journals.

September 24, 1999: JCSO spokesman Steve Davis says it is unlikely Cassie Bernall was asked by the gunmen whether she believed in God before they shot her.

Patrick Ireland named homecoming king of Columbine High.

September 26, 1999: Parents and friends of victims Daniel Rohrbough and Kyle Velasquez march to Littleton's West Bowles Community Church to chop down 2 of the 15 memorial trees the church planted to acknowledge the pain all the affected families were feeling.

September 29, 1999: Governor Bill Owens creates a 14-member Columbine Review Commission to study the tragedy and make recommendations to prevent future shootings.

October 1, 1999: Celine Dion holds a concert at the opening of the Pepsi Center in Denver. She dedicates it to victims and survivors of the Columbine shooting. She gives front-row seats and backstage passes to Principal DeAngelis and several students, some of whom were injured during the tragedy. The Columbine choir sings "Our Hearts Will Go On" with Dion. The concert raises $500,000 which the singer donates to the Colorado Organization of Victim Assistance.

October 4, 1999: The families of Kelly Fleming and Daniel Rohrbough file a federal lawsuit against the school district for removing the memorial tiles they painted on July 20. The tiles were removed

214

because they feature religious themes. The rules of the event stipulated no controversial or religious subjects, or anything that might make returning students feel uncomfortable.

October 12, 1999: *CBS Evening News with Dan Rather* airs a portion of the surveillance tape from the Columbine cafeteria.

October 14, 1999: Carla Hochhalter is released from inpatient mental health care to an outpatient program.

October 17, 1999: The families of 20 Columbine students file notices of intent to sue the sheriff's department and/or the school district. The Klebolds announce their intent to sue Jefferson County for failing to follow up on the Guerra Report they "lost" after the shooting.

October 19, 1999: The evening before the six-month anniversary of the shootings, a 17-year-old Columbine student is arrested on suspicion of threatening to "finish the job".

October 20, 1999: Six-month anniversary of the April 20th shootings. A quarter of CHS students miss school that day; another quarter go home early.

October 22, 1999: Carla Hochhalter enters Alpha Pawn Shop in Englewood and asks to see a gun. While the clerk fills out her background check, she loads the gun with bullets she brought with her and shoots herself in the head in front of 6-10 witnesses. She is pronounced dead at the hospital. Diagnosed with depression before the shootings, the stress of having a daughter paralyzed in the tragedy was too much for her.

October 25, 1999: Wayne and Kathy Harris, parents of shooter Eric Harris, finally agree to meet with investigators.

October 26, 1999: *Duck! The Carbine High Massacre* film is released online. The black comedy is written, produced, directed by, and stars William Hellfire and Joey Smack. After its release, Smack and Hellfire are arrested for possession of weapons on school property. The film is the source of much controversy.

November 1999: Lance Kirklin goes on another hunting trip with his dad. He uses a 12-gauge shotgun, the same type of weapon Klebold shot him with. Lance shoots an aluminum can. Amazed by how the can disintegrates he thinks he must have tough skin to have survived such a blast. The largest fragment of the can is no bigger than a U.S. quarter.

November 2, 1999: Arthur Thomas is charged with three counts of sending threatening letters to people involved with Columbine.

November 12, 1999: Mark Manes is sentenced to 6 years in prison for selling the TEC-DC9 to Harris and Klebold. Robyn Anderson, who bought the other 3 guns, isn't even charged. Neither are the vendors who sold the guns at the Tanner Gun Show or the man who runs the show.

December 1999: Undersheriff John A. Dunaway and Division Commander John Kiekbusch of Jefferson County Sheriff's Office hold a closed hearing based on Sheriff John Stone's representation that his department is engaged in an ongoing investigation. No record is made of the hour-and-a-half meeting. Immediately following the meeting, Sheriff Stone turns over video tapes and other evidence to *TIME* magazine—before the victims' families even see it.

Lance Kirklin's mother Dawn loses her nursing job due to PTSD, which she was diagnosed with a month earlier. Lance has wanted nothing to do with her since the shooting.

December 4, 1999: Columbine's football team beats Cherry Creek High, 21-14, winning the State Varsity title. Adam Kechter,13, is presented with the trophy in honor of his older brother, Matt, who should have played as a defensive lineman. Whether he got to keep it is unclear.

December 13, 1999: JeffCo holds a press viewing of edited versions of the Basement Tapes after reporter Tim Roche lets it leak that he was allowed access to the information for his article in *TIME* magazine. Randy Brown gets word of it and shows up with his wife Judy. Sergeant Webb tells Randy "media only". He pushes his way into the room, saying he has as much right to be there as anyone. The detective doesn't make him leave. Judy joins him.

December 15, 1999: Columbine student Erin Walton receives a threat in an Internet chatroom from "Soup81" (Michael Ian Campbell), warning her not to go to school the next day because he intends to "finish what begun". Campbell lives in Cape Coral, Florida but authorities don't know where he is, so Columbine cancels classes, ending the semester two days early.

December 17, 1999: FBI agents arrest Michael Campbell, who pleads not guilty with the odd defense "Internet intoxication" until prosecution finds evidence he made another threat by telephone 20 months earlier. He changes his plea to guilty. His mother Pam says Campbell's father died from cancer November 1999 and she fears being alone. Campbell faces up to 5 years in prison and a $250,000 fine.

December 16, 1999: Columbine hosts Tim McCloone's Holiday Express celebration on a stage donated by Bruce Springsteen.

December 20, 1999: *TIME* magazine releases an issue featuring excerpts from the "Basement Tapes" made by Harris and Klebold, inciting outrage among the victims' families. They're upset that a media outlet has access to information they don't. After serious pressure from the victims' families, officials agree to let them view the same footage the media saw.

December 22, 1999: Michael Campbell appears in federal court and apologizes for the threat he made on December 15.

2000 — January 11: Arthur Thomas and Michael Campbell indicted for threatening people involved with Columbine.

January 12, 2000: Jefferson County Sheriff John Stone is issued a temporary restraining order for releasing the Basement Tapes.

January 20, 2000: Jefferson County school board votes 4-1 to demolish the old library at Columbine and replace it with an atrium. The vote includes plans to build a new library.

Philip Duran pleads not guilty to the charges against him.

January 21, 2000: Sharon Magness pledges $250,000 to help Columbine build a new school library.

January 27, 2000: The Colorado House Judiciary Committee passes nine bills making tougher gun-buying regulations in Colorado. Robyn Anderson, who legally bought three of the four guns used during the shooting, speaks on behalf of the bills. Legislature rejects a bill that would mandate background checks for buyers at gun shows.

January 28, 2000: Governor Bill Owens signs the order to create the Columbine Review Commission, which will inquire into the shooting and make recommendations about how the event could have been handled better. Sheriff John Stone repeatedly refuses to give the Commission copies of the same evidence and tapes he gave to *TIME* magazine, local media, and others on the grounds that the victims' families are pursuing civil litigation against Jefferson County over prior release of the materials.

January 31, 2000: Isaiah Shoels' family moves to Houston, Texas.

February 2000 — The ESPY Arthur Ashe Courage and Humanitarian award posthumously given to Dave Sanders. Angela Sanders, Dave's daughter, plans "Rebel Yell 2000" concert for the 1st anniversary in Las Vegas to lift spirits.

February 9, 2000: Michael Campbell pleads guilty to communicating a threat across state lines.

February 13, 2000: Columbine students Nicholas Kunselman (15 years old) and Stephanie Hart-Grizell (16) are shot to death at night at a Subway restaurant 2 blocks south of Columbine High School. They were boyfriend and girlfriend. Kunselman was supposed to lock up; Hart-Grizell was there to give him a ride home. Columbine victim Rachel Scott used to work at the Subway with Kunselman.

February 14, 2000: The bodies of Hart-Grizell and Kunselman are discovered at the restaurant at around 1:30 a.m. on Valentine's Day by another Subway employee who noticed the lights were still on when she drove by. Nothing was stolen. Investigators suspect a possible link to drug dealing.

February 19, 2000: Kunselman and Hart-Grizell are buried alongside each other in a joint funeral.

March 2000: Teacher Claudia Abbott and AP English students travel to Dunblane, Scotland, to attend a memorial dedication to 16 students and a teacher were killed at school in 1996 in the UK's deadliest mass shooting.

March 3, 2000: Jefferson County Assistant Attorney Bill Tuthill announces that until litigation concludes, the sheriff's office won't make public any of the shooters' videotapes, diaries, or lists.

March 11, 2000: Stonemasons build a new staircase outside Columbine to replace the one where the shooting started.

March 12, 2000: Dawn Anna is given the Sportswomen of Colorado's award for courage and inspiration.

March 27, 2000: JeffCo Undersheriff John Dunaway announces the official sheriff's office report will be released in May.

March 30, 2000: Bruce Springsteen donates 50 seats at his concert as a fundraiser for HOPE, to help the organization raise money to build the new library at Columbine.

April 5, 2000: The SHOUTS center announces that due to a lack of funding it will close at the end of June.

April 9, 2000: To keep the media away during the upcoming one-year anniversary, Columbine is open to the public for tours.

April 10, 2000: To decide whether to sue Jefferson County Sheriff's Department, the families of Kelly Fleming and Daniel Rohrbough demand the release of the department's investigative report. Lawsuits must be filed by the one-year anniversary of the event according to Colorado law.

April 12, 2000: President Clinton returns to Denver for a SAFE Colorado gun control rally and a town hall meeting with NBC anchor Tom Brokaw. Most of Colorado's congressional delegation declines to meet the President.

April 14, 2000: Families of victims Kelly Fleming and Daniel Rohrbough file a Public Records Act lawsuit against the Jefferson County Sheriff's Office. They want access to the documents the office refuses to release.

April 15, 2000: The shooters' parents issue public apology letters.

April 17, 2000: Colorado District Judge Brooke Jackson rules that the families of Dan Rohrbough and Kelly Fleming can view portions of the sheriff's unreleased report and tapes. They are not allowed to make copies or discuss what they see with the public.

April 18, 2000: Judge Jackson includes all the families of those affected by the shootings in his ruling, allowing them to see the investigative documents. Isaiah Shoels' family is first to file a wrongful death suit against the Sheriff's Office. Nine lawsuits on behalf of 20 students are pending in federal court.

April 19, 2000: Fourteen other families file lawsuits against the sheriff and authorities over the leaked video tapes. Daniel Rohrbough's family alleges he was killed by "friendly fire" after Arapahoe County Sheriff's Deputy James Taylor tells them that's what he saw. Taylor has been a friend of the Rohrboughs for 20 years, so they believe him. Officials deny the accusation.

April 20, 2000: Many Columbine families decide to leave town rather than face the media flooding the area for the one-year anniversary. Half of Columbine's students arrive at the school for a private memorial assembly in the gym while parents gather in the auditorium. Governor Bill Owens leads a state-wide moment of silence at 11:21 a.m. to honor the victims and survivors.

Columbine High opens the library to parents (but not students), to help them cope with the anniversary. At 12:30 p.m. a public remembrance ceremony is held at Clement Park. Thousands of people attend. Heavy foot traffic kills the grass on Rebel Hill where the memorial crosses are set up.

Columbine Rebels girls' soccer team defeats Chatfield 2-0. A candlelight memorial is held at Clement Park amphitheater.

Beth Nimmo and Darrell Scott publish *Rachel's Tears: The Spiritual Journey of Columbine Martyr Rachel Scott*.

April 24, 2000: District Court Judge Brooke Jackson orders the JCSO to release the Columbine investigative report by May 15, 2000.

April 26, 2000: The first records sought by the victims' families are released to the public. Copies of the Columbine "Fire Department training tape" are also released and sold by JeffCo for $25.00. The tape includes a 20-minute walk-through of the school the day after the massacre, with footage of blood-stained furniture in the library and close-ups of evidence cards where dead students were found. The video is produced by Littleton firefighter Chuck Burdick on his own time, set to music including: "I Will Remember You" by Sarah McLachlan, "Friend of Mine (Columbine)" by Jonathan and Stephen Cohen, and "If It Were Up to Me" by Cheryl Wheeler. The tape

220

includes nearly 2 hours of aerial footage shot April 20, 1999, by KCNC-News4.

By the end of the day, all three major networks have broadcast parts of the Basement Tapes and Fire Department tape on the news. The training tape has already been shown 82 times in seminars around the nation.

April 27, 2000: Families of Columbine victims view the Basement and Fire Department evidence tapes for the first time.

Lawyers representing Sarah McLachlan, Cheryl Wheeler, and their labels issue Cease-and-Desist orders to stop Jefferson County selling the training video with unauthorized recordings of their songs. JeffCo officials say they will not remove the music.

April 28, 2000: After labels of Sarah McLachlan and Cheryl Wheeler threaten legal action, Jefferson County officials remove the songs from the tape.

Michael Campbell, who threatened Columbine student Erin Walton in 1999, pleads guilty to transmitting a threat of violence. Campbell faints when he is sentenced to 4 months in prison. His attorney claims sending the 18-year-old to prison would be creating "Columbine victim 14" because his client attempted suicide earlier that month. His mother downplays the internet threat as "just a prank" and accuses the victim of "killing" her son for reporting him. The judge says he believes Campbell is remorseful, but jail time is necessary to deter copycats.

May 1, 2000: Sales of the Fire Department training tape go well even without the songs. After removing previous auctions of tapes containing music eBay allows them to be sold without music.

Tom and Sue Klebold and Wayne and Kathy Harris file a motion to stop items seized from their home after the massacre from being released to the public.

May 2, 2000: ABC News announces they have a draft of the investigative report which details events of April 20, 1999, minute by minute.

HOPE reaches the $3.1 million needed to replace the old library with a new two-story atrium and to build a new library at another location on campus.

May 3, 2000: Corey DePooter is made an honorary Marine during a ceremony at his grave at Chapel Hill Memorial Gardens in Littleton, Colorado.

May 4, 2000: Two weeks after the first anniversary of the shooting, Columbine varsity basketball player Greg Barnes hangs himself. Barnes was a sophomore and was in the school when the shootings occurred. He wasn't injured but saw Coach Dave Sanders die. Victim Matt Kechter was a close friend of his. Barnes' father finds his body in the garage at 12:15 p.m. with a Blink 182 CD repeating "Adam's Song". He leaves no note, but it's believed the suicide was prompted by a recent break-up with his girlfriend.

May 8, 2000: Philip Duran pleads guilty to helping provide the TEC-DC9 to Klebold and Harris, and to possessing a dangerous weapon. His sentencing is set for June 23.

May 9, 2000: Greg Barnes' funeral held at St. Francis Cabrini Catholic Church at 11 a.m.—the same church where the funerals of Kelly Fleming, Matt Kechter, and Daniel Mauser were held.

Colorado state law allows departments and officers 20 days to respond to lawsuits. Victim Mark Taylor's attorney Howard Zucker adds Robyn Anderson, Philip Duran, and Mark Manes to his lawsuit. It is the first time anyone has tried to hold Anderson legally accountable. Officials say she legally purchased the guns so there is no crime. In Colorado, it is legal for an adult to provide a minor with a firearm if it was obtained legally.

May 11, 2000: The Columbine Memorial Committee announces the permanent site in Clement Park at the foot of Rebel Hill close to the school.

In the Colorado Court of Appeals, Jefferson County District Judge Henry Nieto refuses to release 13 of the autopsy reports. The Harrises don't object to the release of Eric's autopsy report. Isaiah Shoels' parents release his autopsy themselves. Jefferson County District Judge Brooke Jackson releases tapes of the Columbine library 911 call to the victims' families, saying the recording is so disturbing, the audio should not be released to the public.

May 15, 2000: By order from Judge Brooke Jackson, Jefferson County Sheriff John Stone releases copies of the long-delayed Columbine Report on CD-ROM. It's made available to the public for $12.00.

May 20, 2000: Columbine High graduation day. Cassie Bernall, Corey DePooter, and Rachel Scott should have been with the graduating class. Survivors Brain Anderson, Richard Castaldo, Jennifer Doyle, Austin Eubanks, Makai Hall, Anne Marie Hochhalter, co-valedictorian Patrick Ireland, Mark Kintgen, and Dan Steepleton all receive their diplomas.

May 23, 2000: Judge Brooke Jackson orders the public release of 8 audio tapes of police radio transmissions and car-to-car communication from April 20, 1999. The tapes are roughly 90 minutes long each. Sheriff's representative Steve Davis says it will take about a week to remove personal information such as caller phone numbers before they can release the information.

May 25, 2000: 1982 Columbine graduate Bill Marshall presents Principal Frank DeAngelis a sculpture of two hands cradling a columbine blossom. DeAngelis says the sculpture will be on display next year in the new library.

May 26, 2000: Judge Jackson orders the public release of a 58-page ballistics report and two video tapes of Columbine's cafeteria surveillance footage from April 20, 1999.

May 30, 2000: Turner Construction tears out Columbine's old library above the cafeteria to make way for the atrium.

The Rohrboughs' attorney Jim Rouse files a suit on their behalf which objects to the fact that the 58-page ballistics report does not identify who shot who, or who fired which fatal shots.

May 31, 2000: All Columbine-related lawsuits filed in Jefferson County courts are merged and will be heard under a single judge.

June 2000: Brian and Lisa Rohrbough are expecting a baby when Lisa is diagnosed with HELLP syndrome, a rare, life-threatening pregnancy complication. Despite the risk to her, Lisa refuses to end the pregnancy. When baby Joshua develops signs of distress, she has a C-section, the only chance of saving his life. Joshua, small enough to fit in Brian's hand, lives for 28 hours. They bury him next to Dan.

223

June 7, 2000: *The Denver Post* files a motion to unseal the autopsies, so they can better understand the shooting and official response. Michigan lawyer Geoffrey Fieger is allowed to represent the families of Mark Taylor and Isaiah Shoels. Fieger was criticized for holding a news conference and releasing copies of the Shoels' lawsuit to the media with monetary amounts in the document, which is against Colorado state law.

The sheriff's office releases the cafeteria surveillance tapes.

June 9, 2000: Randy and Judy Brown start a petition to recall Sheriff John Stone citing his mismanagement of the Columbine tragedy, among other things.

June 23, 2000: Philip Duran pleads guilty to providing a handgun to a juvenile and possessing a sawed-off shotgun. He is sentenced to 4½ years in prison.

July 1, 2000: The families of Jeanna Park, Valeen Schnurr, and Evan Todd file motions in US District Court for a one-month extension, to give their lawyers time to respond to Jefferson County's motion to dismiss the pending lawsuit against them.

Two new state laws, called the "Robyn Anderson Bills" by state legislatures, go into effect in Colorado. One makes it a felony to purchase guns for someone who cannot legally purchase guns on their own. The other makes it a misdemeanor to provide guns to minors without parental consent.

July 5, 2000: In compliance with Judge Jackson's ruling, JCSO releases 45 hours of 911 and dispatch audio recorded during the shooting. 200 volumes of reports and other evidence are still being withheld.

July 7, 2000: Attorneys for Jefferson County say the Klebolds and Harrises, not the authorities, should be liable in lawsuits filed by the victims' families.

July 12, 2000: JCSO Spokesman Steve Davis announces he is resigning on the 30th to take at a position at AleUm International Management Company.

July 13, 2000: Jefferson County is given a two-week extension so they can file additional paperwork in the federal wrongful-death suit filed by Angela Sanders, daughter of victim Dave Sanders.

224

July 18, 2000: Principal Frank DeAngelis, teachers Tom Johnson, Judith Kelly, Garrett Talocco, and a school security director, are added to the lawsuit filed by the families of Isaiah Shoels and Mark Taylor.

Dawn Anna, victim Lauren Townsend's mother, and Linda Mauser, victim Daniel's mom, tour the new atrium being built in the cafeteria of Columbine High. Put together by Turner Construction and the HOPE charity, the atrium will give the impression of looking up in a forest. There are no reminders of the library where so many suffered and died. The same thing goes for every portion of the school that was damaged.

July 25, 2000: North Carolina artist Virginia Wright-Frierson studio creates and ships the large sheets of forest images which will hang above Columbine's cafeteria. Virginia's cousin, a teacher at Columbine, gets permission from HOPE to put together the mural on June 1 and hang it up before students return to school.

August 3, 2000: Unable to acquire the 42,000 signatures they need to get the recall put on the ballot, the petition started by Randy and Judy Brown ends.

August 9, 2000: Brad and Misty Bernall, parents of Cassie, join the federal lawsuits against Sheriff John Stone filed by the families of Kelly Fleming, Matthew Kechter, Dan Rohrbough, Lauren Townsend, and Kyle Velasquez.

Reverend Don Marxhausen, who officiated Dylan Klebold's funeral and helped officiate Greg Barnes' funeral, announces he is leaving St. Philip Lutheran Church. His allowing Klebold's funeral to be held at their church upset his congregation.

August 15, 2000: Columbine High reopens for Fall semester.

August 16, 2000: Dawn Anna participates in a panel discussion at the Democratic National Convention in Los Angeles about violence in schools.

Lawsuits filed by families of Richard Castaldo, Sean Graves, Lance Kirklin, Isaiah Shoels, and Mark Taylor are moved from Jefferson County District Court to federal court, joining the suits filed by families of Cassie Bernall, Kelly Fleming, Matt Kechter, Jeanna Park, Dan Rohrbough, Kacey Ruegsegger, Dave Sanders, Valeen Schnurr, Evan Todd, Lauren Townsend, and Kyle Velasquez in the US District

Court, in Denver. Chief US District Judge Lewis Babcock will preside over the cases.

August 19, 2000: Arthur Thomas sentenced for threatening Columbine with more violence. He is sentenced to 7 months in prison for sending death threats, followed by 7 months of electronically monitored home detention. Thomas has a long record of threats against faculty and students in his area.

August 21, 2000: Michael Campbell is released from Coleman Federal Correctional Institution in Florida.

August 22, 2000: Jefferson County Sheriff's Office, Sheriff John Stone, former Sheriff Ronald Beckham, and seven other officials argue in court to have five lawsuits tossed out that were brought against them by the families of Richard Castaldo, Sean Graves, Lance Kirklin, Mark Taylor, and Isaiah Shoels, saying the suits fail to prove their claims.

August 24, 2000: Principal Frank DeAngelis testifies before the Governor's Columbine Review Commission. He says Harris and Klebold gave no indication of their plans. He requests that the police keep copies of blueprints of all schools in their jurisdiction. JeffCo Coroner Dr. Nancy Bodelson, who performed the gunmen's autopsies, testifies the condition of the corpses prevented her from pinpointing the exact time of their deaths.

September 5, 2000: Judge Brooke Jackson orders Jefferson County Sheriff's Office to release thousands of pages of investigative files the Columbine Report is based on. Jackson spends the next two months reviewing and redacting the files before they are released to the public. JeffCo sells copies through their website.

September 6, 2000: Judge Lewis Babcock moves the five lawsuits filed in Jefferson County to federal court. He will preside over all fourteen cases. The suits were filed by Randall and Natalie Graves, Michael and Vonda Shoels, Mark and Donna Taylor, Richard Castaldo, and Lance Kirklin. The nine lawsuits Judge Babcock already received were filed by Bruce Chapman Beck and Dawn Linda Anna, Joseph and Ann Marie Kechter, Andrew and Michelle Park, Brian Rohrbough and Sue Petrone, Gregory and Darcey Ruegsegger, Angela Sanders, Mark and Sharilyn Schnurr, Dale and Jana Todd, and Albert and Phyllis Velasquez.

226

September 8, 2000: Judge Brooke Jackson orders Jefferson County to release 40 binders of Columbine information they have been holding onto.

Anne Marie Hochhalter and dad Ted sue Porter Adventist Hospital for negligence in the suicide of Anne Marie's mother.

September 12, 2000: Lawyers representing principal Frank DeAngelis and teachers Tom Johnson, Judith Kelly, and Garrett Talocco ask the court to dismiss lawsuits filed against them by families, saying: "The tragedy here originated and ended with Eric Harris and Dylan Klebold."

September 18, 2000: Wayne and Kathy Harris file suit against psychologist Kevin Albert, who treated Eric for depression and obsessive-compulsive disorder. They allege that if Eric even hinted at what he was planning during their sessions, Albert had an obligation to tell someone.

September 20, 2000: Jefferson County Sheriff John Stone agrees to speak at a school crisis seminar in Denver on Friday titled "Mobilization Efforts During the Columbine Shootings." then changes his mind and skips it.

October 2, 2000: Tom and Sue Klebold request that the lawsuit filed against them by the victims' families be thrown out, saying they were not to blame for what their son did.

The Governor's Columbine Review Commission hears public testimony for the first time. Many victims' families speak before the Commission. They say bullying was rampant at CHS, the Trench Coat Mafia was menacing, and the gunmen did show warning signs of what they were plotting. This contradicts Principal Frank DeAngelis' earlier testimony.

Officials refuse to release the Basement Tapes that *TIME* magazine covered in their December 20 issue.

October 6, 2000: Wayne and Kathy Harris appear in federal court. They deny blocking a police search for explosives in their home a year before the Columbine tragedy. They also deny having any prior knowledge their son was planning the assault.

October 11, 2000: Denver Post Attorney Steven Zansberg requests JeffCo District Court Judge Brooke Jackson order the release of the remaining autopsies to determine if Daniel Rohrbough was killed by friendly fire, when Coach Dave Sanders died, and if Dylan Klebold's death was a suicide.

October 23, 2000: U.S. District Judge Lewis Babcock orders all Columbine lawsuits to be clarified except the lawsuit filed by the family of Dave Sanders, whose suit clearly states how they feel the defendants acted in their official capacities or individually.

County Attorney Frank Hutfless sends a letter to the Columbine Review Commission, saying the County will not release the Basement Tapes. He warns if the tapes are released, they could inspire copycat shootings.

October 24, 2000: Richard Castaldo, Sean Graves, Anne Marie Hochhalter, and Patrick Ireland help Craig Hospital dedicate a van with a wheelchair lift, to be used by hospital patients and their families.

November 1, 2000: The Mauser family returns home after spending two weeks in China adopting Madeline HaiXing Mauser, a 1-year-old girl.

November 7, 2000: Colorado voters adopt Amendment 22, which closes the gun-show loophole and requires sellers at gun shows to obtain identification from buyers and run background checks.

November 15, 2000: Jefferson County attorneys argue in court to keep Harris and Klebold's Basement Tapes sealed.

November 21, 2000: JCSO releases 10,973 pages of investigative files to the public. The pages contain violent essays and journals written by the shooters; police interviews with Dylan Klebold's parents; details about Ron Hartmann and James Washington, gun dealers who sold the shotguns and rifle to Robyn Anderson; witness statements, and much more. The report does not include police interviews with the Harrises, medical reports, or autopsy reports. JeffCo makes copies of the report available for public viewing at the Jefferson County Fairgrounds from 9 a.m. to 5 p.m. Monday through Friday. Hard copies of the documents could be ordered by mail for $602 (5.5 cents per page for copying) plus shipping. The Brown case file is included, but nothing about Guerra's investigation of it.

November 28, 2000: Word leaks about a $1.6 million settlement offered by Wayne and Kathy Harris, Tom and Sue Klebold, and Mark Manes to families of the victims. Lawyers fear the leak will jeopardize the settlement talks.

November 30, 2000: Attorneys for *The Denver Post* press Judge Brooke Jackson to unseal the autopsies because they are public record. Only Eric Harris and Isaiah Shoels' autopsies have been released. Attorney James Rouse, representing six families, argues their release will do more harm to the families. Judge Jackson delays his ruling until after the holidays.

December 1, 2000: Regina Huerter, Director of Juvenile Diversion for the Denver District Attorney's Office, commissioned by Governor Owens to investigate the culture at Columbine, tells the Columbine Review Board that "jocks" at the school were not disciplined when they were instigators of bullying. Huerter says she spoke with parents and students who were afraid to testify for themselves.

December 30, 2000: Gun dealers James Washington and Ronald Hartmann, who sold Robyn Anderson guns at the Tanner Gun Show, and Robert Kirgis, owner of Blackjack Pizza where Klebold and Harris worked, are added to lawsuits filed by families of Richard Castaldo, Sean Graves, Lance Kirklin, and Mark Taylor. Hartmann is added to the suits of the families of Cassie Bernall, Kelly Fleming, Matt Kechter, Daniel Rohrbough, Lauren Townsend, Kyle Velasquez. They also claim the sheriff's office has withheld evidence from them.

2001 — After multiple surgeries, Lance Kirkland makes the difficult decision to stop. The stress and recovery are too much to cope with. That same year he learns he is going to be a father.

Theresa Miller, who saved several students during the shooting, is presented with the Teacher of the Year award. She has taught at Columbine for 20 years and has been the head of the Science Department for 2 years.

January 3, 2001: The National Association of Counties appoints JeffCo Sheriff John Stone to help lobby President-elect George W. Bush's team regarding county issues in the US. Critics say he is being rewarded despite his questionable leadership and actions during the Columbine shooting.

January 9, 2001: Robyn Anderson tells a federal court she didn't actually purchase the guns used in the shooting. In her original statement to authorities, she said she went to the Tanner Gun Show in Denver with Eric Harris and Dylan Klebold and purchased the two shotguns and the 9mm carbine rifle from private dealers. She says they went to the gun show because she didn't want a background check run on her. Anderson testifies the shooters asked all the questions and paid for the guns themselves. The only thing she did was show her ID to verify her age.

January 12, 2001: US District Court Judge Lewis T. Babcock denies without prejudice multiple requests to dismiss lawsuits in the Columbine case. The requests are made by Jefferson County Sheriff's Office, the Jefferson County School District, the county commissioners, and the parents of the shooters. The motions to dismiss cannot be refiled. Judge Babcock also refuses to dismiss lawsuits against the owner of Blackjack Pizza where the gunmen worked, Robyn Anderson, Phillip Duran, Mark Manes, the Tanner Gun Show, and the vendors who sold the guns.

January 19, 2001: Attorneys representing Principal Frank DeAngelis, six Columbine teachers, and the JeffCo School District request dismissal of lawsuits brought against their clients. The Federal Court of Appeals ruled earlier public schools were not required to protect students from each other, the basis behind the request for dismissal.

January 30, 2001: Jefferson County District Judge Brooke Jackson orders the release of Daniel Rohrbough's autopsy to clear up questions regarding who shot and killed him. Judge Jackson also orders the release of summaries of the remaining autopsies.

January 31, 2001: Dan Rohrbough's autopsy is released.

February 7, 2001: The remaining 11 autopsy summaries are released to the public. After reviewing the autopsy, pathologists conclude Coach Dave Sanders would have died even if SWAT and medical aid reached him sooner. A bullet tore the carotid artery in his neck and a shot to his back hit the subclavian vein, which leads to the heart.

Dylan Klebold's autopsy is the only one that remains unreleased since the release is being appealed.

230

February 8, 2001: Mark Manes has his lawyers ask for a reduction in his six-year sentence, claiming: "Justice wasn't done. Fairness, reason, and logic were ignored. An opportunity to start a nation's healing process by demonstrating compassion and understanding was passed over."

February 16, 2001: Attorneys representing injured victims Richard Castaldo, Sean Graves, Lance Kirklin, and Mark Taylor claim the relationship between the school and its students required Columbine High and Jefferson County Sheriff's Office to investigate early signs that violence was likely.

Their argument details three things they believe should have been investigated with more diligence. First is the creative writing essay by Klebold. The story is a detailed fictional account of a man in black who parks his car and, armed with guns and a duffel bag full of weapons, waits for a group of popular teens to show up so he can gun them down. It's almost exactly what he did at Columbine just weeks later. Teacher Judith Kelly took the paper to the assistant principal and school counselor, and held a conference with the Klebolds, but the matter went no further. The second item is Harris' websites. Authorities were aware he posted threats and hate-filled rants online. He also posted bomb-making instructions and logs about how he and his friends were out after curfew terrorizing neighbors with explosives and dangerous pranks. The third item is a video made by Harris for audio/video class which features a kid at Columbine enacting violent revenge, shooting jocks and kids who bullied him. The video was filmed at and around Columbine High School. The victims' attorneys file the brief in opposition to attempts of the Sheriff's Office and Columbine staff to dismiss the lawsuits against them.

February 20, 2001: CBS News seeks additional paperwork from JeffCo about the Brown case against the Harrises. Assistant county attorney William Tuthill denies paperwork exists.

February 22, 2001: JCSO releases to the victims' parents the clothing worn by Cassie Bernall, Kelly Fleming, Matthew Kechter, Daniel Rohrbough, Lauren Townsend, and Kyle Velasquez on the day of the shooting.

February 23, 2001: The court releases to the public Dylan Klebold's autopsy summary which shows he died from a self-inflicted large-caliber gunshot wound to the left side of his head.

March 2, 2001: The Columbine Review Commission questions law enforcement's decision to stick to police procedure during the shooting, establishing a perimeter and securing the scene instead of charging into the school and ending the siege.

March 19, 2001: *TIME* magazine releases "The Columbine Effect". *60 Minutes II*, Randy and Judy Brown. and Brian and Lisa Rohrbough go to court to demand the release of missing files and official reports. District Attorney Dave Thomas confirms the Guerra search affidavit exists and claims they mentioned it in the March 30, 1999, press conference; that it's "old news". CBS asks the judge to order it to be released.

March 28, 2001: The parents of the dead and wounded request not to be included in any memorial events on April 20, 2001. Most decline to join the ceremony that JeffCo officials want to hold. The county scales back plans, and considers holding a smaller, low-key memorial instead.

March 29, 2001: The District Attorney admits at the Governor's Commission meeting that the juvenile diversion program is flawed. They allowed Harris and Klebold to participate together, share unchaperoned transportation, and did not have a way for the police to report new complaints or arrests while juveniles are in diversion. The excuse is that they don't have the manpower to follow up on cases.

April 2001: The Columbine Review Commission gets a court order to acquire information from Sheriff John Stone.

April 5, 2001: Columbine students and staff start a program called "The Heart of Columbine" which is inspired by visits from holocaust survivor Gerda Weissman Klein. The service devotes time to hunger prevention and invites other schools to join them.

JeffCo officials announce a small memorial service scheduled two weeks later at the pavilion in Clement Park. The names of the victims will be read, followed by a moment of silence.

Jefferson County District Court Judge Brooke Jackson orders more documents released. The evidence includes four notebooks, and audio recordings and interviews with first responders to the shootings.

April 10, 2001: The above materials are released to the public.

232

April 12, 2001: In a released interview with an Arvada investigator conducted hours after the shooting, Deputy Neil Gardner says he never dealt with Eric Harris before the gunfight on the 20th and didn't recognize a photo of him.

April 13, 2001: JeffCo finally "finds" and releases the search warrant affidavit prepared by detective Guerra for the Harris house, written after the Brown family reported the threats Eric posted on his website. The affidavit is incomplete, and a search never happened. For the past two years, officials denied the meeting took place or that paperwork existed. They accused the Browns of lying for attention.

April 15, 2001: 16-year-old Cory Baadsgaard takes a hunting rifle to school and holds 24 people hostage. He suffers from a rare REM sleep disorder brought on by antidepressants which worsened his mental state. The outburst is out of character for the varsity basketball and baseball player, who claims no memory of the event. Expert doctors testify antidepressants such as Paxil® are proven to make people hostile, homicidal, and suicidal.

April 16, 2001: J. D. Tanner appears in court. The 72-year-old is the manager of the gun show where Robyn Anderson bought three of the guns used in the shooting. He requests dismissal of the lawsuit filed by Richard Castaldo's family. The suit holds Tanner partially responsible for Castaldo's injuries, alleging he provided a place where guns could be sold illegally to minors, and was negligent in his operations of the show. J.D. asserts he had no connection with the gunmen or Richard, and shouldn't be held responsible for something he wasn't directly involved in.

April 17, 2001: *60 Minutes II* airs an episode on the inadequacy of the official response to the Columbine shooting, criticizing the time it took and the methods that were used.

April 18, 2001: Greg Zanis, the Illinois carpenter who crafted the Rebel Hill crosses displayed in Clement Park, files a lawsuit against the Foothills Park and Recreation District. He wants to put the crosses back on the hill for the upcoming anniversary. The District assigned him space on Clement Park's east side.

Interviews with the Brown family on April 22 and 29, 1999, are faxed from the FBI to Jefferson County after an FBI agent reads an article where the Browns mention the "missing" documents. JeffCo states the reason they weren't provided to the Columbine Investigative Task Force was "inadvertent" and "an oversight".

April 19, 2001: The shooters' parents reach a $1.56 million-dollar agreement to settle 30 lawsuits by the families of those killed or injured during the shooting. 36 suits against Philip Duran and Mark Manes settle for $720,000 and $250,000 each. Robyn Anderson is still in negotiations over lawsuits pending against her. Six families who don't agree to settle are those of Cassie Bernall, Kelly Fleming, Matt Kechter, Daniel Rohrbough, Lauren Townsend, and Kyle Velasquez. Shortly after the lawsuits settle Linda Sanders, wife of Dave Sanders, and two of his stepdaughters file a class-action lawsuit against 25 media companies who manufacture or distribute violent video games.

Greg Zanis loses his suit and must display his crosses near the picnic shelter, where the Foothills Park and Recreation originally assigned him.

April 20, 2001: A crowd gathers for the ceremony at Clement Park's amphitheater to honor the victims. JeffCo School District Superintendent Jane Hammond and others speak at the gathering. Rocks are placed on Rebel Hill in Clement Park where Greg Zanis originally placed his crosses. Only 13 rocks are placed though there were originally 15 crosses on the hill. Zanis only displays 13 crosses at the picnic shelter. He crafted a single cross to represent the shooters as well, but public outrage made it impossible for him to display it. The names of those killed at Columbine High are read and a period of silence is held. Ironically, students are not allowed inside the school that day, even though it's a Friday.

April 26, 2001: The six-year sentence Mark Manes received is upheld by the Colorado Court of Appeals. Manes requested a reduction in his sentence because he didn't know the shooters' intentions beforehand, he cooperated with authorities, had no prior criminal record, and was remorseful for his part.

April 27, 2001: Columbine Review Commission Chairman William Erickson, a former Chief Justice of the Colorado Supreme Court, issues a statement that mass murder could have been prevented if authorities had seriously investigated the overwhelming number of clues which surfaced before the shooting. He says lives could have been saved if SWAT had gone in immediately, instead of establishing a perimeter and watching from rooftops across the street.

Assistant Jefferson County Attorney William Tuthill argues that officers should not be held liable for decisions made in chaotic emergencies. Denver U.S. District Judge Lewis Babcock denounces the argument. In reference to how long it took the SWAT team to reach and evacuate Dave Sanders, Tuthill claims they didn't have time to think. The judge contends vehemently: "You had time to think in the third hour!"

Jefferson County School Superintendent Jane Hammond testifies at the meeting, saying the district can't guarantee safety to students, but steps are being taken to decrease the chance of a repeat event. Judge Babcock spends the rest of the day hearing arguments on whether to dismiss nine lawsuits filed by twenty Columbine families against Jefferson County officials and school staff. The Commission holds a final meeting before they prepare their report, to be delivered in May.

May 7, 2001: Lawyers representing Robyn Anderson settle a lawsuit with 36 Columbine families. The terms and amount to be paid are confidential.

May 11, 2001: The Jefferson County Sheriff's Department releases hundreds of pages of official documents to the public.

May 17, 2001: Governor Owens' Columbine Review Commission releases its final report to the public. They find Eric Harris and Dylan Klebold are solely responsible for the tragic events of April 20, 1999. The report is highly critical of the Jefferson County Sheriff's Office, showing they ignored early warning signs, waited too long to engage the gunmen, and were uncooperative during the investigation. They alone refused to provide information and interviews to the Committee. The report calls for every Colorado high school to establish threat-assessment teams and asks the state to offer better training for law enforcement agencies which respond to school violence.

May 19, 2001: Columbine graduation day at Fiddlers Green in the Denver Tech Center. The names of Kelly Fleming, Matt Kechter, Daniel Mauser, John Tomlin, and Kyle Velasquez are printed on the program as they should have graduated. Seats are saved for their families. None of them attend. Survivors Lance Kirklin and Josh Lapp are also in this class. Aaron Brown, graduating senior and younger brother to Brooks, is elected Prom King.

May 21, 2001: The FBI releases 55 pages of official interviews.

May 24, 2001: Brian Rohrbough, father of victim Danny, files suit against JCSO claiming his son was killed by an officer. The complaint is based on statements made by Arapahoe County Deputy James D. Taylor who told them he saw an officer accidentally shoot and kill Danny. Later they reveal Taylor told them the officer responsible was SWAT member Sergeant Dan O'Shea.

May 25, 2001: Jefferson County Sheriff John Stone disagrees strongly with the findings of the Governor's Columbine Review Commission and maintains a defensive stance about official actions during and following the shooting.

June 9, 2001: Dawn Anna leads a group through Columbine's new 13,900-square-foot HOPE Columbine Library. Opened in late May, it is a bright and airy room that bears no resemblance to the old one.

June 12, 2001: Patrick Ireland files a federal lawsuit against the Jefferson County Sheriff's Office, Sheriff John Stone, the Board of County Commissioners, former Sheriff Ronald Beckham, twelve other deputies, and the men who sold guns to Robyn Anderson. He is asking unspecified damages for negligence, failure to act, and violation of his constitutional rights.

June 13, 2001: Tom Mauser is arrested for trespassing outside the National Rifle Association headquarters. When he is taken into custody, he's wearing his son's sneakers—the same shoes Daniel wore the day he was killed. An hour later he posts $250 bail and is released. Later the same day, Tom speaks at the Brady Campaign to Prevent Gun Violence.

June 19, 2001: The courts release 700 more documents to the public, including graphic details of the crime scene.

June 27, 2001: Mark Manes is released on parole to a halfway house in Lakewood, Colorado after serving 75% of his sentence. The move angers some of the victims' families.

June 28, 2001: Columbine survivors Richard Castaldo, Mark Taylor, and Brooks Brown agree to be in a film that director Michael Moore is making. They pressure K-Mart management to stop selling handgun ammunition in its stores. K-Mart CEO Chuck Conaway announces the same day they will stop by fall. It comes out Moore lied to the victims to ensure their participation in *Bowling for Columbine*. Taylor is an

NRA supporter and objects to being characterized as anti-gun. He would not have agreed to be in the film if he knew what Moore's true agenda was.

July 12, 2001: The new Columbine-inspired license plates are in high demand. Created by Mark Schnurr, father of survivor Valeen, and Dale Todd, father of survivor Evan, the plates feature the Rocky Mountains with a columbine blossom centered above the motto: "Respect Life."

Jefferson County officials deny the 32nd annual National Association of School Safety and Law Enforcement Officers conference a tour of Columbine High School.

August 9, 2001: The Jefferson County Sheriff's Office releases 2,651 more pages of evidence to the public. The documents include notes Eric Harris passed to friends.

August 23, 2001: Tom Mauser appears at the Fairfax County Courthouse for his June arrest at NRA headquarters. The arresting officer resigned in the interim and the NRA didn't send a delegate to represent them at the hearing, so Judge Lorraine Nordlund dismisses the case. Mauser returns to NRA headquarters to picket in his son Daniel's shoes an hour later.

August 27, 2001: Midway Home Entertainment asks a federal judge to dismiss a lawsuit filed by Angela Sanders. The company distributes the violent first-person shooter game *Doom*. Midway cites a Kentucky case where Michael Carneal killed three Heath High School students in 1997. The case was thrown out when the judge ruled video games are not subject to product liability laws.

September 2001: The existence of the Guerra documents becomes public knowledge. A series of grand jury investigations are launched into the coverup activities of Jefferson County. Investigators discover some of the documents were "lost" and several computer files having to do with the case were erased during the summer following the shootings.

September 1, 2001: Jacki Tallman, spokesperson for JCSO, says they will release more official documents later that week. More redaction is required to protect witnesses and the families of those killed in the massacre.

September 4, 2001: James Garbarino and Clair Bedard publish their book: *Parents Under Siege: Why You Are the Solution, Not the Problem, in Your Child's Life*. The authors interviewed Tom and Sue Klebold in June 1999, though the Klebolds are not directly quoted in the book. Still, the families of the victims are upset that the gunman's parents would talk to an author about what happened before speaking to them.

September 6, 2001: JCSO releases 242 pages of official materials. Spokesperson Jacki Tallman says no new evidence is uncovered in the documents. Brian Rohrbough is still waiting for details about the outside crime scene where his son died.

October 10, 2001: Sue Petrone, mother of victim Dan Rohrbough, testifies in the Denver U.S. District Court against the Jefferson County School District. She and six other plaintiffs claim their right to free speech and religious expression were suppressed when they were invited in 1999 to paint memorial tiles placed in Columbine High School. They weren't allowed to paint anything that referred to the victims, the shooting, the date, or use any religious symbols. Petrone found such references on 135 accepted tiles the school displayed.

October 15, 2001: U.S. District Judge Wiley Daniel rules the Jefferson County School district had no right to restrict what the Columbine victims' families painted on their memorial tiles. He orders the replacement of 90 tiles which were removed. The school is given 20 days to replace them. He also gives Don and Dee Fleming, parents of slain victim Kelly, 20 days to paint their tiles and give them to the school for placement. School officials consider appealing the decision.

October 17, 2001: $2.85 million has been distributed to 30 Columbine families in a settlement involving the Harrises, the Klebolds, and some people involved in supplying the gunmen with their weapons. The families of surviving victims Richard Castaldo, Sean Graves, Lance Kirklin, and Mark Taylor file motions to dismiss their suits against Wayne and Kathy Harris.

October 19, 2001: The families of Brian Anderson, Corey DePooter, Mark Taylor, Dave Sanders, and Evan Todd file a lawsuit against Solvay Pharmaceuticals, the manufacturer of the antidepressant Luvox that Eric Harris was taking before the shooting. The suit contends Solvay failed to warn Harris' doctor about possible side effects, specifically "emotional blunting or dis-inhibition", which caused the

238

young man "to become manic and psychotic." The families ask for more than $75,000 each. Antidepressants now come with warnings that they may increase emotional and mental problems in young people.

October 28, 2001: On what would have been Stephanie Hart-Grizell's 18th birthday, her mother Kelly Grizzell is charged with harassment and obstruction of an officer. Grizzell was driving home the night of the 27th when she came across three unmarked deputies' cars who had pulled over Columbine survivor Lance Kirklin for a busted headlight. Grizzell got out of her car to find out why they needed six officers for a routine stop. During the confrontation, Grizzell accused them of wasting time harassing her daughter's friends and not doing enough to solve her murder. Police reports say she struck Deputy James Lucas in the stomach. Grizzell claims she just put her hand on his shoulder. Kirklin supports Grizzell's statement, saying he saw the whole thing, but officials support Deputy Lucas. Grizzell was allowed to leave the scene. The charges against her are later settled out of court in July 2002.

November 1, 2001: Jefferson County Public Schools takes Judge Daniels' decision about putting the religious memorial tiles back in Columbine to the 10th Circuit Court of Appeals.

November 2, 2001: Judge Daniels refuses a stay in Jefferson County's appeal. The tiles are required to be in the high school by November 4th.

November 6, 2001: The 10th Circuit Court of Appeals grants a stay that blocks the controversial tiles from being placed in Columbine High until the legalities are thoroughly researched. The decision prevents the Flemings and the Rohrboughs from displaying their tiles.

November 10, 2001: Randy and Judy Brown examine thousands of pages of official documents, including the ballistics and Sheriff's reports. They find evidence Deputy Neil Gardner fired three shots into the library on April 20, 1999. Gardner contests he only fired eight times at the west doors, yet three bullets thought to be his were found in the library.

The official record says police fired 141 shots at the school as cover fire, but as many as 162 rounds may have been fired without targets into windows and doorways. Most bullets aren't on evidence maps though they were found inside the school, sprayed down halls, and in classrooms after the shooters were dead. Hostile fire reported by SWAT after the deaths was likely ricochet from their own volleys. Two of O'Shea's bullets, fired on full automatic setting, went clear down the hall to the east side of the school where the other SWAT team was searching rooms. No one was injured by police fire.

November 27, 2001: U.S. District Judge Lewis Babcock dismisses eight of the lawsuits pending against Jefferson County Sheriff's Office and the Jefferson County School District, citing government immunity. The only lawsuit allowed is one brought by the family of Coach Dave Sanders. The Sanders contend that police gave "Repeated false assurances that help would be there in 10 minutes" to people over the phone who were providing first aid to the fallen teacher. Judge Babcock also rules that portions of lawsuits by Jeanna Park's family and Valeen Schnurr's family can proceed. The suing families claim deputies did not provide medical care outside the school.

December 4, 2001: *Westword* reporter Alan Prendergast releases a report about Eric Harris' journals with examples of his hateful rants and screenshots of his violent drawings. The article includes the court-ordered letter of apology Harris wrote to the owner of the van he and Dylan Klebold broke into in January 1998.

December 5, 2001: Shooters' journals are released to the public.

December 6, 2001: Wayne and Kathy Harris make a rare public statement, saying they are horrified by the release of their son's journals. They also stress they did not leak the documents.

December 10, 2001: Families of Kelly Fleming, Matt Kechter, Daniel Rohrbough, Lauren Townsend, and Kyle Velasquez fire attorney Jim Rouse and hire their former attorney, Barry Arrington. The Bernall family keeps Rouse as their legal counsel. Michael and Vonda Shoels, Isaiah's parents, ask Judge Babcock to reconsider the dismissal of their lawsuit, saying the *Westword* article sheds new light on the case.

December 11, 2001: Families of Jeanna Park, Valeen Schnurr, and Evan Todd request Judge Babcock separate their cases from the rest so they can pursue the claim they should have received medical care sooner, while maintaining the right to appeal later.

240

December 12, 2001: U.S. Chief District Judge Lewis Babcock won't reconsider his dismissal of the lawsuits. Attorney Barry Arrington says he will re-file the request to overturn.

December 26, 2001: The Rohrboughs file lawsuits against JCSO and deputies in connection with their son's death. Attorney Barry Arrington accuses Sheriff John Stone and his department of 29 instances of lying during the investigation over the past 3 years. He names Denver SWAT team member Sergeant Dan O'Shea as the officer who shot and killed Danny. The accusation is based on what Deputy James Taylor told the family earlier that year. Arrington produces evidence of O'Shea tearfully telling a school administrator he hadn't slept in days because he thought he might have shot a student. This confession is later proven the result of "someone" telling O'Shea a "terrible lie about his involvement".

December 27, 2001: Brad and Misty Bernall settle their suit against the Klebolds and Harrises. The terms are kept confidential. The Bernalls have another lawsuit pending against Ronald F. Hartmann for indirectly selling guns to the shooters.

Jefferson County District Attorney Dave Thomas promises the victims' families he will take a second look at threats made by Eric Harris before the shooting, including the one made against Brooks Brown.

December 28, 2001: Jefferson County Sheriff John Stone requests the El Paso County Sheriff's Office to review claims that Sergeant Dan O'Shea killed Daniel Rohrbough. El Paso County Sheriff John Anderson agrees to start an investigation.

2002 — Despite being confined to a wheelchair after being critically injured during the Columbine attack, Anne Marie Hochhalter gets a job at Bath and Body Works.

January 2, 2002: Jefferson County District Judge Brooke Jackson rules Dylan's full autopsy report will not be released to the public.

Arapahoe County Deputy James Taylor issues a 4-page written statement denying he told anyone that victim Dan Rohrbough was shot by an officer. Arapahoe County Sheriff Pat Sullivan contends Taylor was dispatched to the east side of Columbine High on April 20, 1999, and could not have seen what occurred on the south side of the building. Brian Rohrbough and Sue Petrone, Dan's parents, release a recording they made of a conversation with Taylor wherein he told them he saw Dan's fatal shooting. The audio tape was recorded March 2000.

January 3, 2002: Governor Bill Owens petitions Jefferson County District Attorney Dave Thomas to have a grand jury investigate discrepancies and possible cover-ups of officials involved with the Columbine shooting. The judge refuses.

Tom and Sue Klebold ask the Colorado Court of Appeals to overrule Judge Jackson's decision that Jefferson County sheriff's officials can keep the clothing Dylan wore the day he died. This includes his trench coat, baseball cap, black pants and belt, black T-shirt, black combat boots, one black fingerless glove, and a pair of black suspenders.

The Jefferson County Sheriff's Office uses witness statements from Sean Graves, Lance Kirklin, and Mark Opfer (a freshman who was walking up the hill to go to the library) to rebut Brian Rohrbough and Sue Petrone's claim that students were not present when their son Danny was shot.

January 4, 2002: Jefferson County District Attorney Dave Thomas announces he is considering a coroner's inquest to determine the cause of Danny Rohrbough's death.

January 7, 2002: Deputy Jim Taylor admits it's his voice on the recording of the conversation between himself and Sue Petrone, where he tells her he saw an officer shoot Danny. Arapahoe County Sheriff Pat Sullivan says the tape is "misleading".

January 8, 2002: Arapahoe County releases 800 pages of new information about the Columbine shooting to Randy Brown.

Attorney Barry Arrington asks U.S. Attorney John Suthers to convene a grand jury investigation into the cover-up of potential violations of federal law by the Jefferson County Sheriff's Department. William Erickson, head of the Governor's Columbine Review Commission, announces the commission will meet again soon.

January 9, 2002: Arapahoe County fires Jim Taylor after he admits to lying to the Rohrboughs about what he saw during the shooting. Taylor attempts to explain himself by telling Inspector Grant Reed from the Arapahoe County Sheriff's Office of Professional Standards:

"I think emotionally I just got too attached to the whole thing. I guess I got overloaded."

Sheriff Sullivan tells Brian Rohrbough and his attorney they can request additional documents if they need, that the office hasn't destroyed anything. However, when Rohrbough asks for documents a few weeks later, Sullivan claims there is no other paperwork, and the dispatch tapes have all been recycled to save money. Rohrbough tells *Westword*:

> "This is the worst school shooting in the country, and they destroy the primary record of what their officers did that day? They don't save a copy for anybody? I find that really hard to believe."

January 11, 2002: William Erickson says the court system, not the Columbine Review Commission, is the appropriate forum to fully investigate the incident at Columbine.

January 14, 2002: Denver Police Sergeant Dan O'Shea's attorney David Bruno says his client did not shoot anyone at Columbine. District Attorney Dave Thomas requests County Coroner Carl Belsch do an inquest into the death of Daniel Rohrbough.

January 15, 2002: Colorado State Representative Don Lee, R-Littleton, says he will push to create a legislative panel to investigate the Columbine shooting if a federal grand jury doesn't.

January 16, 2002: Jefferson County Coroner Carl Blesch announces he will not hold an inquest into the death of victim Daniel Rohrbough, saying:

> "Because an inquest is confined to the manner and cause of death, at least some of the issues that have been raised in the Columbine tragedy cannot be reached by a coroner's inquest at all."

Danny's father Brian told CNN a coroner's inquest was too narrow a focus, that his family wanted an investigation that looks at all of Columbine. A legislative commission or grand jury investigation would be preferable.

That same day, Mark Manes, who sold the shooters the TEC-DC9 semiautomatic handgun, is denied parole. He continues to live in a halfway house in Lakewood to finish his sentence.

January 20, 2002: Sergeant Dan O'Shea claims his statement to a school staff member about friendly fire at Columbine has been wrongly interpreted as evidence that he shot and killed Daniel Rohrbough, which he denies doing.

January 21, 2002: Frank DeAngelis announces he will remain Columbine's principal indefinitely. He previously said he would step down from the role along with the graduating class of 2002. They are the last class of students who attended Columbine on April 20, 1999.

January 23, 2002: After viewing aerial footage from Denver's Channel 7, Sergeant Dan O'Shea says it shows Dan Rohrbough was already on the ground before he fired his weapon. That footage hasn't been released to the public.

U.S. District Judge Lewis Babcock refuses to reinstate lawsuits from families of 15 students injured or killed during the shooting.

January 25, 2002: Officials postpone a court hearing that will decide whether the evidence seized in the Columbine case will be released to the public. They want to hear expert testimony regarding the potential effect such a release might have on society and on copycats.

January 27, 2002: The *Denver Post* announces Sergeant Dan O'Shea used a type of ammunition sold only to law enforcement agencies: Speer +P 9mm Gold Dot Hollow Point bullets. The bullet's shape and jacket are proprietary and have several distinct features which can easily be tested for to determine if the bullet removed from Daniel Rohrbough's body came from O'Shea's weapon or from Harris or Klebold's guns. Such tests have not been performed by the Colorado Bureau of Investigation.

January 30, 2002: Seven Columbine families go to the Colorado State Capital to request a legislative probe of the shooting. They're hoping for a thorough, unbiased investigation. Patricia DePooter, mother of slain victim Corey, wants another test of a bullet that passed through her son's arm and lodged in his backpack. The bullet was only compared against law enforcement weapons, not the guns the shooters carried.

January 31, 2002: Pat Ireland, who survived the shooting, carries the Olympic flame down Pierce Street to Columbine High where he hands it to Principal Frank DeAngelis. They travel 2/10 of a mile to hand it to John Tomlin Sr., father of slain victim John. The three walk together to the next hand-off.

Colorado U.S. Attorney John Suthers refuses to convene a federal grand jury probe into Columbine or claims that authorities covered up information which could have prevented the shooting.

February 1, 2002: Jefferson County School District asks the 10th Circuit Court to appeal a lower court's decision requiring Columbine to display eight religious tiles painted by relatives of two of the victims of the shooting. The district's lawyer Stuart Stuller tells the court that forcing the school to display memorial tiles with religious messages will open the door for others to express anti-religious ideas.

Jefferson County Sheriff's Office sends the bullet from Corey DePooter's backpack to the CBI for more testing.

February 4, 2002: CBI finds that Eric Harris fired the shot that went through Corey's arm and lodged in his backpack.

February 5, 2002: Families of Kelly Fleming, Matthew Kechter, Jeana Park, Daniel Rohrbough, Valeen Schnurr, Evan Todd, Lauren Townsend, and Kyle Velasquez give formal notification to federal courts that they will appeal the dismissal of their civil suits against the Jefferson County Sheriff's Office and Jefferson County Public Schools.

February 7, 2002: Colorado House Speaker Doug Dean announces a legislative commission probe into the Columbine shooting will not commence until summer, to allow the commission the time they need to investigate.

February 12, 2002: Colorado Attorney General and Jefferson County District Attorney Dave Thomas announce they will release all the information about the Columbine shooting in an orderly and controlled manner, for those who need closure.

February 18, 2002: Colorado State Representative Don Lee, R-Littleton, proposes a legislative commission with subpoena powers to investigate the mass shooting. Survivors will have the chance to opt-out if they aren't comfortable being interviewed. If approved, the report will be finished by December 1, 2002.

February 22, 2002: Four students are arrested for starting a food fight in Columbine's cafeteria. Administrators knew beforehand the food fight was going to happen and asked the students to stage it outside, instead of preventing it.

March 4, 2002: Several classified crime scene photos from the Columbine shooting are leaked to the public, over 60 images of the destruction inside the school. Some show bodies of the victims and gunmen in grisly detail. The Columbine families are outraged, even those of the shooters who are unprepared to see color photos of their dead children on tabloid covers. Jefferson County launches an investigation into how the photos were leaked to news outlets and individuals without their knowledge.

U.S. District Judge Lewis Babcock dismisses a wrongful death lawsuit brought against the manufacturers and distributors of violent media by Linda Sanders, victim Dave's wife, and his daughters. The suit claims the deadly spree would not have occurred were it not for the games and films which made violence "pleasurable and attractive and disconnected the violence from the natural consequences".

March 5, 2002: Jefferson County Sheriff John Stone and Undersheriff John Dunaway are the first officials to undergo polygraph tests. The county will test all its employees to learn who leaked the crime scene photos to the public.

March 6, 2002: U.S. District Judge Clarence Brimmer has the Basement Tapes and other evidence sealed and stored in the Denver federal courthouse to prevent more leaks.

March 7, 2002: The Colorado House of Representatives Civil Justice and Judiciary Committee votes 7-2 against a proposal to launch a commission with subpoena power to investigate the Columbine shooting. The committee was the last hope of the victims' families for an honest investigation.

March 8, 2002: Attorney Bruce Jones, representing Dave Sanders' family, tells U.S. District Judge Lewis Babcock he wants to interview officials of the 34 agencies involved in handling the assault before setting up depositions in which they must appear and testify. The judge sets a hearing date of May 10 to decide who will be formally questioned first.

March 11, 2002: Colorado State Representative Don Lee, R-Littleton, announces he will submit a new proposal in the quest for answers about the Columbine shooting.

March 19, 2002: Jefferson County Sheriff John Stone asks a federal judge to allow his office to distribute the Basement Tapes. Neither the Harrises nor the Klebolds want the video tapes released. To prevent their release, they claim copyright ownership. The sheriff's office counter-claims ownership of the tapes because they are evidence.

March 20, 2002: U.S. District Court Judge Lewis Babcock dismisses five of the lawsuits against the gun show vendors, allowing one to continue. That lawsuit is brought by four families whose kids were injured or killed by shotgun fire. The suit claims vendor Ronald Hartmann sold a shotgun to Robyn Anderson when it was clear she was buying it for Harris and Klebold. Robyn legally purchased the gun at the Tanner Gun Show.

March 22, 2002: Jefferson County Sheriff's Office releases updated digital crime scene diagrams from the shooting on CD-ROM. The disc contains information omitted by the FBI earlier.

March 26, 2002: U.S. District Judge Lewis Babcock dismisses Pat Ireland's lawsuits against law enforcement and school officials. The judge allows his case against Ronald Hartmann and James Washington to continue. The two men sold guns to Robyn Anderson before the shooting.

April 1, 2002: Randy and Judy Brown ask the Columbine Open Records Task Force for copies of all the materials Jefferson County District Attorney Dave Thomas provided to *A&E Investigative Reports* for their upcoming show titled *Columbine: Understanding Why* which will air April 15th. A&E asks the Browns to participate in the show, which they do. The Task Force adds John Ireland, Pat's father, to the team. Dawn Anna declines to join them.

April 4, 2002: Representative Don Lee, R-Littleton, introduces Colorado House Bill 1418. The bill would create a bipartisan group of six lawmakers to find answers to specific questions about the Columbine shooting. The bill is a revised, more focused version of the bill which failed earlier.

April 5, 2002: Sheriff John Stone announces he will not seek re-election. He calls Columbine a "tar baby" he cannot shake.

April 10, 2002: Jefferson County officials receive a 1,200-page report from the El Paso County Sheriff's Office reviewing the death of student Danny Rohrbough. Jefferson County District Attorney Dave Thomas says he will not release the report until after the three-year anniversary.

April 11, 2002: Patrick Ireland requests U.S. District Court Judge Lewis Babcock reconsider his ruling which cleared Jefferson County officials and the Tanner Gun Show of responsibility for his injuries. Pat's motion includes a sealed affidavit which includes a private "document of a sensitive nature".

Rocky Mountain News announces the results of the El Paso County Sheriff's independent review of Daniel Rohrbough's death. The report shows Rohrbough was not killed by Dylan Klebold at close range, as stated in the official JCSO report released May 15, 2000. The review also finds that Rohrbough wasn't shot by Sergeant O'Shea, who hadn't yet arrived when the boy was killed. The report concludes the fatal bullet was a "textbook match" to Eric Harris' gun and Rohrbough's death was undeniably caused by Harris.

Jefferson County authorities ask Judge Babcock to review 5,000 additional pages of Columbine documents to be released to the public. The documents include an index of the Columbine Report's contents, with witness names and page numbers where their interviews begin.

April 12, 2002: *Home Room* debuts. The film is about the aftermath of a school shooting that leaves 9 people dead including the shooter.

April 13, 2002: Jefferson County District Attorney Dave Thomas announces the El Paso County Sheriff Office's report will be released by Wednesday or Thursday of the next week, instead of waiting until after the anniversary as stated earlier.

April 15, 2002: *A&E's Investigative Reports* airs an episode about the Columbine tragedy which includes a "psychiatric autopsy" of Eric Harris and Dylan Klebold. One parent calls the show "shallow at best".

April 16, 2002: The Columbine Review Task Force adds Randy Brown to their panel.

April 17, 2002: Jefferson County District Attorney Dave Thomas releases the El Paso County Sheriff's Office report to the public at a news conference.

April 18, 2002: Colorado State Representative Don Lee, R-Littleton, brings House Bill 1418 before the Colorado State Veterans and Military Affairs Committee to create a probe with subpoena powers, to investigate the Columbine shooting. The bill passes 8-1, though Lee expects it will die in the House Appropriations Committee if he can't prove that private donations and lawyers working pro bono will cover the $300,000 cost.

April 19, 2002: Greg Zanis unveils a proposal for a permanent Christian memorial to those who died at Columbine with thirteen marble and wood crosses in his hometown.

April 20, 2002: For the third anniversary of the shooting a memorial service is held at Clement Park at 11:00 a.m.

April 22, 2002: In a press meeting Brian Rohrbough offers a public apology to Sergeant Dan O'Shea for blaming him for his son's death. Rorhbough told the media: "We're sorry for the pain and frustration we have caused him."

Several members of the Columbine Task Force support public release of the Basement Tapes and crime scene photos. Some members do not agree.

April 24, 2002: The Colorado Bureau of Investigation releases 3,221 pages of Columbine documents to the public

April 30, 2002: The Colorado House Appropriations Committee approves a modified version of Representative Don Lee's HB1418. The object of the probe is to investigate official response on April 20, 1999, to prepare for similar terrorist-type attacks on schools or other public places.

May 3, 2002: Colorado House of Representatives approves HB1418, 39-24. They pass the bill to the Colorado Senate.

May 6, 2002: The Senate Judiciary Committee kills HB1418, 4-3 against.

May 7, 2002: Solvay Pharmaceuticals, manufacturer of Luvox, the antidepressant drug prescribed to Eric Harris, asks the U.S. district judge to remove Donna Taylor, the mother of survivor Mark, from the lawsuit pending against the company.

May 10, 2002: After a year of legal battles, attorneys for the *Denver Post* get the 1999 search warrants for the Harris and Klebold homes released. The sealed warrants use information from the 1998 police report the Browns filed – the same filing (Guerra documents) JeffCo claimed up until April 2001 didn't exist. Judge Nieto, the person who signed the 1999 search warrants, is the same one who sealed them.

May 15, 2002: Jefferson County School Superintendent Jane Hammond resigns for a position in California focusing on student performance.

May 17, 2002: Michael Moore's film, *Bowling for Columbine*, premiers at the 55th Cannes Film Festival. It's the first documentary in 46 years to compete for the top prize, the Palm d'Or. Moore tricked Columbine victims Richard Castaldo and Mark Taylor, along with Brooks Brown, into participating by misrepresenting what he was doing.

May 18, 2002: 457 Columbine students graduate at Fiddler's Green Amphitheatre in Denver. They are the last group of students who attended Columbine during the 1999 shooting. The class tassel has four colors to represent the dead who should have graduated that year: Steve Curnow and Danny Rohrbough who died during the shooting and Stephanie Hart-Grizell and Nick Kunselman who were killed in the Subway shooting.

Craig Scott, survivor and brother of victim Rachel, decorates his girlfriend's room to surprise her when he asks her to prom. Evan Todd and Sean Graves graduate. Sean gets up out of his wheelchair and uses a single crutch to help him cross the stage to collect his diploma.

May 20, 2002: U.S. District Court Judge Lewis Babcock unseals survivor Pat Ireland's appeal of the dismissal of his case. In it, Ireland claims law enforcement knew injured students were in the library but did nothing to expedite rescue efforts—just like the Dave Sanders case which Judge Babcock let stand. Ireland wants to amend his case with new photo and video evidence. Judge Babcock agrees to conduct a hearing in July.

250

May 21, 2002: *National Enquirer* interviews Brian Rohrbough. They tell him they intend to publish the leaked photos of the gunmen dead in the library.

May 24, 2002: The *National Enquirer* publishes the leaked photos of Harris' and Klebold's bodies. Colorado grocery stores refuse to display the issue. Other surrounding states such as Arizona refuse to carry the issue as well.

May 28, 2002: The Columbine Task Force formally requests the Colorado Court of Appeals to unseal Klebold's autopsy.

June 4, 2002: A group of Columbine survivors and their families, led by Pastor Bruce Porter, head to Erfurt, Germany, to help those affected by the April 26, 2002, shooting there.

June 6, 2002: The 13 Columbine families settle lawsuits with Jefferson County School District and the Jefferson County Sheriff's Office. They reach a $285,000 deal. Each family will receive roughly $15,000.

June 7, 2002: Pastor Bruce Porter's Columbine group present the Erfurt shooting survivors with a torch, wreath, and plaque.

June 17, 2002: The Acts of Kindness Association posthumously awards Rachel Scott the title of Student of the Year for leading an honorable life of intentional kindness.

Jefferson County lawyers argue in court that the suit filed by Angela Sanders should be thrown out because the Columbine shooting was unprecedented; law enforcement could not have known what they were dealing with, nor could they have anticipated the legal implications of their actions.

June 24, 2002: The Columbine Task Force reviews 1,800 additional pages of information. They find Dylan Klebold harassed Mark Kintgen at Columbine six months before the shooting and a journal entry by Eric Harris that says he wants to rob a gun collector and has enough explosives to kill 100 people.

Michael and Vonda Shoels, victim Isaiah's parents, want their lawsuit against the shooters' parents moved back to state court.

Luvox, the drug Harris was prescribed and stopped taking before the shooting, is removed from pharmacy shelves.

251

June 27, 2002: The 10th Circuit Court of Appeals rules the Jefferson County School District acted properly when it banned religious themed tiles from display at Columbine. The Flemings and Rohrboughs will appeal the decision before the U.S. Supreme Court.

July 12, 2002: The shooters' parents ask U.S. District Court Judge Lewis Babcock to order Michael and Vonda Shoels to sign settlement papers and dismiss their lawsuit. This follows the April decision to disburse $1.5 million to the victims' families.

July 15, 2002: Jefferson County officials remove themselves from the Columbine Open Records Task Force due to a lawsuit filed by the Task Force against JCSO seeking official records.

July 17, 2002: Pat Ireland's lawyer Stephen Peters asks Judge Babcock to hear Ireland's suit again based on new photo evidence which shows that despite having a clear view into the library during the events of April 20, 1999, law enforcement did nothing to aid survivors for hours after the shooting ended. Judge Babcock will consider the request.

July 24, 2002: The Columbine Task Force asks for public release of Harris and Klebold's juvenile records. Some were previously released but the committee wants to see all of them.

August 18, 2002: Columbine High School readies for the new school year. Nearly 60% of the staff have left the school since the tragedy of 1999.

August 20, 2002: Angela Sanders's lawsuit against Jefferson County settles for $1.5 million. The suit claims officials stopped students and faculty from rescuing Sanders even after they knew the gunmen were dead. Despite receiving desperate and repeat 911 calls about his worsening condition, aid that arrived at the school at 2:30 p.m. did not reach Sanders until 4 p.m. Angela is satisfied officials have changed their policies on how they handle mass shootings. She blames the commanders, not the officers and deputies, for her father's death. Judge Lewis Babcock says the sheriff's officials showed deliberate indifference toward the wounded Dave Sanders.

The county announces it will pay $15,000 settlements to the 11 other families who sued. County Attorney Bill Tuthill says it's better to heal than fight. The Rohrboughs accept the offer and say they hope

Attorney General Ken Salazar will succeed in making the investigative documents public.

August 26, 2002: Jefferson County Sheriff John Stone refuses to allow the Columbine Records Review Task Force access to his department's Columbine files. In a letter to State Solicitor General Alan Gilber, assistant Jefferson County Attorney Lily Oeffler says Stone will have to release the documents to the public if he gives them to the Task Force.

September 3, 2002: Mark Taylor's lawsuit against Solvay Pharmaceuticals is given a trial date of March 2004.

September 4, 2002: Brian Rohrbough and Sue Petrone file a lawsuit against former Arapahoe County Deputy James Taylor for defamation and outrageous conduct. Taylor falsely told them he witnessed another officer shoot their son.

Sunday, September 15, 2002: Tom and Sue Klebold receive an anonymous message on their unlisted telephone number from a young man who promises a copycat attack at his school sometime after 11 p.m. Jefferson County schools are put on heightened alert Monday, but students are not told about the potential threat. The day passes without incident.

September 16, 2002: The Columbine Task Force files suit against Jefferson County, claiming public safety outweighs privacy concerns when it comes to releasing the juvenile diversion records of Eric Harris and Dylan Klebold. The Task Force wants to see the records of the gunmen's participation in the diversion program after they were caught breaking into a van in 1998.

September 17, 2002: The FBI takes over investigation of the threatening phone call the Klebolds received earlier that week.

October 1: Brooks Brown and Rob Merritt publish *No Easy Answers: The Truth Behind Death at Columbine High School*.

October 5, 2002: The *Rocky Mountain News* reports that, a year and 13 days before the shooting at Columbine, Eric Harris told his juvenile probation officer he had homicidal and suicidal thoughts and had issues with anxiety and controlling his temper. He said he often cried and blew up when angered. The probation officer assigned him to anger management class.

October 6, 2002: Lawyer for the Harris family C. Michael Montgomery files a response with the JeffCo Court that says they will not oppose the release of their son's juvenile diversion files.

Greg Zanis wants to raise $650,000 for a permanent memorial at Roxborough State Park. The 13 eight-foot-tall crosses he made that are displayed in the park have deteriorated over time. Zanis wants to replace them with new ones in marble and glass.

October 8, 2002: The Klebolds' lawyers C. Michael Montgomery and Gregg Kay request that portions of the civil trial where their son's videos and journals will be viewed be held in secret. They are concerned public display may glorify Dylan's actions and encourage copycats.

October 11, 2002: Film-maker Michael Moore releases his controversial film *Bowling for Columbine* to the public

A judge rules 4 videotapes made by Harris and Klebold can be removed from the courthouse by lawyers working on a lawsuit related to the attack, despite the risk of leaks.

October 19, 2002: Lisa Van Syckel contributes $31,000 to survivor Mark Taylor's lawsuit against Solvay Pharmaceuticals. Van Syckel's daughter had a violent reaction to Paxil®, an antidepressant like Luvox, the drug Eric Harris was prescribed. Four other Columbine families involved in the suit drop out due to financial reasons.

October 21, 2002: The Columbine Task Force petitions again for the release of Harris and Klebold's juvenile probation records.

October 25, 2002: Michael Moore's *Bowling for Columbine* opens in mainstream theaters across the USA.

October 29, 2002: The *Rocky Mountain News* asks the Colorado Court of Appeals to overturn a January 2 court order by District Judge Brooke Jackson to unseal the autopsy of Dylan Klebold.

October 30, 2002: Judge Brooke Jackson orders the release of the juvenile diversion program records. The judge contends public scrutiny may help determine if officials missed warning signs in months prior to the shooting.

October 31, 2002: Dr. Peter Breggin and Dr. Donald Marks, experts Mark Taylor intends to use in his lawsuit against Solvay Pharmaceuticals, are limited in what they can say in court. Mark Kennedy, attorney for Solvay, claims the doctors must look at thousands of Columbine materials, released and unreleased, to form a sound opinion on the shooting. U.S. District Judge Clarence Brimmer is angered the experts failed to view the evidence before but denies Solvay's motion for sanctions against Taylor's legal team. The judge says the medical experts will not be allowed to review the evidence since the deadline has passed. They are only allowed to testify about matters mentioned in their established reports. Breggin testifies: "Eric Harris was suffering from a substance induced (Luvox) mood disorder with depressive and manic features that had reached a psychotic level of violence and suicide. Absent persistent exposure to Luvox, Eric Harris probably would not have committed violence and suicide." The judge rejects the argument.

November 4, 2002: Jefferson County District Attorney Dave Thomas releases Eric Harris's juvenile diversion file to the public. Dylan Klebold's record is ordered to be released as well but is being held while his parents consider appealing Judge Brooke Jackson's decision.

November 12, 2002: Attorney Jim Rouse, lawyer for the families of Kelly Fleming and Daniel Rohrbough, asks the Supreme Court to hear their case against the Jefferson County School District for not displaying their religious memorial tiles in Columbine's halls. The 10th Circuit Court of Appeals rules against the families, citing separation of church and state.

November 13, 2002: U.S. District Judge Richard Matsch accuses Jefferson County officials and the shooters' families of making a deal that would keep audio and videotapes made by Harris and Klebold from public release. The deal would return the tapes to the families, released only for scientific research. Judge Matsch refuses to approve the agreement. The judge gives the Harris lawyer ten days to file additional arguments.

November 14, 2002: Klebold family attorneys request District Judge Brooke Jackson remove some of the information in Dylan's juvenile probation file before releasing it to the public.

November 19, 2002: JeffCo District Attorney's office announces the Columbine shooters' "prosecution files" will remain sealed. The files are independent from the diversion records. There was no request filed specifically for them. The Columbine Task Force will pursue release of the prosecution files.

November 21, 2002: The Colorado Court of Appeals orders Jefferson County District Judge Brooke Jackson to reconsider his refusal to release Dylan Klebold's autopsy report to the public.

November 22, 2002: Dylan Klebold's diversion file released to the public.

December 4, 2002: Columbine teacher Theresa Miller dies from cancer at age 44. She saved several students and assisted Dave Sanders after he was shot.

December 11, 2002: U.S. District Judge Richard Matsch rules the parents of the Columbine gunmen cannot use copyright laws to suppress recordings their sons made before the shooting. The parents assert they own the copyright and have reached an out-of-court settlement with Sheriff John Stone to keep the tapes locked up. Judge Matsch's decision does not provide public release of the recordings.

2003 — January: Michael Moore's *Bowling for Columbine* website is hacked by someone who doesn't approve of the film.

January 8, 2003: Jefferson County Sheriff's Office releases 9,736 more pages of Columbine documents to the public on CD-ROM. The pages include school assignments written by Klebold and Harris, and notes written by individuals who were trapped inside Columbine waiting to be rescued.

January 10, 2003: The Klebolds release their son's full autopsy report to the public, to dispel questions about whether he committed suicide or was murdered. They announce in a press statement that Dylan was left-handed, debunking conspiracy theories about why he was shot in the left temple.

January 13, 2003: The US Supreme Court refuses to hear an appeal by the families of Kelly Fleming and Daniel Rohrbough against the Jefferson County School District regarding the memorial tiles Columbine refuses to display.

January 15, 2003: Mark Taylor appears in a television interview with Wahluke High School hostage instigator Cory Baadsgaard to raise awareness about adverse reactions when children are forced onto drugs. The show promotes a documentary by Gary Null about the rising tendency to overmedicate children. Solvay Pharmaceuticals denounces Null and Taylor as conspiracy theorists performing a "pseudo-scientific crusade".

January 24, 2003: Columbine survivor Jonathan Ross Ladd, 21 years old, dies when the single-engine Cessna 172 Skyhawk he is piloting collides with a twin-engine Piper Cheyenne II plane. The airplanes crash in a Denver neighborhood, killing four other people along with the pilots. Jonathan was a junior at Columbine and was in the school on the day of the attack. He was a student assistant in the Tech Lab who aided Rich Long and Peggy Dodd.

January 31, 2003: The families of Cassie Bernall, Kelly Fleming, Daniel Rohrbough, Matthew Kechter, and Kyle Velasquez settle their claims against Ronald Hartmann, one of the vendors who sold Robyn Anderson three guns used by the shooters. Survivors Patrick Ireland and Lance Kirklin also settle their suits against Hartmann and James Washington, the other vendor.

February 6, 2003: Mark Taylor drops his lawsuit against Solvay on the promise they will donate $10,000 to the American Cancer Society. He later tells the media he did not want to settle, and the money never materialized. He went through three lawyers, two of whom pressured him to settle. With the third, he was not allowed to have his mother present during proceedings. According to Taylor, Solvay told him they would countersue, and he could end up in jail if he didn't settle.

February 19, 2003: Denver attorneys release 309 pages of Columbine files. Some of the documents released include the "spy files," documents that name 75 teens initially thought to be associated with the Trench Coat Mafia, and the results of a computer check that was run on them.

March 4, 2003: A 14-year-old boy from Eden Prairie, Minnesota, is arrested after he uses an online service for the hearing impaired to threaten that he is going to blow up Columbine High.

March 12, 2003: Judge Lewis Babcock rules in favor of five of the Columbine families, allowing them the right to question the parents of Eric Harris and Dylan Klebold. Attorneys and families of Kelly

Fleming, Matthew Kechter, Daniel Rohrbough, Lauren Townsend, and Kyle Velasquez are allowed to question up to 15 people under oath.

March 13, 2003: Jefferson County Sheriff's Office releases over seven hours of Denver police dispatch tapes from April 20, 1999.

March 14, 2003: The Harrises and Klebolds ask U.S. District Court Judge Robert Blackburn to enforce the terms of the $1.6 million settlement agreement from summer 2001.This will prevent Isaiah Shoels' family from pursuing a civil lawsuit against them. Judge Blackburn says he will make a decision as soon as possible.

April 2, 2003: The Columbine Task Force votes to stay together and continue their work, saying the Jefferson County Sheriff's Office still holds over 6,300 unreleased items related to the shooting at Columbine.

April 7, 2003: The Columbine families announce a permanent memorial will be built in Clement Park for the five-year anniversary next year.

April 20, 2003: The fourth anniversary of the Columbine tragedy falls on Easter Sunday. There is no official ceremony.

May 9, 2003: Columbine is put on modified lockdown after three threatening notes are found on campus. Half of the students are in class that day.

May 12, 2003: Jefferson County District Attorney Dave Thomas releases his "prosecutor's files" that show Klebold and Harris coasted through a 12-month juvenile diversion course and were released early from the program.

June 9, 2003: The Jefferson County Sheriff's Office releases another 200+ pages of documents related to Harris, Klebold, and their associates.

June 25, 2003: U.S. District Judge Robert Blackburn orders the Shoels to accept a $366,000 settlement for the wrongful death of their son Isaiah. Their lawyer, Geoffrey Feiger, claims the acceptance paperwork was filed by mistake, which the judge says isn't credible based on the evidence.

July 8, 2003: Federal District Judge Clarence Brimmer opens a case for survivor Mark Taylor, who is seeking a refund from his first lawyer, John DeCamp. Taylor questions the amount of work the attorney did in his dismissed suit against Solvay Pharmaceuticals. Taylor's new attorney Ron Miller claims DeCamp violated Colorado law which requires a written fee agreement between an attorney and a client. Judge Brimmer gives DeCamp 10 days to submit a thorough accounting of the work he did on Taylor's lawsuit.

July 28, 2003: The shooters' parents give depositions at the Denver federal courthouse to attorneys of the families of Kelly Fleming, Matthew Kechter, Danny Rohrbough, Lauren Townsend, and Kyle Velasquez in their wrongful death lawsuits. U.S. District Judge Lewis Babcock reviews the depositions and allows the lawsuits to proceed.

August 12, 2003: Families of Kelly Fleming, Matthew Kechter, Lauren Townsend, and Kyle Velasquez settle their lawsuits against the Harrises and Klebolds.

August 21, 2003: Dawn Anna, victim Lauren Townsend's mother, wants the depositions from the shooters' parents be made public to help other schools and parents see the signs that were missed in the Columbine tragedy.

September 2003: Production and sale of Luvox is stopped.

September 3, 2003: Film *Zero Day* opens in New York. Inspired by the Columbine shooting, it features security camera style footage that is mistaken for Columbine footage when people post clips of it to the Internet, spawning a new barrage of conspiracy theories about Columbine.

September 8, 2003: Judge Lewis Babcock denies a request by Valeen Schnurr to file an amended lawsuit against law enforcement as the statute of limitations has been reached.

September 9, 2003: Brian and Lisa Rohrbough return from a trip to Ukraine to adopt Rachel (2 years) and Isaac (1).

September 23, 2003: Judge Patricia Coan issues an order to clean out the Columbine evidence room in the Denver federal courthouse since the lawsuits are settled. She orders the evidence destroyed including depositions by the parents of Klebold and Harris. Attorney Barry Arrington says he will appeal.

October 2, 2003: Michael and Vonda Shoels file a motion objecting to the order to destroy the files in the Columbine evidence room.

October 7, 2003: Colorado Attorney General Ken Salazar files a motion asking Judge Patricia Coan to preserve files in the Columbine evidence room. Salazar asks for an inventory of all records that have ever been in the room.

October 14, 2003: Deputy Attorney General F. Michael Goodbee reviews over 22,000 pages of Columbine material and finds 406 more pages can be released. The pages include police reports, text from Eric's websites, maps of the crime scene, and more.

October 15, 2003: Judge Lewis Babcock gives the Harrises and Klebolds 20 days to respond to the motions filed about preserving the files in the Columbine evidence room. He allows the National Archives and Records Administration to file friend-of-the-court briefings allowing Columbine files to be stored in Washington, D.C.

The Jefferson County Sheriff's Office announces it will release the *Rampart Range* video tape made by Harris and Klebold as they tested their new weapons on March 6, 1999.

October 22, 2003: *Rampart Range* video released to the public.

October 23, 2003: The complaint filed against Eric Harris by the Browns about his threatening website is found in a three-ring binder unrelated to the investigation. JeffCo Sheriff Ted Mink asks Colorado Attorney General Ken Salazar to investigate why the documents were overlooked for so long. The files are called the "Guerra file" in the Columbine Documents.

November 1, 2003: Jefferson County District Judge James D. Zimmerman allows the lawsuit from Brian Rohrbough and Sue Petrone to pursue damages against former Arapahoe Deputy Sheriff James Taylor for negligent and outrageous conduct. In it, the family accuse Taylor of defamation, negligence, and outrageous conduct for telling them he saw Dan run from the school only to be gunned down by Sergeant Dan O'Shea's "friendly fire".

November 3, 2003: Colorado Attorney General Ken Salazar asks U.S. District Court Judge Lewis Babcock to allow Delbert Elliott, director of the Center for the Study and Prevention of Violence at the University of Colorado, to review dozens of withheld Columbine

260

documents and issue a public report on his findings. Jefferson County Sheriff Ted Mink files a motion allowing him to intervene in the court fight over the destruction of Columbine documents ordered by U.S. Magistrate Judge Patricia Coan.

November 8, 2003: Philip Duran, who sold the Columbine shooters the TEC-DC9, is released from electronic monitoring and placed on parole.

November 14: Gus Van Sant's film *Elephant* opens. Inspired by the Columbine shooting, the main characters are gay, reigniting rumors that Harris and Klebold were gay.

November 20, 2003: During a School Board meeting, a group of Columbine parents ask JeffCo to release the sealed report of the shooting which was compiled for district attorneys as they prepared for lawsuits.

December 18, 2003: Former Jefferson County Sheriff's Deputy John Hicks speaks with two investigators from the Colorado Attorney's Office at his home in Rock Hill, South Carolina. The investigators seek answers about why the complaint against Eric Harris (Guerra file) was exempt from the investigation.

December 26, 2003: JeffCo District Attorney Dave Thomas and his wife Shirley announce they are creating a nonprofit charity, Helen's Hope, to support local shelters that cater to abused women. The charity is named in honor of Shirley's sister Helen who was murdered by her husband Arthur.

2004 — January 14: The Jefferson County Sheriff's Office debates releasing over 70 video tapes collected during the investigation, some of which were made by the gunmen.

January 20, 2004: Jefferson County Sheriff Ted Mink says the results of the investigation about contact between the Columbine shooters and local law enforcement will be released next month. The results are based on interviews with former deputy John Hicks and others two years before the shootings.

January 23, 2004: Judge Lewis Babcock rules those who oppose the destruction of the sworn statements from the Harrises and Klebolds cannot intervene, but their arguments against the case will be considered by the court.

January 30, 2004: *The Denver Post* calls for release of the records once investigation ends. The Colorado Court of Appeals announces some of the Columbine evidence might be released to the public, including journals and videotapes seized at the Harris home.

February 20, 2004: Jefferson County sheriff's office announces the evidence will be released to the public February 26, 2004.

February 24, 2004: Investigators end a four-month probe and conclude Randy and Judy Brown were the source of an anonymous August 7, 1997, report to the Jefferson County sheriff's office about Eric Harris. However, the Browns say they don't remember making the report. There are several inconsistencies in the Directed 1997 Report investigation.

February 24-25, 2004: Jefferson County holds a public exhibition of the released Columbine evidence at the Jefferson County Fairgrounds Auditorium. A grim display of morbid artifacts, the exhibit includes boxes of personal belongings, photographs, weapons, remnants of the damaged school, maps, reports, and more. The event attracts a large crowd, including family members of slain victim Coach Dave Sanders.

February 26, 2004: Colorado Attorney General Ken Salazar reveals law enforcement had at least 15 encounters with Harris and Klebold before April 20, 1999, but finds no evidence of negligence on the part of Jefferson County Sheriff's Office. After the press conference the public is allowed to view the evidence. Two video tapes are available for sale: One is 34 minutes long and shows the crowd in Clement Park the day of the shootings. The second tape is 94 minutes long and contains videos the gunmen made for A/V class.

February 29, 2004: Jefferson County Sheriff's Office settles the lawsuit brought by victim Patrick Ireland, for $117,500 The case was dismissed in 2002 on the grounds of governmental immunity, but Ireland appealed and won. The sheriff's office assumes no liability in the settlement. This is the last federal case against them. Isaiah Shoels' family still has an unsettled lawsuit pending against the shooters' parents.

March 10, 2004: Attorney Geoffrey Fieger asks a 3-judge panel from the 10th U.S. Circuit Court of Appeals to review the mistyped letter filed by Fieger's secretary which says the Shoels accept $366,000 from the 2001 settlement. If the court finds in their favor, the Shoels will be allowed out of the deal so they can continue a wrongful death suit against the Harrises and Klebolds.

March 30, 2004: Chairman of the Columbine Memorial Committee Bob Easton announces construction of the Columbine Memorial will be delayed until more funds are raised. They have less than a quarter of the $2.5 million needed, dashing the hope to have the memorial built by the 5th anniversary.

April 6, 2004: The newly-released book *Surviving Columbine: How Faith Helps Us Find Peace When Tragedy Strikes*, which includes the stories of three Columbine survivors — Liz Carlston, Amber Huntington, and Michael Johnson — is promoted by Mike Johnson in Salt Lake City, Utah.

April 17, 2004: Tom Mauser walks in his son Daniel's shoes to the NRA national convention in Pittsburgh. Vice-President Dick Cheney is delivering the keynote speech Saturday night at the convention. Tom wants to challenge him to discuss extending the assault weapons ban which expires in September. He's not allowed into the convention.

April 20, 2004: 5th anniversary of the Columbine tragedy. Columbine High closes completely. People gather that evening at Clement Park amphitheater for a candlelight memorial. A fighter jet fly-over at 6:00 p.m. starts the evening. Survivor Anne Marie Hochhalter gives a speech about moving forward; The Cohen brothers perform their song "Friend of Mine" again. Dawn Anna speaks on behalf of the victims' families. The ceremony ends with Principal Frank DeAngelis reading the names of those who were killed, followed by a moment of silence.

That same day, Dave Cullen's article "The Depressive and the Psychopath" is posted to Slate.com. In it, FBI Supervisory Special Agent and psychologist Wayne Fuselier and psychiatrist Dr. Frank Ochberg diagnose Eric Harris as a psychopath based on his rants in his journals. They surmise Dylan Klebold was the one prone to fits of rage and Harris calmed him down. Witnesses say the exact opposite was true: Harris would fly off the handle and Klebold would defuse him. It isn't known if their diagnosis considers the fact that Harris was on SSRIs.

July 20, 2004: Former President Bill Clinton promises to assist fund-raising for a permanent memorial to be built in Clement Park. A $250-per-plate dinner raises $350K, along with a $100K donation from the

Coors family (Al Velasquez worked at Coors). The Columbine Memorial has raised $1 million.

September 2004: The final grand jury investigation of the "lost" Guerra documents is released. They "cannot determine whether the absence of original official records, any handwritten notes, the complete working file and all electronic documents is tied to a particular person or the result of a particular crime." Randy Brown declares it collusion and criminal conspiracy.

October 12, 2004: *Duck! The Carbine High Massacre* is released on DVD with deleted scenes and other extras.

November 29, 2004: Parents of victim Danny Rohrbough settle out of court with James Taylor one day before the jury trial of their lawsuit against him.

2005 — The play *Columbinus* world premiere in Silver Spring, Maryland. Inspired by the Columbine shooting, it focuses on alienation, social pressure, and hostility in high school. The play doesn't exploit or satire the event.

January 10, 2005: *Dawn Anna* Lifetime TV movie is released. The film stars Debra Winger and chronicles the struggles Dawn Anna has endured, including losing her daughter in the shooting.

August 26, 2005: Tiffany Lien, 21, is shot and killed by her boyfriend in Tempe, Arizona. Lien was a freshman at Columbine and was outside when the shooting started. She and her friend Tessa Anderson saw one of the gunmen shoot two people before the girls ran and hid in a bathroom.

September 23, 2005: Joseph D. Stair, father of Amanda and Joe Stair, passes away at age 46.

November 2005: The Supreme Court allows Jefferson County Sheriff Ted Mink to decide whether to release to the public the Basement Tapes and Columbine documents including Wayne Harris' diary. He calls in advisors and questions the families of the victims about the matter but won't reach a decision about the tapes until next year.

2006 — January: Wayne Harris, father of shooter Eric, petitions the high court for a rehearing. He doesn't want the public to see what he wrote in his journal prior to the shooting, maintaining the writings are his private property.

March 5, 2006: Survivor Crystal Woodman Miller publishes *Marked for Life: Choosing Hope and Discovering Purpose After Earth-Shattering Tragedy.*

Early April 2006: Roy Miller, grandfather of Joe and Amanda Stair, passes away at age 67.

Spring 2006: 1st annual Run for Remembrance charity race is held. Future charity events will take place each spring.

June 2006: Groundbreaking ceremony for the Columbine Memorial. Bill Clinton helps raise money and makes a personal donation to ensure the memorial will be built.

July 6, 2006: Jefferson County Sheriff Ted Mink decides not to release the Basement Tapes. Instead, he releases the Columbine documents: 946 pages of additional reports and scans of the shooters' journals and other papers. Wayne Harris' writings are included after the courts overturn his appeal.

September 10, 2006: Reporter Tim Roche, who wrote the Basement Tapes article for *TIME* magazine, dies following multiple strokes at age 38.

October 6, 2006: Governor Bill Owens commissions Director of Juvenile Diversion Regina Herter to report on the "Culture of Columbine". The report is referenced in producing the final report of the Columbine Review Commission. Huerter confidentially interviews 34 parents, faculty, and students from October 14th to November 29th. The interviews focus on the culture of the school with bullying as a major focus.

October 24, 2006: Victim Mark Taylor's book *I Asked, God Answered: A Columbine Miracle* is published.

2007 — January: Chief Judge Lewis T. Babcock of the U.S. District Court in Denver suggests the depositions of the shooters' parents be transferred to the National Archives and kept sealed for 25 years instead of being destroyed.

April 4: Judge Babcock orders sealed for 20 years the statements made by the Klebolds and Harrises to the police after the shootings, to settle concerns that their release would encourage copycats. Columbine families disagree. They believe the documents could help others stop similar situations. The judge also rejects a request from the Harrises and Klebolds to release the depositions in redacted form.

March 1, 2007: Someone calls a bomb threat into Columbine High. The school is evacuated, and students sent home. Classes resume the next day.

April 16, 2007: Lone gunman 23-year-old Seung-Hui Cho goes on a shooting spree at Virginia Tech college in Blacksburg, Virginia. He kills 32 people and injures 25 before killing himself. It is the deadliest school shooting in US history. In videos he made shortly before the shooting, Cho mentions becoming a martyr "like Eric and Dylan".

The Columbine Memorial reaches its $2.2 million goal. This includes $400K in donated materials as well as a $50K donation from former President Clinton, who visited Colorado twice to raise money for the cause. The final donation comes from an anonymous source which is downplayed as it occurs the same day as the Virginia Tech shooting. The Columbine Memorial Committee sends out dedication ceremony invitations.

September 21, 2007: The Columbine Memorial is finished. The memorial is situated at the base of Rebel Hill in Clement Park. Patrick Ireland is a guest speaker at the dedication ceremony.

September 23, 2007: 27-year-old Joseph Stair, a founder of the TCM, hangs himself in his family's Colorado print shop. Joe suffered from depression. He leaves behind his wife, a 6-year-old daughter, and 1-year-old son. His sister Amanda was in the library during the shooting. In YouTube videos she tells the public her brother's suicide wasn't related to Columbine.

2008 — June 12: Patrick Ireland is doing well for himself. He is employed as a financial rep and has a wife, Kacie.

September 20, 2008: Brian Anderson, now 26 years old, has moved on with his life. He still tries to make sense of that fateful day at Columbine High. He hasn't set foot into any library nor does he like the sound of helicopters or fire alarms. Brian would like to go back to Columbine and see the new library. He hopes to find more closure.

2009 — Anne Marie Hochhalter is now a manager at Bath and Body Works.

February 2009: Two years after Tom Mauser sent them an angry letter, the Harrises agree to meet with the Mauser family to discuss Eric killing Danny.

March 25, 2009: *Columbine: A True Crime Story* by Jeff Kass is published.

April 15, 2009: Film *Reunion* debuts. It imagines what life would have been like for the 13 victims if they had lived.

April 18, 2009: Film *April Showers* debuts, written and directed by Andrew Robinson who was a senior at Columbine during the shootings. A friend of Rachel Scott, he also wrote the school play she starred in prior to the shooting, *The Smoke in the Room*.

April 20, 2009: 10th year memorial held. Alumni from 1999 to 2005 are invited to breakfast. It's the first time the Class of '99 is together in the building since the day they had to come back and collect the belongings they left behind during the shooting,

Oprah films an episode that features an interview with Principal Frank DeAngelis. It focuses on the trauma rather than the healing. After he expresses concern that it will only add to the hurt the victims and their families suffered, Oprah makes the executive decision not to air the show.

September 2009: Solvay sells its pharmaceuticals division to Abbott Labs for €4.5 billion ($6.2 billion).

October 20, 2009: After turning down repeat requests for interviews over the years, Susan Klebold writes an essay for Oprah Winfrey's *O Magazine*. She describes the morning of April 20th, 1999, and says she had no idea how sick and suicidal Dylan was until she read his journals after his death.

November 14, 2009: Sean Graves marries long-time girlfriend Kara Dehart. Sean works in financial services in Denver and is an ambassador for the Christopher and Dana Reeve Foundation, which advocates research and improving the quality of life of individuals with spinal cord injuries. Sean is working toward a degree to enable him to become a crime scene investigator.

2010 — Richard Castaldo runs for Congress, representing the Peace and Freedom Party. He doesn't win.

January 13, 2010: Former Chief Justice William Erickson dies at age 85. He served on the Supreme Court for 25 years and was married to his wife Dorie for 56 years. He tried very hard to get to the truth behind the Columbine shooting coverup and was upset by the investigation.

March 3, 2010: *Columbine* by Dave Cullen is published.

2011 — December: Former Arapahoe County Sheriff Pat Sullivan arrested for soliciting male prostitutes in a meth-for-sex drug trafficking scandal. One man Sullivan was with was found dead. Sullivan defended former Deputy Jim Taylor back when the Rohrboughs accused him of lying about their son's death. Sullivan was an active participant in state and local meth task forces in 2007 and 2008. He admits to smoking meth and giving a man "date rape drug" before taking sexual advantage of him. He pleads guilty and is sentenced to 38 days in jail with 8 days credit for time served, and 2 years of probation.

February 3, 2011: Former District Attorney Dave Thomas, out of politics since it was discovered he was part of the coverup of the Guerra documents, runs for president of the school board. No one else runs. He wins by default.

April 28, 2011: 15-year-old Ryan Kile is in a car wreck that paralyzes him. He is visited at Craig Hospital by Sean Graves, who was also 15 when he was paralyzed in the Columbine shooting. Graves worked to walk at his graduation 3 years later. Inspired, in 2014 Kile defeats the odds and walks at his graduation. He said: "Sean could do this. Why can't I?" Graves keeps a clipping of the newspaper article in his wallet.

2012 — April 12: Tom Mauser announces his intention to publish his book, *Walking in Daniel's Shoes*.

April 20, 2012: Tom Mauser's book is published, detailing the family's experiences from the day of Daniel's death to what they've dealt with over the years. Mauser says he referenced *aColumbineSite.com* to establish the timeline used in his book.

May 2012: *13 Families: Life After Columbine* is released. Directed by Nicole Corbin, Mark Katchur, and Steven Lukanic, it focuses on the families of those who were killed and how they have healed. It also emphasizes gun control.

July 20, 2012: During the premier of *The Dark Knight Rises* at a theater in Aurora, Colorado, James Holmes sets off teargas and opens fire on the audience. 12 people are killed. A group of Columbine survivors band together to assist the survivors. Holmes, who was taking Zoloft at the time of the shooting, is later found guilty of 165 charges and receives a life sentence without possibility for parole.

November 2012: Sue Klebold speaks at length for the first time about her son Dylan's role in the shootings in the book *Far from the Tree: Parents, Children and the Search for Identity*.

Wells Fargo forecloses on Richard Castaldo's Los Angeles home during the housing crisis. The 31-year-old turns to Occupy Los Angeles to keep his handicap-enabled condo. He still loses his house and ends up homeless.

2013 — April 8: Of the total donations received by Mile High United Way and McCormick Tribune Foundation, 58% ($2.6 million) made it to the victims. The rest goes to the Jefferson Center for mental health and violence prevention ($1 million), to "services to Columbine community" ($560,000), and to the Colorado Organization for Victim Assistance ($294,000).

April 10, 2013: Craig Scott, brother of victim Rachel Scott and a survivor, returns to the school for the 14th anniversary of the shooting.

June 15, 2013: 30-year-old Matthew Depew, who was a sophomore hiding in the kitchen during the Columbine shooting, dies while working on power lines for Xcel Energy in Carlsbad, New Mexico.

November 14, 2013: Dawn Anna publishes the book *Heaven's Flower*, inspired by her daughter.

2014 — Susan and Thomas Klebold divorce, citing differences in how they dealt with their grief, and that they don't have any views in common about what happened with Dylan.

February 15, 2014: Jefferson County Ted Mink announces the department destroyed the Basement Tapes in 2011. The rest of the evidence from the Columbine shootings was deemed too inflammatory and was also destroyed, according to his statement.

April 30, 2014: Documentary television series *Killing Spree* airs an episode called "Columbine Massacre". It features Sean Graves, Craig Scott, Tom Mauser, Randy and Judy Brown, Frank DeAngelis, and others.

May 2014: Frank DeAngelis officiates his last Columbine graduation before he retires after 35 years. He will go on to speak at many public events about Columbine and healing after tragedy.

June 19, 2014: Former Sheriff Pat Sullivan arrested for probation violations. Sullivan missed 36 urine tests and tested positive for meth and alcohol 10 times in over two years of probation. He is sentenced to 15 months in prison.

2015 — May 21: Director PJ Paparelli dies in a car crash in Scotland at age 40. He co-wrote the critically acclaimed play, *Columbinus*.

2016 — Sean and Kara Graves have a daughter, Olivia.

Sue Klebold publishes *A Mother's Reckoning: Living in the Aftermath of Tragedy* against the wishes of ex-husband Tom and son Byron. She donates the proceeds to mental illness and suicide prevention organizations.

February 12, 2016: Sue Klebold speaks with Diane Sawyer on *20/20* in the broadcast: "Silence Broken: A Mother's Reckoning".

2018 — February 14: 19-year-old Nikolas Cruz, a former student of Marjory Stoneman Douglas High School, goes to the campus in Parkland, Florida, where he shoots and kills 17 people. He injures 17 more. He escapes by with the fleeing students but is arrested an hour later. He is given life in prison without parole. News footage looks like that from Columbine, sparking adverse reactions in many survivors.

October 7, 2018: The Columbine Memorial Foundation works to raise funds to undo the toll nature and traffic has taken on the memorial. The Foundation estimates annual upkeep to cost roughly $10,000.

2019 — March 31: Frank DeAngelis publishes his book: *They Call Me Mr. De: The Story of Columbine's Heart, Resilience, and Recovery.*

Patrick Ireland and wife have three children. The oldest is 8 years old. He remains close to many of his Columbine friends, some were at his wedding.

April 16, 2019: Obsessed with the Columbine shootings, 18-year-old Sol Pais flies from Florida to Denver, Colorado where she purchases a pump-action shotgun and ammunition. She had professed her infatuation for the tragedy and the gunmen. 22 schools in the area go into lockdown shortly after noon.

April 17, 2019: Sol Pais is found dead at the base of Mount Evans west of Denver. Cause of death is self-inflicted gunshot wound using the shotgun she purchased the previous day.

April 18, 2019: *Ripples of Columbine*, a documentary created by Rocky Mountain PBS, airs in honor of the 20th anniversary of the shooting. It features survivors including Lance Kirklin, Makai Hall, and Diwata Perez Quach.

April 20, 2019: 20 years since the Columbine shooting. Frank DeAngelis still says a morning mantra of the names of the victims who were killed. Dawn Anna still saves a seat when she goes to the movies for her slain daughter, Lauren Townsend.

April 24, 2019: Morgan County District Court convicts Ronald Graff of solicitation to commit first-degree murder. Graff tried to hire someone to kill Eric "Rick" Dendorfer, his former business partner. The "hitman" was a CBI agent. Graff claimed Dendorfer and son Matt sexually assaulted his wife. Neither Dendorfer was charged. Rick was in Hawaii with his own wife when the rape supposedly occurred in June 2008. The men's relationship soured over a business investment gone wrong. Graff is sentenced to 16 years in prison. Matt was a freshman at CHS at the time of the shooting. Rick's daughter Erika was a junior.

April 26, 2019: Kacey Ruegsegger Johnson, a survivor of the Columbine shooting, publishes her book *Over My Shoulder*.

May 18, 2019: Weeks after the 20th anniversary of the shooting, Columbine survivor Austin Eubanks dies from accidental heroin overdose at age 37.

2020 — February: CBS4 reports help is being organized for survivor Richard Castaldo after Hollye Dexter found him living in a convalescent home, sick with a MERSA infection. He is taken to the hospital and treated. A GoFundMe account raises over $20,000 to help get him a new wheelchair and housing. Stuart Zimring provides him with free legal counsel and is one of the organizers helping him get resituated.

June 8, 2020: Catherine Marguerite Chouzenoux Lutz dies at age 77. She was the French teacher Dylan Klebold disrespected. By all accounts she was an amazing teacher and person. Her stepchildren considered her their mother. Because of COVID, her funeral service is postponed. Her family asks people to donate to the Breast Cancer Foundation, Denver Hospice, or Service Dogs of America in her honor.

June 14, 2020: Randy Brown publishes his book *The Inside Story of Columbine: Lies. Coverups. Ballistics. Lessons.*

2021 – January 1: Survivor Crystal Woodman Miller publishes *A Kids Book About School Shootings.*

June 8, 2021: Former Arapahoe Sheriff Patrick Sullivan dies at age 78.

July 19, 2021: Thomas "T.J." Johnson, Eric Harris and Dylan Klebold's philosophy teacher, passes away at age 71. His family encourages well-wishers to donate to the Frank DeAngelis Columbine Academic Foundation.

2024 – January 31: Coach Andrew "Andy" Lowry receives the NFL's Coach of the Year award for 2023. Lowry, who has been with Columbine for 30 years, receives $15,000 for the football program, a $10,000 personal award, and an all-expenses paid trip to the Pro Bowl and Super Bowl LVIII.

April 20, 2024: The 25th anniversary of the shooting is observed with a private memorial at the school and a public candlelight vigil in Denver. Dawn Anna, Craig Scott, and his family are in attendance. The school also plays host to the 8th Annual Day of Service where people come together to do projects to benefit the community. The general sentiment in the larger Columbine family is that it's time to stop looking back and instead move forward, to heal and to hope.

SECTION III
FACTS & STATISTICS

WHO

There were a lot of "who"s in this case. The survivors, the victims, and their families. The first responders and assistance agencies. The school faculty. The community. The gunmen. Their parents and friends. The people who helped arm the shooters. The authorities and journalists who investigated afterward. The people who got involved after the fact.

This section looks at some specific individuals and groups having to do with the event. You can find more information in the timeline, on *aColumbineSite.com*, and in *A Columbine Book: 25 Years of Healing*.

VICTIMS

The victims are those whose lives were disrupted or ended by the shooting. In addition to those who were killed or injured and their families, this group includes uninjured survivors and their loved ones. There were approximately 1,495 students and 200 faculty at Columbine that day who suffered trauma. They were first responders who dodged bullets and saved lives. Students and teachers who hid for hours waiting to be saved. Counselors who assisted anxious and grieving individuals. The list goes on.

The people who died were complex individuals with dreams and goals cut short in a brutal, senseless way. The wounded will forever bear the scars of the tragedy. Survivors without physical injury have scars that can't be seen but are just as real. This tragic event has impacted others, too. People all over the world have shed tears for Columbine.

The Columbine families have forged on, aspiring to make some good come from the horror. Memorials and scholarships dedicated to victims carry their names. Some survivors became public speakers. Others became health care workers or first responders. They all deserve kindness and understanding. Surviving a brutal catastrophe which killed and injured so many isn't something a person can just shake off. It takes years for the full impact to take shape.

BY THE NUMBERS

Homicides: 12 students: Cassie Bernall, Steven Curnow, Corey DePooter, Kelly Fleming, Matthew Kechter, Daniel Mauser, Daniel Rohrbough, Rachel Scott, Isaiah Shoels, John Tomlin, Lauren Townsend, Kyle Velasquez. 1 teacher: Coach William "Dave" Sanders

Injured: 24 students and teachers: Brian Anderson, Richard Castaldo, Jennifer Doyle, Stephen "Austin" Eubanks, Nicholas Foss, Sean Graves, Makai Hall, Anne Marie Hochhalter, Patrick Ireland, Michael Johnson, Joyce Jankowski, Mark Kintgen, Lisa Kreutz, Lance Kirklin, Adam Kyler, Stephanie Munson, Patricia "Patti" Nielson, Nicole Nowlen, Jeanna Park, Kacey Ruegsegger, Valeen Schnurr, Daniel Steepleton, Evan Todd, Mark Taylor

Suicides: 2 during event (the gunmen); 3 following – Carla Hochhalter, Anne Marie's mother, who shot herself in a gun store in October 1999; Columbine varsity basketball player Greg Barnes who hung himself in May 2000 (he witnessed Coach Sanders get shot); and Joseph Stair, a founding member of the Trench Coat Mafia, who hung himself in 2007. Austin Eubanks could also be counted as a suicide due to accidental overdose May 18th, 2019, shortly after the 20th anniversary of the shooting.

THOSE WHO DIED

The information that follows is public knowledge, sourced from the families. It is included here to provide a better understanding of who these individuals were. Some entries are longer because their families have shared more about them over the years.

Cassie René Bernall

Born November 6, 1981, Cassie was a 17-year-old junior at Columbine. Her parents Misty and Brad Bernall called her "Bunny Rabbit". She grew up in an evangelical Christian home with her younger brother Chris. Though she had strayed from her roots in the past, things had gotten better for her in recent months. She loved to go rock climbing in Breckinridge and recently visited Great Britain. She enjoyed swimming and going on bike rides with her dad. Her favorite movie was *Braveheart*.

Pastor Dave McPherson, who presided at her funeral, said there were 47 members of the Christian youth group trapped in Columbine during the shooting, 4 of them in the library. All except Cassie escaped without injury.

For a long time, it was believed she was the girl in the library who was asked at gunpoint: "Do you believe in God?". It was thought the gunman shot her because she said "Yes". The idea was inspiring to many, including her mother, who wrote a book titled *She Said Yes: The Unlikely Martyrdom of Cassie Bernall* (Sept. 1, 1999). Eventually it came out that the conversation occurred between the shooter and victim Valeen Schnurr. Emily Wyant was hiding beside Cassie during the shooting and told the FBI and *Rocky Mountain News* the real story, but they withheld it so as not to make things difficult for the Bernalls. It wasn't until *Salon.com* reporter Dave Cullen broke the story that news outlets ran the true version. By then it didn't matter. The idea of standing strong in the face of adversity was too compelling. The exchange might not have been real, but the inspiration the idea brought to others was. Even though she didn't say anything to either of the gunmen, the story of the girl who said "yes" still inspires people all over the world. Her family prefers to think of her as that girl.

Over 2,000 people attended Cassie's funeral at West Bowles Community Church, including Governor Bill Owens. Attendees signed her coffin. She was laid to rest in Golden Cemetery in Golden, Colorado.

Steven Robert Curnow

Born August 26, 1984, Steve was a 14-year-old freshman. The youngest victim, he dreamed of being a Navy top gun pilot. He was close with his mom Susan (Susie) and his father Robert (Bob) even though his parents were divorced. Weeks before the shooting, he told his father he forgave him for mistakes made which led to the breakup.

Steve loved soccer. He started playing at age 5 with the YMCA. He later played for Club Columbine. His father encouraged him to be a referee and helped him train for the position. Being a part-time referee helped Steve learn the game better and he earned money while he did it. His favorite classes were Spanish, technology, and gym because he got to play sports. He dreamed of becoming an aviator after discovering the joy of flight during a family vacation to England. A huge fan of the *Star Wars* series, he watched the films so many times, he could recite the dialogue along with the actors. Science fiction fans nationwide put together a "Go to Star Wars" day in his honor when *Star Wars I: the Phantom Menace* premiered in theaters on May 19th, 1999. He had been anxiously awaiting its release.

His funeral was held at Trinity Christian Center, the fourth funeral of a Columbine victim held in five days. Members of his soccer team were among the mourners. *"Every time we'd play, he'd have a huge smile on his face,"* Justin Norman, a former teammate, said at the funeral. He was among a dozen friends who offered eulogies for Steve.

His mom wrote a note to Steve that was read at his funeral: *"Thank you for that special moment two weeks ago when you said, 'Mom, I bet there aren't many guys who can discuss things with their moms like we do.'"*

Steve was buried in Fort Logan National Cemetery in Denver, Colorado.

Corey Tyler DePooter

Born March 3, 1982, Corey was a 17-year-old former wrestler who loved to hike, golf, hunt, and fish. He enjoyed golf and in-line skating, but fishing was his passion. Someone Corey used to fish with said: *"It was the times we didn't do well that his personality really shined."*

A junior at the time of the shootings, Corey was an all-American kid who put schoolwork above everything: He had his wisdom teeth removed that year and was upset that the procedure forced him to miss school. His sister Jena was a freshman at Columbine when he died. He taught her how to fly fish and they hiked together along the mountain stream at their family's favorite camping spot near Buena Vista. To cope with the loss, Jena said she liked to imagine her brother was doing something he loved. The day he died Corey was supposed to go to the bank with his father Neal to get a loan for a used Mustang.

"Corey would have told us to move on. He would not like us moping around," his mother Patricia told the Denver Post.

Corey's best friend Austin Eubanks was with him in the library when he was killed. Austin later said about Corey: *"People said he was the kind of guy people like to be around. I know I sure did. Corey was always able to pick our spirits up in a gloomy situation."*

The DePooters received thousands of cards and letters from around the world after Corey's death. They read every one, though they couldn't personally respond to them all. They grew close to other victims' families, meeting weekly and gathering monthly for potluck meals. By engaging in community projects together and leaning on each other they found true friendship.

Corey's funeral was held at Trinity Christian Center. His grandmother, Fern Hamilton, contacted the Marine Corps about holding a ceremony for Corey because he'd always wanted to be a Marine. On May 3, 2000, Corey was granted that dream during a ceremony at his gravesite in Chapel Hill Memorial Gardens in Littleton, Colorado, where he was made an honorary Marine.

Kelly Ann Fleming

Born January 6, 1983. 16-year-old Kelly and her family moved to Littleton from Phoenix, Arizona 18 months before the shooting. Her father Don and mother Dee scoured the area for a good neighborhood where Kelly and her older sister Erin would be safe.

Kelly was a sweet, creative girl who loved Halloween. Born with a jaw that was too small, she recently underwent surgeries to remove her tonsils, wisdom teeth, and adenoids and was put in braces to prepare her for surgery to correct the problem. The process was supposed to be finished by Christmas 1999. She told her father: *"Dad, I'm going to start running next year because I'll be able to breathe."*

She was learning to drive and wanted a job at a day care center to save money to buy a Mustang or Corvette and return to Phoenix to visit. She loved to read, especially books about vampires. An aspiring songwriter and author, she wrote poems and short stories based on her life and the struggles she faced. The stories often had happy endings. She'd been writing an autobiography that started with the moment her mother's water broke and had gotten as far as her fifth year. She regularly went to Columbine's library to write. Jud Blatchford, Kelly's math teacher at CHS in 1999, said: *"She was one of the kindest students I've ever had. She was really shy. She would never read them [her stories] to me."* She would hand him the paper and let him read it himself. He served as a pallbearer at her funeral.

278

Kelly's funeral was held at the same time as Daniel Mauser's at the St. Frances Cabrini Catholic Church. She was buried with two teddy bears in her arms. At the funeral home, her parents were given the choice to have her braces removed, which they agreed to because Kelly was looking forward to when they would come off. Her grave is at Mount Olivet Cemetery in Wheat Ridge, Colorado. After Kelly's death, the Flemings' neighbors brought them pizza, bagels, flowers, and food trays. They shoveled snow from the Flemings' sidewalk. Kelly's father said he and his family felt as safe as ever in the community.

Matthew Joseph Kechter

Born February 19, 1983, Matt was a sturdy 210-pound sophomore. The 16-year-old played on both the offensive and defensive lines of the football team. He's remembered for his ready laugh. He was a weightlifter and was always getting good grades in school.

"He was always in the library studying," said sophomore basketball player and close friend Greg Barnes. *"He always put academics first. He had straight A's, but he would never brag about it. I kinda looked up to him because of it. He was never in a bad mood; he was consistently happy."*

Other friends described Matt as a sweet, shy guy. Neighbors remembered him as a good student who had "tons of friends" and often played basketball in the family driveway with his younger brother Adam.

"He was a wonderful role model for his little brother," his parents wrote in a statement read at his funeral at St. Frances Cabrini Catholic Church on April 27. *"Their brotherhood had just recently developed into a bonding friendship. In Matt's heart, there was always enough room for everyone to be victorious."*

For days after the shooting, his mother Ann slept in his dirty clothes just to feel close to her son. In 2001, she and Matt's dad Joe fostered an 8-year-old girl. Two years later, they adopted her. Matt's mother said: *"We were not trying to replace Matt, but we have a lot of love to give. We feel more complete as a family."*

The University of Colorado, the college Matt planned to attend, sent Adam a jerseys bearing his brother's name, and the number Matt wore on Columbine's football team, #70. The Columbine High School football team wore ribbons bearing his jersey number at his funeral service and were asked to dedicate the next season to Matt's memory. Matt was buried in Mount Olivet Cemetery in Wheat Ridge, Colorado. In September of 1999, he was posthumously accepted into the National Honor Society.

Daniel Conner Mauser

Born June 25, 1983, Daniel was a 15-year-old who excelled in math and science. He got straight "A"s the last two grading periods and posthumously won the "Stretch for Excellence" award for top sophomore Biology student at CHS. Dan was shy but didn't let that stop him joining the debate team. And though he wasn't a natural athlete, he was on the cross-country team. Daniel just returned from a two-week trip to Paris with the French club.

His family described him as lovable and loving. His dad Tom remembered him as a smart young man unafraid of challenges and unashamed to hug his parents. Dan was close with his sister Christine. He liked pepperoni pizza, playing video and computer games, and shows such as *The Simpsons* and *X-Files*. He was fond of trivia games, swimming, skiing, camping, and hiking. He volunteered at the Swedish Hospital. He would have been Confirmed at St. Frances Cabrini Church two weeks after the date of his death. His class put a plaque in the teen room in his honor. Daniel wanted to get his driver's license in 2000. Concerned with gun safety, just two weeks before he was killed, he asked his father if he knew there were loopholes in the Brady Bill. Dan was shot with a gun bought through one of the loopholes he pointed out. Tom is now an active protester of the NRA and campaigns for stricter gun laws.

Dan's funeral was held with Kelly Fleming's at St. Frances Cabrini Catholic Church. He was buried in Mount Olivet Cemetery in Wheat Ridge, Colorado. Daniel was posthumously accepted into the National Honor Society in September of 1999.

Soon after the shooting, his family and other Columbine families learned the school district was planning to reopen the library where Dan and the others died. They were going to make cosmetic changes: removing carpet, repainting, replacing bullet-riddled shelves. The Mausers and other parents and volunteers founded HOPE (Healing of People Everywhere) and convinced the district to tear out the old library and replace it.

Daniel Lee Rohrbough

Daniel was born March 2, 1984. The quiet 15-year-old freshman enjoyed electronics and computer games. He was getting his driver's permit soon. Friends remembered Dan as a fun, zany guy who wore shorts in winter. He helped at his father Brian's stereo business Excalibur Sound Systems every day after school. In the summer he worked on his grandfather's farm in Kansas harvesting wheat, which he'd done since he was 3. He used his paycheck to buy Christmas presents for his family.

His parents were divorced, but made a pact that raising Dan was their #1 priority. His mother Sue married Rich Petrone, whose daughter Nicole became Dan's stepsister. His father Brian married Lisa. Danny spent time with both families. Sue didn't often see Dan in the mornings but April 20th, they met up for a brief chat. For months he had forgotten to bring home his school pictures from fall. That morning, he pulled one out of his backpack and gave it to her. They hugged. His mom kissed him and said she loved him.

Dad Brian knew something was wrong when his son failed to show up at the shop after school. His family agonized for hours waiting to hear what happened to Danny. They learned the truth when Sue recognized her son's body in a heart-breaking photo on the *Rocky Mountain News* the next morning. Dan was known in media reports as "the boy who held the door open" for friends so they could escape during the assault. It's a heroic notion but it isn't supported by the evidence or witness statements. Chances are his story was conflated with that of Sean Graves, who was stuck in the doorway of the cafeteria, paralyzed.

In December 1999 Sue and Rich were treated to a video recording of Danny being interviewed in 1998 while sitting on the stairs on the southwest side of Columbine. They had never seen the footage. The video came from a tape Bethanee Scott found when she and her family were looking through their home videos. Bethanee is the sister of victim Rachel Scott, who likely filmed the interview. When Bethanee recognized Dan, she called Sue. She and Rich hurried over to see the tape. Ironically, Danny was wearing the same shirt he wore when he was killed. The video footage they Bethanee gave them was "the best Christmas present ever".

Dan's funeral was held at Grace Presbyterian Church. He was buried in Littleton Cemetery in Littleton, Colorado. Brian and Lisa Rohrbough adopted two toddlers from Ukraine, Rachel and Isaac, on September 9, 2003.

Rachel Joy Scott

Born August 5, 1981, Rachel was a vibrant 17-year-old junior at Columbine. A straight-forward individual, she wasn't afraid to stand up for what she believed in. She was close with her younger brother Craig but had trouble connecting with her father Darrell in the months before the shooting. The week before her death, Rachel and her dad had a long. bonding discussion that would give him comfort when dealing with her death.

Rachel liked photography, produced her own videos, and dreamed of being a film director. An aspiring writer and actress, she was "made for the camera" according to her father. She was writing a play for her senior year about a piano player in the '20's who made his own songs in an impromptu fashion because he couldn't read music. He took his talent for granted and lost everything. Her friend Sarah Arzola said Rachel wrote music the same impromptu way.

Throughout her life Rachel was an incredibly spiritual person. She was active in the Celebration Christian Fellowship church and the Orchard Road Christian Center. She often wrote to God in her diaries about wanting to "reach the unreached". She begged Him for a chance to show others the way, to let her life have purpose. After her death, her family started Rachel's Challenge, an outreach program with a mission to teach others conflict resolution through love.

Rachel's car was turned into a makeshift memorial by her friends. They hugged the fenders and kissed the windows. Huddled together, they chanted: "We are COLUMBINE! We are COLUMBINE!"

"In my eyes, she was just one of those kinds of people you know you won't ever meet again. She was the kind of person only born once," Rachel's friend Lauren Beachem said of her.

Rachel was buried at Chapel Hill Memorial Gardens in the Columbine Memorial Garden in Littleton, Colorado.

Isaiah Eamon Shoels

Isaiah was born August 4, 1980. The 18-year-old senior had a congenital heart defect at birth that required two surgeries when he was little. His parents said he was a fighter who overcame his disability and went on to play football and wrestle. He played cornerback the previous year on the football team, but his father Michael said he quit the team due to racial intimidation. Isaiah wanted to be a comedian and dreamed of becoming a music executive. Isaiah also played keyboards and wanted to become a record producer like his father, who was the president of Notorious Records and Ft. Knox Entertainment, a firm Michael started to promote black musicians in the Denver area. Isaiah planned to attend the Denver Institute of the Arts.

He was a popular boy. Columbine principal Frank DeAngelis said his classmates would compete to work on projects with him. He said at Isaiah's funeral:

"Isaiah Shoels, thank you for having such a positive impact on our school and on our family. You will be greatly missed, and I love you, my dear child."

"He's smiling down on us. I know he is,." classmate and friend Nick Foss said.

Isaiah's brother Anthony was a freshman at Columbine who was outside the school when the shooting started. He was able to get away safely.

Isaiah was the only person of color killed at Columbine. The last of the victims to be buried, Isaiah was laid to rest in Fairmount Cemetery in Denver, Colorado. Martin Luther King III, son of Martin Luther King, Jr., spoke at his funeral at the Heritage Christian Center.

John Robert Tomlin

Born September 1, 1982, John was a 16-year-old sophomore at Columbine who enjoyed lifting weights. He wanted to join the Army when he graduated. A native of Wisconsin, his family moved to Colorado in 1995 when his father John Michael got a job with a heating firm. Shy and lonely, John found the move difficult at first. He soon made friends with Jacob Youngblood and Brandon Sokol. Both spoke at his funeral.

John was gentle and kind. He loved church. He attended Foothills Bible Church and belonged to the Riverside Baptist Church South youth group where he met his girlfriend, Michelle Oetter. His sister Ashley said the pair, who were together 7 months, were nearly inseparable. Michelle said of John: *"He treated me like the queen of the world."*

His family and friends remember his energy and the warmth of his smile. His mother Doreen said: *"He had such a sense of humor. He was always making goofy faces."*

John loved Chevrolet trucks and off-roading in the Rocky Mountains. He worked after school and weekends at Arapahoe Acres Nursery to save for the Chevy 4x4 truck he bought just before his 16th birthday. He always wore the same thing to work: Carpenter pants, mud-caked boots, a blue cap, and a jacket from his favorite team, the Green Bay Packers. His truck became a memorial in the parking lot. Thursday following the shootings, his family gathered around the truck even though it was raining. His bible was sitting on the dashboard, where he always left it hoping it would bring someone closer to God. His family took turns sitting in the truck. John's father said:

"He was as close to a perfect son as you could get. He was just good. You'd ask him to wash a car, and he'd wash both cars."

The first of the victims' funerals, his was held at Foothills Bible Church. He was buried in his hometown of Waterford, Wisconsin, in Saint Peters Cemetery. His coffin was lined with green and gold satin, embroidered with Chevy trucks. After his death, Habitat for Humanity built and dedicated a Lakewood home in his name. Columbine students and other schools helped with the project. Later, his family found his "to do" list for his truck. You can find out about how Chevrolet fixed it up in Sean Reavie's book *Keys to the Kingdom*.

Lauren Dawn Townsend

Born January 17, 1981, 18-year-old senior Lauren was captain of the girls' varsity volleyball team, which her mother, Dawn Anna, coached. She was a National Honor Society member and a candidate for valedictorian. Lauren was a talented sketch artist. A straight "A" student, she never got a "B". Her 4.0 grade point average earned her President Clinton's Award for Education Excellence. She volunteered at a local animal shelter and planned to major in biology at Colorado State University when she graduated.

Lauren's funeral was held at Foothills Bible Church where her brother Josh played a tribute video filled with moments from her life. Many of her teachers spoke at her funeral, commending her gentle nature and loving spirit as well as her academic excellence. Her coffin was a white one that attendees could write on, much like signing a yearbook. Her father wrote: *"Lulu, you'll always be my baby."* She was buried in Littleton Cemetery in Littleton, Colorado.

The 5th year after the shooting, her family decided they wanted their daughter and the other victims to be remembered for more than their deaths at Columbine. They petitioned the governor to declare April 20th a Day of Service. Lauren's father Rick Townsend helped grow the *Never Forgotten Fund* to provide 12 scholarships and one teacher annually. As of 2024, over $1.5 million has been awarded. The family set up and supports the Denver Foundation Lauren Townsend Wildlife Fund which grants roughly $20,000 annually to nonprofit organizations that focus on animal welfare or wildlife preservation.

At the Columbine Memorial groundbreaking ceremony, the day was stormy while Dawn Anna gave a moving speech that began with: *"They're here. Can you feel them? Our angels."* At the end of the event, the clouds parted, and a beautiful rainbow appeared over Rebel Hill. Principal Frank DeAngelis has a picture of that rainbow at Columbine High. Her quote is featured on a plaque at the Columbine Memorial.

Kyle Velasquez

Born May 5, 1989, Kyle was a 16-year-old sophomore at Columbine. Neighbors and relatives say he enjoyed chores and family activities. He was 6 feet tall when he died but to those who knew he was a little boy at heart. Affectionate and sincere, he loved nothing more than helping his dad, Al, around the house putting up shelves, mowing the lawn, washing the car. Every day he would kiss his mom, Phyllis, on the cheek and tell her he loved her. He loved his brother Daniel and the family cats. He enjoyed playing with computers and eating ice cream. And he dreamed of joining the Navy like his dad or becoming a firefighter.

Kyle suffered a stroke as a baby which left him mentally disabled. He also had severe asthma. As a "special needs" child, he was often ignored, avoided, and teased while growing up. Due to his disabilities, his parents were prepared to spend the rest of their lives with him. He went everywhere with his mother while she ran errands. Kyle's last words to her were: *"Goodbye. I love you, mom."*

A shy teen, he was just beginning to come out of his shell. Kyle very much wanted to "be normal" and went through speech therapy and worked on his fine motor skills to offset the damage the stroke did. He had just started staying at the school through lunch; a few weeks earlier and he would've been on his way home when the shooting started. Friends and relatives brought food, hugs, and love to the Velasquez home following his death. They described the family as tight knit.

Since his dad was a Navy veteran, Kyle was buried with full military color guard honors in Fort Logan National Cemetery in Denver, Colorado. His parents were given the flags from his coffin and the one that was flown at half-mast in Kyle's honor at the state Capitol.

Coach William "Dave" Sanders

Born October 22, 1951, 47-year-old Dave was a computer and business teacher at Columbine for 25 years, and coach for the girls' basketball and softball teams. He left behind his wife, four children, and five grandchildren. His students said he was a mentor, a friend, and an inspiration. He was good friends with the other coaches and with Principal Frank DeAngelis, who he aided back when DeAngelis was Columbine's baseball coach. When the gunmen opened fire outside, he ran through the cafeteria and sounded the alarm.

Along with two of the school's janitors, he helped get hundreds of students out of the path of danger. His quick actions saved untold numbers of lives that day.

Dave's daughter Angela said at his funeral: *"What you did in that school on Tuesday was an amazing act of heroism. Even after you were hurt, you continued to be the brave, selfless man we all know you are."*

By the time the gunmen entered the cafeteria, it was nearly empty. Sanders was in the upstairs hall trying to get students safely hidden in classrooms when he was gunned down. With assistance from teacher Rich Long, he managed to get to a science classroom. Despite first aid from students and faculty, Sanders bled to death while waiting for emergency assistance that took too long to arrive.

Dave was buried in Littleton's Chapel Hill Memorial Gardens. Since his death, a softball field at Columbine and a scholarship have been named after him and he posthumously received the Arthur Ashe Award for Courage. A highway also bears his name.

THE INJURED

For the sake of privacy, I have not included the birthdates of the injured. I only included information relevant to the focus of this section, which is to explain who the survivors are and how they adjusted to life following the tragedy. Some sections are shorter than others because there have been no other public updates about their situations. I wish all their stories were successes, but sadly they're not. However, every individual has truly tried to move on with life. Each has faced their own unique challenges on the long road to recovery.

Brian Anderson

Brian, a junior, was in the school, heading out the west entrance when he was shot at. He was injured but managed to flee to the library where he hid in the periodicals room until he could escape. He was treated for injuries from bullet fragments and shattered glass when Eric shot at him through the windows of the west-exit. Brian was released from the hospital April 20, 1999, and graduated from Columbine on May 20, 2000.

In 2008 a friend of his, Dewayne Johnson, said Brian had moved on with his life. He owned his own trucking company in the Littleton, Colorado area and was still trying to make sense of what happened that fateful day at Columbine High School. Brian lost his good friend Corey DePooter in the shooting and said there were times when he thought of him and all the fun times they had in school. Brian said "there is one person that means a lot" to him and will always have a place in his heart because in his eyes she's a HERO: Teacher Patti Nielson.

Richard Castaldo

Richard was a junior and a saxophone player in Columbine's marching band. He was friends with Rachel Scott. They were eating lunch outside when the shooters opened fire on them. His near-fatal injuries left him paralyzed from the chest down. He was moved from the Swedish Medical Center to Craig

Hospital June 1, 1999, for spinal cord rehabilitation. Doctors put two 14-inch metal rods in on either side of his backbone. He was released August 21, 1999; the last of the injured to go home. He remains in a wheelchair.

He got his driver's license in February 2000, and drove a van modified for his wheelchair. Featured in Michael Moore's *Bowling for Columbine* film along with victim Mark Taylor and survivor Brooks Brown, he convinced K-mart to stop selling ammunition. It came out later that Moore was dishonest regarding his intentions, but Richard was glad some good came from it. That same year his father Rick made a congressional testimony about Project Exile: The Safe Streets and Neighborhoods Act of 2000. He and Richard didn't blame guns for what happened. They felt making more laws wouldn't help— 17 federal laws were already broken during the shooting. Instead, they wanted the government to focus on prosecuting the laws already in place.

On January 31, 2002, the Olympic torch was passed along Pierce Street, from survivor Patrick Ireland to Richard Castaldo, to Columbine principal Frank DeAngelis. DeAngelis handed it off to John Tomlin Sr, father of victim John Tomlin. In 2020, Richard lost his apartment after succumbing to a bad infection. A team of volunteers kept him fed and sheltered and helped him search for a new home. In 2023, Richard worked in the music department on the film *The Uncanny*.

Jennifer Doyle

Jennifer, a junior, was sitting at a table in the library when Patti Nielson hollered for everyone to get down. Jennifer was going to get under the table she shared with Mark Kintgen, but she was concerned it wasn't big enough to hide her. She ran to a table in the back of the library where she hid with Peter Ball, Austin Eubanks, and Corey DePooter.

Jennifer was injured but survived and was able to escape with Austin. Released from the hospital on April 24, 1999, she has a metal plate and screws holding her ring finger together. She graduated from Columbine High School on May 20, 2000, and went on to attend the University of Colorado that fall.

Stephen "Austin" Eubanks

Austin was a junior at Columbine. He with his best friend Corey DePooter in the library during the shooting. When teacher Patti Nielson told everyone to get down, he, Corey, Jennifer Doyle, and Peter Ball hid under the same table. Austin was injured when the gunmen shot at them. After the shooters left the library, he had to leave Corey behind when he and the other survivors fled. He was shuttled to triage for his injuries and released from the hospital the same day. Though he never got over Corey's death, he graduated from Columbine on May 20, 2000.

While recovering from his injuries Austin became addicted to opioids. In 2006, he switched to narcotics such as heroin. He entered three different residential treatment programs starting in 2006. He married at age 25 and had two sons. He divorced 4 years later. In 2011, Austin woke in jail with no memory of how he got there. After that, he got serious about getting clean and became a motivational speaker. From 2015 to 2019, he was the Chief Operating Officer for the Foundry Treatment Center in Steamboat Springs, Colorado. He celebrated 5 years of sobriety in 2016. Those who knew him said the 2018 Parkland shooting had a profound impact on him. He was quoted in a news article saying: *"...students running out with their hands above them, the armored vehicles and the police cars and ambulances on the grass... this one is really close to home."*

On May 18, 2019, shortly after the 20th anniversary of the Columbine shooting, Austin died from an accidental heroin overdose. His family set up the Triumph Over Tragedy memorial fund in his honor.

Nicholas "Nick" Foss

Nick, a senior, was in the cafeteria when he heard a girl shout: *"Someone's shooting! Someone's shooting!"* He and his friend Tim Kastle hid in the teachers' lounge bathroom with

Joyce Jankowski and three other school employees. According to statements he gave investigators, Nick suggested they try to escape through the ceiling ventilation shaft. When Nick went up, he fell through the ceiling into the lounge. He was able to run from the building to police officers outside.

His twin brother Adam was also in the school at the time of the shootings. Trapped in an office, Adam helped other students up into the ceiling where the air wasn't so stuffy so they could breathe easier while they hid.

Nick was treated for injuries and released April 20, 1999. He graduated from Columbine in May 1999.

Sean Graves

Sean was a freshman who was outside with his friends Dan Rohrbourgh and Lance Kirklin when they were all shot. He spent a long time lying in the doorway of the cafeteria too injured to move. Sean was also best friends with fellow victim Patrick Ireland. Since the shooting, Sean and Lance haven't spoken much about that day. Sean said he gets too emotional to talk to him in person, preferring email correspondence as of 1999. Before the attack on Columbine Sean used to have nightmares about being shot. Those nightmares stopped after the shooting.

Sean's wound was deemed an 'incomplete spinal injury' by doctors, meaning he was paralyzed below the injury level but retained some feeling and movement. He was later moved to Craig Hospital for spinal cord rehabilitation. On June 20th, 1999, he took his first steps. He was released from Craig Hospital on July 7th, 1999.

His house was rebuilt to accommodate the wheelchair he was using. Donations from people around the world paid for a home gym to assist with his personal therapy. When he turned 16, Sean's father Randy purchased him a used pick-up truck when the teen proved he could get in and out of it unassisted. Sean graduated from Columbine in 2002, using only a crutch to walk across the stage to receive his diploma. He went back to

Columbine for the 5th anniversary of the tragedy and placed a cigar on the ground where Danny was killed. He said:

"Watching my friend die is still traumatic, but it is in the past. I'm not trying to be mean. I just have to focus on today and looking at the positive and the future."

As of 2023, Sean was married to longtime girlfriend Kara and had a daughter, Olivia. He still lived just six miles from Columbine. When asked if he ever considered moving from the area, he told interviewers: *"No. This is my home."*

Makai Hall

Makai, a junior, was sitting with his friends in the library when the shooting began. He hid under a table with Daniel Steepleton and Patrick Ireland. Makai held Dan back when the killers demanded all "white hats" stand up. He was injured when they shot at his table. One of gunmen threw a home-made CO_2 bomb under their table and Makai saved them by throwing it back out. Three days after the tragic event he was interviewed by CNN. He was quite modest when asked to discuss his act of heroism.

He underwent surgery and was released April 23, 1999. Makai graduated from Columbine on May 20, 2000, and studied business finance at Colorado State University where he met his future wife on the first day. He decided to pursue a career in healthcare because of the kindness shown to him by those who helped him. He got a job working as a nurse with UCHealth where his coworkers provided him comfort. Makai told UCHealth in a 2019 interview:

"If you find yourself after an experience like this or having experienced violence in a bad place, it's not hopeless. There's a way to kind of come back to the light."

That same year Makai was featured in the Rocky Mountain PBS documentary *Ripples of Columbine*. At the time he was married and had three children.

Anne Marie Hochhalter

Anne Marie, a junior, was outside on the grassy knoll with her friends when the gunmen opened fire. She was paralyzed by a bullet that severed her spinal cord. When she was rescued by paramedic John Aylward, she had virtually no blood pressure. If rescue hadn't reached her when they did, she would have died. Doctors called her a "miracle girl".

Anne Marie spent four months in the hospital in rehabilitative therapy with fellow survivor Patrick Ireland. She went back to Columbine on September 9, 1999, and had a Physics class with him. With the help of the Colorado Homebuilders Foundation her family bought a house with wheelchair ramps and lifts. The following is Anne Marie's open letter to the public the day she was released from the hospital and is unedited:

"To all the people who have cared about me from the day I was hurt:

I am leaving Craig Hospital today and didn't want to have a press conference but wanted to write my own press release. I have wanted to be private during my recovery, and I appreciate the media's respect for my wishes.

I have many thanks to share. First, I wish to thank my family who has loved and supported me all through my recovery. I would like to thank the paramedics and staff at Swedish Medical Center who saved my life. I want to thank the Craig Hospital staff who taught me the skills to be independent again. I want to thank my many friends who have visited me and cared about my well-being from the very beginning.

Thanks also to the families who have brought meals to my family every night, and to all the caring people across the country who prayed for me, and who sent wonderful gifts and cards. They meant a lot to me. Your loving care and support have helped me tremendously to get through my recovery.

I still have many obstacles to overcome, but I know that I can do it, and God will give me strength along the way.

Once again, I give my thanks to all of you."

Anne Marie Hochhalter

August 12, 1999

Her younger brother Nathan was a freshman at Columbine and was in trapped in one of the science rooms for four hours. When they were freed by SWAT, he and the others were frisked five times before they were hustled out with their hands on their heads.

Two months after the shooting their mother Carla committed suicide. She struggled with depression for at least three years before the shooting. People who knew her (including Richard Castaldo's mother Connie Michalik) said they saw how the tragedy affected her. Anne Marie's father Ted was married to Carla for 22 years. A year after her death, he married Katherine Zocco, who had been his grief counselor. He became a school safety activist who trained parents how to respond to crisis.

At age 18, Anne Marie attended Columbine part time and helped in the nurse's office. She wanted to go to community college after graduation but took the summer of 2000 off to "be a teen" since she'd lost that time the previous summer. Anne Marie earned her business degree from the University of Colorado and bought a townhouse in Westminster. In 2002 she was working at Westminster Bath and Body Works. She was promoted to Manager in 2009.

Patrick Ireland

Patrick was a junior who was in the library and was shot while trying to render first aid to Makai Hall. Pat passed in and out of consciousness for two hours on the floor before he was eventually able to pull himself up onto the ledge of a broken second floor window. He rolled out into the arms of SWAT members. The rescue was captured by news crews and Pat was dubbed "the boy in the window" who survived the shooting against all odds.

He was treated at multiple hospitals and rehab clinics. He returned to Columbine High that fall, using a cane to help support him. September 25, 1999, he was elected Columbine's homecoming king. He graduated May 20, 2000, as a co-valedictorian. In 2004, Jefferson County settled with Pat for $117,500 though they assumed no liability settling the lawsuit.

In 2009 he was doing well for himself working as a financial rep and had married sweetheart Kacie. By 2012, he had 2 daughters and was managing director for Northwestern Mutual Financial Network. He became a public speaker and spoke at the 2019 National Summit on School Safety hosted by the Safe and Sound Schools organization.

Michael Johnson

Mike, a sophomore, was outside with his friends Denny Rowe, Mark Taylor, John Cook, and Adam Thomas. He was one of the first victims shot and was in intensive care for 8 days. He was released April 28, 1999. Though doctors thought he might lose his leg Mike can now run and held a job at the Mann Theater. His parents Kathy and Gary went through a lot, but felt the ordeal made them closer as a family.

He served a Mormon mission in California and studied at the Metropolitan State College of Denver. In 2004, Mike's story was published in the book *Surviving Columbine* (Deseret Book) along with those of Liz and Kathy Carlston and Amber Huntington, all of whom belong the Church of Jesus Christ of Latter-day Saints. The message of the book is you shouldn't be surprised by the problems you can handle with the support of God. Mike told Deseret.com:

"You don't realize what you can go through until you have to. It's all about doing what you have to do to get through. Trials change you. You can't go into a trial and leave unchanged — for better or worse. That's your choice."

296

Joyce Jankowski

When the shooting started Joyce Jankowski, a teacher at Columbine, was in the faculty lounge. She hid in the bathroom with three other staff members and three students. At one point, Tim Kastle headed up into the ceiling to escape. Jankowski followed, but she fell through and ran back to the bathroom. About 40 minutes after the attack began, a student poked his head down and told her and the others it was safe to run. Jankowski and the rest escaped through the cafeteria to a police unit near the school. She was treated for injuries sustained in her fall and was released April 20, 1999.

Mark Kintgen

Assigned to "B" lunch, junior Mark's fifth period was free. He usually spent it in the library and was there when the shooters entered. Mark later remembered hearing a male voice ask someone: *"Do you believe in God?"*. The next thing he knew, he was waking up covered in splinters, afraid he was going to die. He crawled out from under the table and followed student Patti Blair out of the library to the safety of the patrol cars outside the school. He was treated and released from Denver Health on April 23, 1999.

Mark has cerebral palsy. His twin brother Mike also attended Columbine. Their mother Kay hopes their family will one day find closure. Mark graduated on May 20, 2000, and got his bachelor's degree at Colorado State University with a Major in History and a Minor in Business. He was in the CSU Marketing Club for 3 years. As of 2024, he was working as a Library Assistant at the University of Denver.

Lance Kirklin

Sophomore Lance had "A" Lunch with Dan Rohrbough and Sean Graves. He was shot on the stairs outside when the three of them left the cafeteria so he could have a cigarette. He was released from St. Anthony Central Hospital on May 15, 1999. On May 21, 1999, he went with investigators to Columbine to do a walk-through of the crime scene in hopes of remembering more details about that tragic day. Seriously injured, Lance underwent 9 operations over the course of 3 years. He should have had more, but procedure fatigue and the pending birth of his first child led him to quit in 2001.

He returned to Columbine in fall of 1999 but was suspended due to sporadic attendance. He continued to hunt with his dad Mike and spoke for gun rights April 2000 at a Denver town meeting about guns President Bill Clinton attended. Lance and his father moved into a new house with their puppy Hunter. In 2019, Lance was featured in the Rocky Mountain PBS *Ripples of Columbine* documentary. Lance Kirklin's family wrote this letter to the public:

"Lance has worked hard to overcome adversity. He believes in treating others as he would want to be treated. He is sensitive, caring and able to put the needs of others before his own. Though he is unable to speak at this time due to the nature of his injuries, he has indicated tremendous sadness and concern for the others affected by this tragedy. Knowing Lance, he would want to be available to comfort others and is moved by the outpouring of love and support he has received. We know that Lance has many challenges to address, and we count on and ask for your continued prayers and support in the months ahead for all students and families affected.

Lance is an outdoorsman and loves to fish. He likes the opportunity to be in the mountains with family and friends. We know that his sadness will be lightened when he is again able to go to the mountains. On behalf of Lance, we would like to thank all involved in Lance's rescue, Littleton and other communities throughout Colorado, across the country and worldwide for their prayers, support and love extended to Lance and his family. Especially all Lance's family in Scotts Bluff, Nebraska, we appreciate your prayers and love. We would also like to thank Denver Health administrators, Surgical Intensive Care staff, Emergency Department staff, surgeons and everyone for caring for Lance and our family."

Dawn, Mike, and Amanda Kirklin

Lisa Kreutz

Senior Lisa usually spent "A" lunch in the library or going out to eat with friends Jessica Holliday and Bethany Koch. On April 20th she sat with Jeanna Park, Lauren Townsend, Valeen Schnurr, and Diwata Perez on the east side of the library. When the shooting started, she hid under the table with her friends.

Severely injured by gunfire, she was unable to leave the library on her own. Officials eventually rescued her. She was the last survivor in the library and was released from the hospital April 28, 1999.

Lisa graduated from Columbine High on May 23, 1999, wheeled to the podium in a wheelchair with a cast on her leg and a sling on her arm. Her parents Ken and Sheryl were in attendance. She received a scholarship to Regis University but later attended the University of Colorado. She has never spoken publicly about what happened to her on April 20, 1999.

Adam Kyler

Adam, a sophomore, was in the cafeteria with his friend Kyle Velasquez, both Special Needs students. Adam hid under his table when he heard Coach Dave Sanders yell for students to get down. He was injured when he got up later to run to a better hiding place. A chair struck him in the chest.

Sophomore Dusty Hoffschneider helped him up and they ran to the kitchen. Adam hid in the kitchen storage area where he and 18 other people, including sophomore Matthew Depew, barricaded the doors. They hid there until the SWAT team came to evacuate them hours later.

He was treated for abdominal pain at Centura Littleton Adventist Hospital and released April 20, 1999. In an interview after the shooting, Adam spoke about how Rachel Scott once stood up for him when he was being bullied.

Stephanie Munson

Junior Stephanie transferred to Columbine four months before the shooting. As she and her friend Melissa Walker were fleeing the school, Stephanie was shot in the foot. Melissa helped her to Leawood Park. An ambulance took Stephanie to Centura Littleton Adventist Hospital. She was treated and released the same day.

Stephanie's younger sister Jennifer was a Columbine freshman who escaped the cafeteria when the shooting started. Stephanie and Jennifer designed a commemorative Columbine stuffed bear to raise money and honor the victims. It was made available shortly after the shooting. One of the bears was put inside the shuttle Endeavor for an 11-day mission before it was returned to the Munsons. When classes resumed in fall of 1999, Stephanie returned to Columbine High.

She was the subject of a conspiracy theory about the shooting being a hoax. Some people believed she was in a photo on the cover of *Newsweek* magazine which showed four girls outside of Columbine crying. The blonde in the center was supported by the others yet appeared uninjured. This was because the photo was of Jessica Holliday, who was in the library during the shooting. She was uninjured but traumatized by what she witnessed.

How Stephanie was mistaken for Jessica is unknown as none of the articles say who was in the photo. You can read more about this and other Columbine conspiracy theories in my book *We Are All Columbine: 25 Years of Healing*.

Patricia "Patti" Nielson

Patti Nielson, a substitute art teacher, was the first Columbine staff member to encounter and be injured by one of the gunmen. She alerted people in the library of the danger. Nielson placed a 911 call from under the circulation desk that lasted over 20 minutes during which she repeatedly told kids in the room to stay hidden. After the gunmen left the library, she hid in the library kitchen until SWAT rescued her. She was treated at Pierce Street triage and then was then taken to the hospital. She was released on April 20, 1999.

Nielson, a mother of three, finished out the rest of the school year when classes resumed at Chatfield. She went back for the first two months of the new school year at Columbine when it reopened in fall of 1999 then took a much-needed leave. While Nielson eventually returned to teaching, she switched to elementary classes at another school. She continued to pursue her master's degree, though her focus had shifted to family first. She didn't want her career path to come between her and time with her kids.

In 2004, Patti told NBC news: *"I can't change whatever went wrong with those boys. And I probably will never have an answer to what went wrong."*

Nicole Nowlen

Sophomore Nicole typically spent her lunch break in the library so she could do homework. When Patti Nielson came in and told everyone to get down, Nicole hid under her table, but didn't feel safe and asked John Tomlin if she could join him. As the gunfire got closer John held her hand to comfort her.

Doctors called her a "miracle girl" because she survived a close-range shotgun blast. She was treated at Lutheran Medical Center and released April 21, 1999, with five pellets still in her body. She went back to Columbine that fall, refusing to let the gunmen "win" by chasing her out of her school. She took a part-time job at an appliance store in her junior year and did outreach work for the Rachel's Challenge movement.

In 2001, she moved to Tennessee. By 2003, she was living in Franklin, TN where she was a circulation assistant for Board Member Magazine. In 2006, Rachel's Challenge brought her on part time to help spread their mission of compassion and kindness. Nicole spoke at events all over the USA and Canada. In 2007 she was working for them full-time and had spoken at over 80 schools. She told an audience that when she arrived at the emergency room on April 20th, a doctor told her the probable reason she survived was because she was overweight, which stopped the shotgun pellets from reaching vital organs. She laughed about it, saying: *"You see? The thing you dislike the most about yourself may just be the thing that saves your life."*

Her mother Shawna Anderson said of her: *"I am very proud of her. Nicole had a bad situation, and she turned it into a way to help other people."*

Jeanna Park

Columbine senior Jeanna was hiding under a table in the library with Lauren Townsend, Lisa Kreutz, Diwata Perez, and Valeen Schnurr during the shooting. Her friends had to hold her back because her younger sister Kathy was hiding somewhere else in the room, and she wanted to be sure she was okay. Jeanna was nearly killed by the gunmen. Despite her critical injuries, she was able to muster the strength to escape after the gunmen left the library.

She was released from Denver Health Medical Center on April 26, 1999. Jeanna returned to Columbine when she was well enough and graduated from Columbine High with honors on May 23, 1999, at Fiddler's Green Amphitheatre. She had a sling on her right arm. She planned to attend an out-of-state college that fall, with hopes of becoming a pediatrician. She told the Denver Post: *"I have a lot more respect for the profession now. The doctors I had were really great."*

Kacey Ruegsegger

Kacey, a junior, was in the library and survived a point-blank shotgun blast while hiding under a computer table. After the gunmen left, Craig Scott and Amanda Stair helped her up. She made it out of the building and to the police who rushed her to triage. She went through several surgeries and lengthy physical therapy before she was released from St. Anthony Central Hospital on May 1, 1999.

She attended Colorado State University and eventually married and had children of her own. Though sending them to school was difficult, she knew it was best for their development

302

not to let her trauma stop them living a full life. Her experience led her to become a public speaker. She has spoken at several events over the years. Kacey wrote a book, *Over My Shoulder: A Columbine Survivor's Story of Resilience, Hope, and a Life Reclaimed*, which she published Mar. 22, 2019. It's her hope that by sharing her story others will find purpose and healing in their own lives. She told Denver7 it took her 20 years to come to terms with what happened.

Following the Uvalde shooting in 2022, her message to the survivors was that they somehow had to "turn pain into purpose" by finding hope in tomorrow.

Valeen Schnurr

When senior Valeen was shot in the library, she cried out *"Oh, my God!"*, which prompted one of the gunmen to ask her if she believed in God. It was first reported Cassie Bernall was asked this question, and she died because she said "yes". When Salon.com set the record straight, people accused Val and her family of lying. They called her a copycat. But she wasn't interested in martyrdom and never pushed anyone to give up their ideal of Cassie, especially not the girl's parents.

Mark and Shari Schnurr, Valeen's parents, found it difficult but understood the situation was complicated. Val was spiritual enough that it didn't matter to her. If Cassie's example brought others to God or gave them comfort, that was fine by her. She preferred to try to live as normally as possible rather than be known as a hero. When Misty Bernall published her book about Cassie, she met with the Schnurrs and asked if she could include Valeen. Val agreed only to a brief mention.

Val was treated at Swedish Hospital and released on April 27. She graduated from Columbine on May 23, 1999. That fall she started at the University of North Colorado, majoring in Psychology. She was one of five students who received a scholarship from the Grand Master Masons in the name of Coach Dave Sanders.

Daniel Steepleton

Daniel was in the library hiding with his friends Patrick Ireland and Makai Hall when the shooters called for jocks to stand up. Dan almost did but his friend Makai Hall stopped him. All three boys were injured during the shooting. Dan was able to escape, but he regretted not being able to help his friend Pat.

Dan was treated and released from the hospital before April 24, 1999. He graduated from Columbine on May 20, 2000, and went on to teach science in the Jefferson County Public School system from 2008-2012. In 2022, he was working as an Aerospace Instructor with Littleton Public Schools.

Evan Todd

Evan was injured in the library when one gunman opened fire from the doorway. He ducked behind a copy counter and was safe for a few minutes, then was face-to-face with both killers. They threatened him but ultimately let him live. He escaped the school after they left the library and helped provide first aid to victims in worse shape than he was. Evan never went to the hospital though he did go to a nearby clinic where he was treated for abrasions. He was released the same day.

The last of the survivors to be identified; he was listed in local papers as 'Unnamed Boy'. He returned to Columbine that fall and played on the Columbine Rebels' state championship football team. He held a 27-10 wrestling record on the varsity squad and made Eagle Scout in 2000. At one point he wanted to become a law enforcement officer.

Evan testified at the Colorado state house in favor of allowing faculty to carry guns on school grounds because he believed an armed teacher might have made the difference at Columbine. He has also done some public speaking on the topic. In 2019, Evan said: *"We need to respect the dignity of life and humans."*

Mark Taylor

Freshman Mark survived incredible odds after he was shot multiple times. He was treated and released April 30, 1999, and later readmitted for infection. He was in and out of the hospital three times. He never returned to Columbine, instead enrolling in Dove Christian School.

He and his family created a "Ten Commandments Bear" to honor those who died in the massacre. A born-again Christian, Mark spoke at several churches in 2000. In 2001, he sued Solvay Pharmaceuticals claiming their antidepressant made Eric Harris psychotic and violent. The Taylors also sued the shooters' parents.

The Solvay suit was dropped in 2003 (see the Timeline for more info). In 2002 Mark appeared in Michael Moore's film *Bowling for Columbine* with Richard Castaldo and Brooks Brown. Mark later said Moore used him and the other Columbine victims. In Mark's words: *"I had no idea what Moore's agenda was. And he had an agenda. He had it all planned out, completely. I believe that every American has the right to have a gun. We should have the right to protect ourselves."*

In 2006 Mark ghost-wrote a book, *I Asked, God Answered- A Columbine Miracle*, but was "not in a state to promote it" according to the publisher. His suit against the Harris and Klebold families was settled in 2007.

Dr. William Deagle was the Taylor family physician from the beginning of Mark's recovery. He was a conspiracy theorist and born-again Christian who showed up at tragedies such as the Oklahoma City bombing to offer his services to victims' families.

Deagle's medical license was suspended in 2004 due to the death of a patient he overprescribed medication to. Deagle was sued again after the suspicious death of another patient. Donna Taylor, Mark's mother, broke off contact with Deagle due to concerns he was overprescribing medication to Mark. In 2007, the Colorado state board revoked Deagle's medical license for 6 more overprescribing cases.

In 2008, Mark was put into Aspen Pointe hospital in Colorado Springs after an alleged meltdown at a bookstore. When he was released, he was not the same person. After two consecutive stays in the ward, he was unable to form coherent answers when he was interviewed in 2009. In 2021, family friends put together a GoFundMe to help Mark. According to Donna, her son was living in a group home, was being drugged, and wanted out.

UNINJURED SURVIVORS

There were roughly 1,500 students and faculty at Columbine High during the shooting. Though they were not physically injured, they were traumatized. Many were locked in classrooms and closets for hours hearing bombs, gunshots, and screams. Some outran the gunmen who chased them down the halls. Others fled just moments before a shooter came by or had the misfortune to witness others get gunned down.

Many of these survivors have expressed feeling forgotten afterward. One said she was told at a memorial that she wasn't a victim because she wasn't hurt. She was in the library and saw her friends die. Coni Sanders, the daughter of slain victim Coach Dave, was told that her loss wasn't as great as others because she didn't lose a child.

Survivors endure similar post-trauma emotional side effects as the injured. They suffer anxiety, panic attacks, paranoia, fear of crowds and loud sounds. Fire drills and closed-in places are triggers. Several victims of the Columbine shooting, injured or not, have had issues sending their own children to school or had anxiety attacks while attending college.

Though some of the faculty and students never returned to Columbine, many did. Some kids who survived the assault later got jobs at CHS. Guidance counselor Noel Sudano did. A sophomore in 1999, she was in class when the shooting started. She was one of hundreds of people who flooded out of the school. You can learn more about some of these individuals and their paths to a "new normal" in my book *A Columbine Book: We Are All Columbine – 25 Years of Healing.*

PATIENT INFORMATION

4 TRIAGE AREAS	PATIENTS TRANSPORTED
• 160+ Patients Triaged for injuries	• 10 Patients Transported in first hour
• 24 Patients Transported	• 10 Patients transported in second hour
• 6 Hospitals Utilized	• Last 4 Patients transported by 3:45 pm

HOSPITALS USED	PATIENT STATUS
• 4 Patients to Swedish Hospital	• 4 Critical Condition
• 4 Patients to St. Anthony Hospital	• 6 Serious Condition
• 9 Patients to Littleton Hospital	• 3 Fair Condition
• 4 Patients to Denver Health	• 2 Good Condition
• 2 Patients to Lutheran Hospital	• 9 Treated and Released
• 1 Patient to University Hospital	

+ Brian Anderson	+ Makai Hall	+ Lisa Kreutz	+ Jeanna Park
+ Richard Castaldo	+ Anne Marie Hochhalter	+ Lance Kirklin	+ Kacey Ruegsegger
+ Jennifer Doyle	+ Patrick Ireland	+ Adam Kyler	+ Valeen Schnurr
+ Stephen 'Austin' Eubanks	+ Michael Johnson	+ Stephanie Munson	+ Daniel Steepleton
+ Nicholas 'Nick' Foss	+ Joyce Jankowski	+ Patricia 'Patti' Nielson	+ Evan Todd
+ Sean Graves	+ Mark Kintgen	+ Nicole Nowlen	+ Mark Taylor

NAME	DOB	LOCATION	INJURIES	WEAPON	SHOOTER
FERNALL, CASSIE	11/6/81	Library	1 shot through finger and right side of head	PUMP SG PELLETS	HARRIS
CURNOW, STEVEN	8/26/84	Library	1 shot through right shoulder and neck	PUMP SLUG	HARRIS
DEPOOTER, COREY	3/3/82	Library	1 shot left shoulder, through lung out neck / 3 shots neck, back, arm	9MM TEC-9 / 9MM HI-POINT	KLEBOLD / HARRIS
FLEMING, KELLY	1/6/83	Library	shot to lower back	PUMP SG PELLETS	HARRIS
KECHTER, MATTHEW	2/19/83	Library	1 shot to left shoulder through neck, lung, right arm	DBL BARREL SLUG	KLEBOLD
MAUSER, DANIEL	6/25/83	Library	1 shot (graze) behind ear, 1 shot to nose, through neck	9MM HI-POINT	HARRIS
ROHRBOUGH, DANIEL	3/2/84	Outside	1 shot to leg / 1 shot to stomach, 1 shot to chest	9MM HI-POINT / 9MM TEC-9	HARRIS / KLEBOLD
SANDERS, DAVE	10/22/51	Hallway	2 shots to back, out front	9MM HI-POINT	HARRIS
SCOTT, RACHEL	8/5/81	Outside	4 shots to arm, ribcage, temple, leg	9MM HI-POINT	HARRIS
SHOELS, ISAIAH	8/4/80	Library	1 shot to left arm through armpit, heart, right arm	PUMP SG SLUG	HARRIS
TOMLIN, JOHN	9/1/82	Library	1 shot to chest (graze) / 3 shots to head, 1 shot to back	PUMP SG PELLETS / 9MM TEC-9	HARRIS / KLEBOLD
TOWNSEND, LAUREN	1/17/81	Library	6 wounds to back torso / 3 wounds to front torso, graze to head	9MM TEC-9 / PUMP SG PELLETS	KLEBOLD / HARRIS
VELASQUEZ, KYLE	5/5/82	Library	shot to back left shoulder, 1 to head	DBL BARREL PELLETS	KLEBOLD

TRENCH COAT MAFIA

The Trench Coat Mafia (also known as Trenchcoat Mafia or TCM) was a group of misfit teens at Columbine who hung around the cafeteria stairwell starting in 1994—a year before Dylan Klebold and Eric Harris attended. Several members claimed to have been the founder and the first to wear a trench coat. The original group consisted of Charles "Chuck" Phillips Jr , Patrick McDuffee, Chris Morris, Joseph "Joe" Stair, and Thaddeus "Tad" Boles. The teens became friends over a shared interest in video and roleplaying games, movies, and bowling.

They were an informal group, not a sanctioned club. Described by Boles' mother as a "tiny clique of boys who had long been losers, finally finding a place", they used to hang out at Amazing Fantasy Comics in Littleton. According to store owner Shawn Carey they stopped when they got interested in paintball and girls. The group was anywhere from 7 to 20 people, depending on who was asked.

Research shows Tad Boles was the first to wear a long coat. He received the black duster as a Christmas gift in 1996. His mother bought it because it was on sale for $99 at Miller Stockholm western wear. Roughly a week later Chris Morris got one. In their freshman and sophomore years, they and their friends wore the coats at school as a statement of individuality and to intimidate students who had picked on them. This inspired some girls at Columbine to jokingly call them the "Trench Coat Mafia". Instead of being insulted, the boys adopted the name. Before that, kids called them "Freaks".

In fall of 1997, Eric Harris and Dylan Klebold met Morris, then a junior, in video production class. The three became close friends, playing games and bowling together. Chris stopped wearing his long coat around the same time the gunmen started wearing their black leather dusters in 1998. He felt the look had gotten too popular. Klebold and Harris met the TCM through him. The three teens sometimes went over to Cory

Friesen's house to shoot pool, but the gunmen weren't friends with everyone in the group or even considered part of it by most.

In 1998, Harris, Klebold, and Zach Heckler executed the "missions" Harris mentions online. That December, he had a school assignment to create a company. He named it "Hitmen for Hire" and called the employees the "Trench Coat Mafia". He handed in the paper just days after he and Klebold filmed *Hitmen for Hire*. Originally called *Revenge for Hire*, it was a short video in which their characters threatened people with guns that looked suspiciously like the ones they used in the massacre.

When news broke about the shooting at Columbine, several students blamed the Trench Coat Mafia. Klebold and Harris wore their dusters all the time at school, regardless of the weather. They also wore them during the assault. The gunmen were seen at a distance or a glance as the witness was trying to get away. Many just saw the coats and assumed they were TCM. However, while the shooters were friends with some members, by fall 1998 most of the original group had graduated, transferred to another school, or dropped out.

They had staked claim on the Trench Coat Mafia name, but by 1999 it was used by students as a general term to describe any outcast who wore a long black coat. The media latched onto the Trench Coat Mafia name, sensationalizing the "gang" until TCM members came forward to disavow responsibility. When officials questioned them—an investigation that included lie detector tests and background checks—they ruled them out as accomplices. The group wasn't responsible for the shooting, regardless of association or friendship with the gunmen.

MEMBERS OF THE TCM

Chuck Phillips Jr.

He was suspended several times for fighting before he graduated from Columbine High in 1998. He met Harris and Klebold in a theatre production at school and later worked with them at Blackjack Pizza, though he didn't work there long. He was working at Video City the night before the shootings.

Eric Dutro

Attended CHS until 1997 when he switched schools. He told investigators he left because he was being teased by students and faculty, specifically football coaches and principal Frank DeAngelis. He said students called him "freak" and "faggot" and threw things at him. While at Columbine, he and Joe Stair "made out" in front of the jocks to harass them. He and Stair were friends since 8th grade, though he hadn't seen anyone from the TCM for a year before the shooting. He didn't know Harris or Klebold well and said they were not Trench Coat Mafia members. His parents bought his trench coat 3 years prior at Sam's Club, and he wore it often, even while the police interviewed him.

Chris Morris

A CHS senior in 1999, he was at Cory Friesen's house during the shooting. Morris was known to have a bad temper and often wore a beret. He was arrested the day of the shooting after he called to tell police he suspected Harris and Klebold were involved. Initially a suspect, Morris told investigators he had no clue what his friends were planning that day. If he had, he never would have let his girlfriend, Nicole Markham, or her younger brother Christopher go to school. Morris was cooperative with authorities and cleared of charges. He later helped with the investigation of Philip Duran, who illegally sold a gun to the shooters.

311

Cory Friesen

Graduated from Columbine in 1997. He met Klebold and Harris
through Chris Morris. They all went to his house several times.
He started to disassociate from the group in 1998, though he took
the famous Trench Coat Mafia '98 yearbook photo and attended
Harris' 18th birthday party on April 9. Chris Morris was with him
at the Friesen residence during the shootings. Cory's father Kent
was a science teacher at Columbine and spent hours trying to
keep the fatally wounded Dave Sanders alive. Cory told
investigators he wouldn't have been sitting around playing video
games if he knew there was going to be a shooting where his dad
worked.

Robert Perry

One of the first to wear a long coat, he was the only one with true
trench coat. He couldn't afford the oiled Australian leather
dusters the other boys wore. He met Klebold and Harris in 1998
through Morris. A self-described Goth who wore colorful tie-dye
t-shirts, he was teased for "acting gay". Perry stopped associating
with the TCM in August 1998 after Morris put him in a headlock
and pulled a knife, threatening to kill him over something Perry's
sister Lydie said. Perry dropped out of Columbine his senior
year, a couple of months before the shooting. Perry and Klebold
had similar features. Some who didn't know them well mistook
them when talking to authorities. This led some to suspect he
was a third gunman, but several witnesses supported his alibi,
including many who were not affiliated with Perry.

Joe Stair

Graduated from Columbine in 1998. His younger sister Amanda
was in the library during the shooting. Stair last saw the gunmen
in December 1998. When police searched his home, they found a
news article on his mirror about Robert Craig, a 1997 Columbine
senior who killed his stepfather and then himself. Stair told
officials he met Harris and Klebold through Morris roughly two
years prior and only hung out with them occasionally, never
outside of school. Stair committed suicide in 2007. Amanda said
online that his death was unrelated to Columbine.

Tad Boles

Dropped out of Columbine and got his GED in fall of 1998. He once dated Robyn Anderson, the girl who bought guns for the shooters. Individual senior photos were taken in late summer before school started, so his picture appears in the 1999 yearbook even though he dropped out. He knew Klebold from Ken Caryl and met him through Chris Morris. He told investigators Harris and Klebold joined the TCM in 1997, but then also said he didn't meet Harris until he attended classes with him in 1998. Boles' He worked the night before the shooting was at home in bed during the massacre. He told officials that following the shooting he spoke with Morris and Brian Sargent. Morris was angry because he was worried about his girlfriend. Sargent was "in a panic" because he couldn't find a friend of his who was at the school.

Brian Sargent

A junior at Columbine at the time of the shooting. He bought his trench coat from Chris. He worked at Blackjack Pizza with the gunmen for a time. While he used to hang out with the people in the yearbook picture, scheduling conflicts reduced them to hallway acquaintances starting in 1998. The last time he saw Klebold and Harris was the day before the shooting when they left Columbine at 11:10 a.m. with Nate Dykeman. Sargent was off campus for lunch break when the shooting started.

Patrick McDuffee

Graduated from Columbine in 1998. He got in with the TCM in May 1997 and started associating with Klebold and Harris around that time. Under the username "ROMEO" he communicated via AOL with Chris Morris ("GRUNT") and Harris ("REB"). Klebold wasn't on AOL but went by "VoDkA" on other online platforms. McDuffee got his duster from Morris and was in Chess Club with Klebold. He stopped wearing his coat in his last semester in 1998.

313

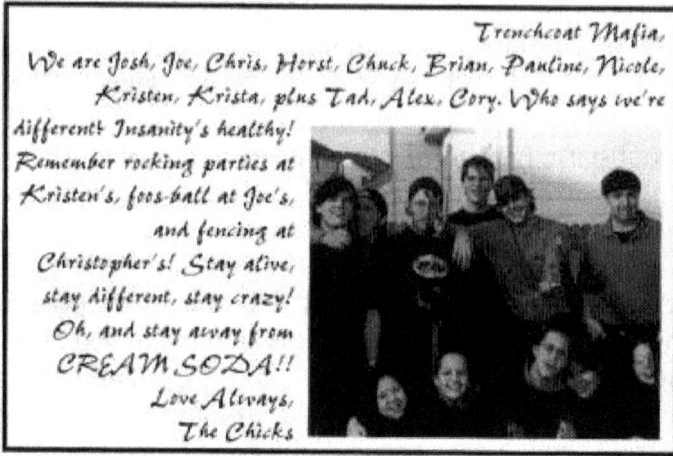

> *Trenchcoat Mafia,*
> *We are Josh, Joe, Chris, Horst, Chuck, Brian, Pauline, Nicole, Kristen, Krista, plus Tad, Alex, Cory. Who says we're different? Insanity's healthy! Remember rocking parties at Kristen's, foos-ball at Joe's, and fencing at Christopher's! Stay alive, stay different, stay crazy! Oh, and stay away from CREAM SODA!! Love Always, The Chicks*

OTHER ASSOCIATES

Some TCM members said Harris and Klebold were not members of the group. Others said they were "associates"—people who hung around the group but weren't considered core members. Some of the others said the shooters were only around because of their friendship with Chris Morris. Some claimed Klebold and Harris joined the group in 1997. It was a loose knit group, so who "belonged" depended on who was asked.

Known TCM associates included Josh Barnes, Horst Rossmueller, Eric Jackson, Andy Thomas, Robyn Anderson, Nate Dykeman, Pauline Colby, Kristen Theibault, Krista Hanley, Alex Marsh, Devon Adams, Erin Adams, Nicole Markham, Jessica Rusch, Nicole Dickey, Abigail Boles, Zach Heckler, Chris Tibaldo, Kristi Epling, and Nate Epling.

Whatever their affiliation, the gunmen had a lot in common with the Trench Coat Mafia: They were all known for their short tempers and their alcohol and drug use (particularly marijuana and tobacco). They shared a negative view of people and school. They played paintball, games, and bowled. The gunmen played pool at Friesen's house and practiced fencing with bamboo swords at Morris' home. But association doesn't mean their friends helped them or even knew what they were up to. In their writing and videos, the shooters never mention anyone else being a part of the plan. Only he and Klebold appear on the Basement Tapes. The only help they describe having is in the vandalism "missions" they did months before the shooting and the people who got them their weapons.

Ultimately the courts ruled the Trench Coat Mafia were not responsible for the shootings. It wasn't the fault of Columbine High School or the shooters' parents. The people responsible were Eric Harris and Dylan Klebold.

HARRIS AND KLEBOLD

Much of who they were is already detailed in this manuscript, but the "Who" section would be incomplete without mentioning them. You can find more details about the gunmen online at *aColumbineSite.com.*

Dylan and Eric both spent a great deal of time playing violent video games, watching violent films, and acting in violent home videos. Those who knew them suggested that this deliberate oversaturation combined with bully culture desensitized both to the violence they planned and engaged in at Columbine High on April 20, 1999.

ERIC HARRIS AND FAMILY

The Harris family included Wayne (father), Kathy (mother), older brother Kevin, and Eric. Wayne was a decorated Air Force pilot before his retirement, which meant the family moved a lot. Once they settled in Colorado, Wayne took a job with a company that made flight simulators and had a sideline buying and fixing up old BMWs. Kathy was a part-time caterer. Kevin, 3 years older than Eric, was a popular athlete at Columbine before graduating in 1996. Some who knew him said Eric's parents wanted him to be like his brother, but he wasn't, and they couldn't accept that. Eric was close with his brother and attended his sports games. He called Kevin his favorite relative. But Eric resented moving so much as it interfered with his social life and his ability to make lasting friendships.

He had a medical condition, funnel breast (*pectus excavatum*) where the chest is concave. The defect didn't stop him playing sports though. He played Little League baseball in the Columbine Sports group, but didn't fit in. Kids in the Columbine Sports Association were given preference in school over kids in community programs or not in sports. CSA kids would go on to become athletes and jocks at Columbine. Eric underwent corrective surgery in 1994 and played for the Columbine soccer team in his freshman and sophomore years. He also played with the local club, Colorado Rush, until 1998. Though he grew to hate the people in it, Harris ironically seemed attached to Columbine. He used the nickname "REB" and called his *Quake* group "Rebel Clan". Columbine's mascot is the Rebel (whose musket was removed following the shooting). He even styled his website title after the title graphic that was once on the high school's website.

Eric's parents were described as "nice" and caring individuals. They were good people who trusted their younger child too much. Eric was allowed to have the basement level largely to himself and got away with stowing bomb-making materials and weapons in plain sight. He also kept alcohol stashed down there. Eric often tried to charm and lie to people. If that didn't work, he was known to lose his temper. These outbursts got more violent and frequent in late 1998 and early 1999, when his Luvox dosage was up to 100mg.

His father caught him with explosives more than once. The Brown family tried to tell the Harrises that Eric was using them to commit vandalism, and that he was threatening Brooks. This was while Eric was on probation, yet his parents did little to monitor or intervene in their son's activities. Following the shooting, the Harris garage was so toxic with fumes from explosives the gunmen made that the bomb squad had to evacuate and air it out before the investigation could continue.

The Harrises essentially disappeared after the legal dust settled. They gave no media interviews and moved someplace where the press couldn't find them. Media reports say Kevin studied kinesiology at the University of Colorado, then joined the Army. While enlisted, he got his master's degree. Around 2018, he got married and had children of his own.

DYLAN KLEBOLD AND FAMILY

The Klebold family included Thomas (dad), Susan (mom), older brother Byron, and Dylan. Tom was a geophysicist, and Sue was helped disabled people find employment. They also ran a company that bought and restored houses. Byron, 3 years older than Dylan, was a popular young man at Columbine before his graduation in 1996.

Friends of Dylan said he and his brother didn't get along. Byron told investigators that he and Dylan were "not close". He moved out of the Klebold home in 1997 and worked as a lot technician for a local auto dealership. People who knew them described Tom and Sue as nice people, friendly and "normal", though not overtly affectionate with their sons. They expected their children to be moral, motivated achievers. Tom was close with Dylan, whom several described as his "best friend". Like the Harrises, the Klebolds let things slide with their "trustworthy" son. Though he was underage, Dylan had a poster on his wall detailing how to make cocktails. He drank and smoked. When investigators searched his room after the shooting, they found the sawed-off barrel of his shotgun on his dresser in plain sight.

Dylan was shy and awkward. Moving out to the country away from easy access to friends didn't help. Though smart and good at academics, he suffered from low self-esteem and was a persistent wallflower, traits that weighed against him in the competitive community he was in. But he also had a quick and volatile temper like his father and an aggressive, violent streak that would show when he was thwarted or embarrassed. After he and Eric became friends, he adopted a meaner, indifferent, and lazy attitude about school and life. He also grew more depressed.

After the fallout from the shooting, Sue went on to write books, do interviews, and worked as a public speaker talking about her experiences as the mother of a mass murderer. She was diagnosed with breast cancer in 2001 which was in remission in 2016. Tom and Sue divorced in 2014. As of 2024, Byron was married with children and was a manager at the same auto dealership he worked at since 1997.

AGENCIES AND ORGANIZATIONS

* Arvada Police Department, Boulder Police Department, Brighton Police Department, Castle Rock Police Department, Columbine Valley Police Department, Commerce City Police Department, Denver Police Department District 4, Edgewater Police Department, Federal Heights Police Department, Greeley Police Department, Greenwood Village Police Department, Lakewood Police Department, Littleton Police Department, Longmont Police Department, Northglenn Police Department, Sheridan Police Department, Thornton Police Department, Westminster Police Department
* Littleton EMS and Fire
* Adams County Sheriff's Office, Arapahoe County Sheriff's Office, Boulder County Sheriff's Office, Clear Creek County Sheriff's Office, Douglas County Sheriff's Office, Gilpin County Sheriff's Office, Jefferson County Sheriff's Office
* Denver Homicide, SWAT
* Cites of Golden, Blackhawk, Central City
* Englewood Department of Safety Services
* CBI, FBI, ATF, DEA / HIDTA
* Colorado State Patrol
* National Guard
* Attorney General's Office
* Denver District Attorney's Office
* State Court Administrators Office
* Division of Criminal Justice
* Boulder County Crisis Intervention Team
* Victim Services Unit of the Jefferson County Sheriff's Office
* Victim Outreach Information
* Wings Foundation
* Colorado Organization for Victim Assistance
* Children's Advocacy Center
* Women in Crisis
* Salvation Army

* Mile High United Way Healing Fund
* Jefferson Foundation
* McCormick Tribune Foundation
* The Academic Foundation
* HOPE
* Bill Clinton
* Celine Dion
* Rosie O'Donnell
* Columbine Public Library
* Leawood Elementary School
* Chatfield High School
* Coroner – Boulder, Arapahoe Co, Denver, Jefferson County

LAW ENFORCEMENT AND EMS

In addition to the 6 deputies who were the first responders to the scene, 35 law enforcement agencies and 11 EMS and fire agencies mustered nearly 1,000 officials and emergency personnel. Even more participated in the subsequent investigations.

You can see in the narrative what specific individuals did or didn't do. Some were amazing saviors, risking their lives to rescue survivors and championing the truth about what happened. Some officials failed the Columbine families so badly over the years, their actions only added to the tragedy. You can learn more about that in books such as Kacey Ruegsegger's *Over My Shoulder*, Randy Brown's *The Inside Story of Columbine*, and Sue Klebold's *A Mother's Reckoning*.

MEDICAL CENTERS

Centura Littleton Adventist Hospital

Denver Health Center

Lutheran Medical Center

St. Anthony Central Hospital

Swedish Medical Center

University Hospital

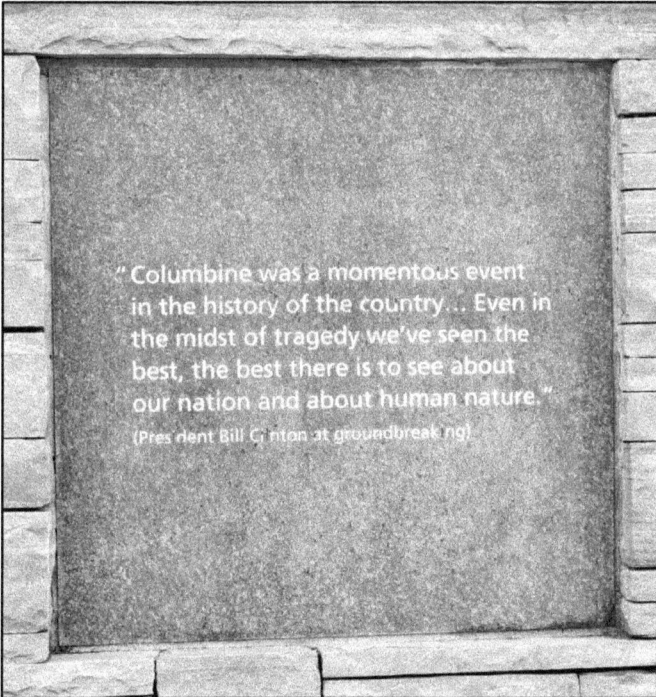

"Columbine was a momentous event in the history of the country... Even in the midst of tragedy we've seen the best, the best there is to see about our nation and about human nature."
(President Bill Clinton at groundbreaking)

WHAT

This section deals with the physical evidence and some of the issues with the investigation that followed the shooting. Between media misinformation, public conspiracy theories, official confusion and cover-up, it can be difficult to know what the truth is. You can learn more about the gear and weapons involved at *aColumbineSite.com*, as well as find the official reports, follow-up independent investigations, and much more that would make this book too long if it were included.

DISCREPANCIES

The investigation was plagued with discrepancies before and after the shooting. Unfortunately, there were several bad actors. Witnesses who gave inaccurate interviews or lied to investigators and reporters. Officials who lied and covered things up. News agencies that knew the truth and hid it or else leaked sensitive, sometimes inaccurate information that hurt the victims. Between deliberate misinformation and the natural human inclination to make errors with numbers and memory, it is difficult to say for certain what the real story is. The best we can do is look at the bigger picture and apply Occam's Razor: The simplest explanation is probably correct.

TIME

There are several timelines in the Columbine shooting. There was no synchronization between official agencies, and clocks at Columbine were also off. The cafeteria cash register that logged a purchase by Rachel Scott at 11:32 a.m. was at least 10 minutes off from the rest of the school. The surveillance cameras were running on a different time from both. The Columbine High fire alarm was 3 minutes slower than the cameras. The Littleton Fire Department was 4 minutes slow. Jefferson County Sheriff's Office 911 dispatch was 2 minutes and 46 seconds faster than that.

Witnesses who reported times were either speaking in general terms, guessing, or were referring to their own watches which were not synched with any of the other times. News agencies were running on their own clocks as well. This makes it difficult to say when a given event took place. Timestamps from any source are best looked at as a "plus or minus" situation and not used as solid evidence of whether something might or might not have happened. The times in this book are for tracking rather than to assert that was the exact time something happened.

WITNESS RECALL

Eyewitness accounts are generally considered unreliable in investigations. Even when we're at ease and trying to pay attention, details can be hard to recall. Remembering the order of things can be difficult under the best circumstances. When stress and fear are added, it's even trickier. Loud noises, flashing lights, weapons, and crowd movement can interfere as can the emotional state of the witness. Not having enough time to see a perpetrator or situation can lead to mistaken identity and recalling details that aren't real as the mind tries to fill in the blanks. Prejudice and memory degradation play a part as does suggestibility. People hear other versions of what happened. They get information from outside sources which can become

324

indistinguishable from memory, as can speculation, embellishment, and even dreams.

The National Institutes of Health, the United States' medical research agency, establishes that "seeing" something is comprised of several things. Vision, which is the detection of light and basic image extraction. Sensation, of which only a small portion is ever perceived to prevent sensory overload. Attention, the filtering process by which information is sensed, and vision is selected (over hearing, smelling, etc.). Perception, where visual information is integrated and linked to what's around, and made coherent through meaning, value, and emotional response. All of this goes into visual memory, which is why people in high stress, unexpected situations with lots of sensory input (witnessing a car wreck, being shot at) misidentify basic details such as colors, speed and time, or descriptions of people and things.

Observer bias is the tendency of people to see what they expect to see. Lighting, shadows, smoke, distance, and more create uncertainty. Uncertainty is resolved by bias. Victims often report their attacker was "big" regardless of their true size. Bank robbers are said to have a gun, even if one isn't present. Subjective confidence can add to bias, where someone trusts their memory to the point where they are certain they experienced something even if they did not. Memory isn't concrete. It's encoded with our prejudices and influenced by things taken in from the news, law enforcement, friends, family, even strangers. Worse, there was deliberate coverup going on which forced false narratives and some people to change their stories.

In the Columbine shooting, most of what we know comes from witness statements. Over time, many stories have proven to be flawed for a variety of reasons. No one person's account is completely reliable. Stories that have changed over the years are even less so. As such, the best approach to finding the "true story" is to look at where multiple accounts say similar things.

MASKS

More than 30 witnesses told investigators they saw one or both gunmen wearing some sort of balaclava or ski mask for a portion of the shooting. Masks are not mentioned in this book's narrative because it's impossible to tell which of the shooters wore them, when they took them off, and whether they put them back on. It isn't vital to understanding the bigger picture of what happened, but it is worth mentioning that this played a factor in people identifying the shooters and how many gunmen they thought they saw.

MULTIPLE GUNMEN

In their plans, Harris and Klebold only talk about the two of them being involved in "NBK" day. Some have speculated that their friends might have helped them transport and plant explosives (such as the field bombs and the one in Columbine's kitchen). However, most of them were either in school that day or had family members and friends who were. Why would they endanger themselves and people they cared about?

Another factor that weighed in on the impression of more shooters was cover fire from the authorities. Twelve officers shot at and into the school, even after the gunmen were dead. At least 141 (possibly more than 162) law enforcement rounds went through windows and doors, and bounced off the walls back at officials, making them think they were being fired on. It's possible some of the shots kids ran from were fired by authorities, as bullets from police weapons traveled all the way down the northern hall to the east side of the building.

Harris and Klebold's friends weren't people the authorities would need to cover for. Only Harris had a military parent of note who might be worth the risk of a coverup. If any of their associates were involved, chances are law enforcement would have been glad to offer them up for the public to focus on. As it was, in initial reports authorities mistakenly identified

Brooks Brown, Robert Perry, and others as being involved because investigators wrote things down wrong and because witnesses who didn't know them misidentified them. All those falsely accused were eventually cleared of any wrongdoing.

Regardless of whether anyone else knew or suspected something was up, experts, authorities, and the evidence agree that Eric Harris and Dylan Klebold were the only gunmen responsible for the tragedy of April 20, 1999.

DEPUTY GARDNER

According to the Columbine Report, Gardner fired 8 shots. 8 casings were found on the ground at the spot where he was shooting at Eric Harris. However, 3 rounds that seem to be matched to his gun were also found in the library, including an unfired round.

Gardner wasn't wearing his prescription glasses during the shooting but instead a pair of non-prescription sunglasses. However, his vision was good enough that he could drive without them and was able to accurately describe Eric Harris and his weapon. It's possible that he merely needed reading glasses, but there is very little information on what his prescription was.

One inconsistency that is puzzling has to do with a victim outside. When Carole Weld looked out the west windows before the shooters entered the library, she said she saw a student dragging another kid who had been shot in the hip. The victim was being dragged toward the athletic shed. According to Gardner, once the shooting stopped after noon, he spent an hour in his squad car with a boy who had been shot in the hip. He stayed with him until SWAT evacuated them from the south parking lot. However, there are no victims on record who were shot in the hip. Also, SRO Andy Marton's report said he and Gardner held their position until 3:00 p.m. when they were ordered to the command post.

DYLAN'S DEATH

This is a discrepancy that has sparked many theories. The official story is that Klebold killed himself. This is something even his own parents agreed with. The autopsy shows that he died from a "large caliber" gunshot wound to the head, with the entry on the left side and the exit on the right. Which would make sense given that Klebold was left-handed.

However, in the CBI report prepared by Agent Tom J. Griffin, Library Team 2 Leader, Klebold was found with the TEC-9 "in his right hand under his right leg". This detail spawned many a theory. It would not be possible to shoot oneself in the left temple with that type of gun held in the right hand. Which would suggest on the surface that Harris or someone else killed him. But this is more complicated than it seems.

The bodies of the shooters were moved by investigators. So, nothing can be taken for granted where their positioning in the leaked photos is concerned. Which leaves the crime scene diagrams. The TEC-9 was attached with a strap to Klebold's body, which freed Klebold to switch to his shotgun without having to holster the gun. The way his body was lying on the TEC-9, the gun was not in a position that he could have been holding it to shoot himself with, specifically it was upside down relative to the positioning of his hand.

Even still, how could this be ruled a suicide? First, there was DNA/blood found in the muzzle of the TEC-DC9, which was loaded with a magazine and had a round in the chamber. The blood was found in a drawback flow pattern extending roughly one inch into the barrel, which is only possible if the weapon was fired at close range. There is little doubt based on forensics that this weapon killed Klebold. Harris' rifle, which was found between them, had no such evidence on it and it was completely unloaded. The forensic evidence also shows that Klebold died shortly after Harris did. I don't want to get into grislier details, but the way the remains were found, and the splatter patterns indicate this. Which rules out Harris having killed him.

328

The TEC-DC9 has a magazine in front of the grip, which puts more weight on the front of the gun. To hold it to one's temple and fire, one would most likely need to stabilize it by gripping the magazine.

When I worked in the mall, I pierced the cartilage of my own ear. I used a light-weight ear piercing gun and could not get my hand to fire it. I had to use both hands to overcome the shaky grip and strange bout of nervousness that made me freeze up. I can imagine how much worse this might be if it were a real gun. It isn't difficult to imagine Klebold would need to steady a front-heavy weapon with his off-hand to fire it. Once fired, his grip would relax instantly as he fell. The strap on the weapon would control where it dropped. It would also come into play when the body was moved by investigators.

According to the Columbine Report, the Library Team cut the strap of the TEC-9 and removed it at 3:30 p.m., under the direction of the Jefferson County Coroner's Office Chief Deputy Coroner Treina Harper. Harper told them the rest of the weapons could be collected later in the day. Why did they remove the TEC-9 first? Chances are they were treating it like the bombs that were removed. A TEC-DC9 can be converted to fully automatic, which means an accidental brush with the trigger could fire it. They had no way of knowing if the weapon was modified, so it was removed along with the crickets and pipe bombs.

SHOTS FIRED

DYLAN KLEBOLD

Intratec TEC-DC9 9mm semi-automatic pistol

Outside the school: 3   Inside the school: 31   In the library: 21

    (total 55)

Double barrel Savage Arms Stevens 311D 12-gauge shotgun

Outside the school: 2   Inside the school: 4   In the library: 6

    (total 12)

TOTAL ROUNDS FIRED BY KLEBOLD: **67**

ERIC HARRIS

9mm semi-automatic Hi-Point model 995 carbine rifle

Outside the school: 47   Inside the school: 36   In the library: 13

    (total 96)

Single barrel Savage-Springfield 67H 12-gauge shotgun

Inside the school: 4   In the library: 21

    (total 25)

TOTAL ROUNDS FIRED BY HARRIS: **121**

TOTAL ROUNDS FIRED:

Shotgun: 37 9mm: 151   **TOTAL: 188**

BOMBS

(most info is from the Littleton Fire Department Columbine Review
Commission report to Governor Bill Owens)

48 – Carbon dioxide ("cricket") bombs

27 – Pipe bombs

7 – Gas/napalm bombs

11 – 1.5 gallon propane containers

2 – 20-pound propane bombs in cafeteria

1 – 20-pound propane and gasoline bomb in kitchen

2 – Backpack time bombs

2 – Time bombs in the shooters' cars

40+ gallons of flammable liquid

Exploded:

Outside – 13

Library – 5

Classrooms/Hallways – 6

Cafeteria – 6

Not Detonated:

Outside – 2

Library – 26

Classroom/Hallway – 14

Cafeteria – 4

Klebold car – 12

Harris car – 1

Klebold home – 6

Harris home – 2

WHERE

COLUMBINE HIGH SCHOOL

6201 S. Pierce Street, Littleton, Colorado 80123

Named after Colorado's state flower, CHS opened in 1973. Located in the Columbine area in Jefferson County, it has an average enrollment of 2,000. The building is roughly 250,000 square feet with 75 classrooms. In 1995, it underwent a $15 million dollar makeover. An opening ceremony in August of that year welcomed Eric Harris, Dylan Klebold, and the rest of the student body to a brand-new cafeteria, student entrance, and hallways. It was the first facelift Columbine had since the 1970's.

Less than four years after renovation, the school would need costly repairs to fix the damages inflicted on it on April 20, 1999, by Harris and Klebold during their fatal attack. Frank DeAngelis, who had been with the school for 19 years as a coach and teacher, was principal for 3 years before the shooting. He stayed on as principal until his retirement in 2016.

In 2018, the school board explored whether to allocate $15 million in bonds to the renovation of the school or to "scrape and rebuild" the school for roughly $60 million. While it would be more cost-effective to renovate the 40-year-old school, rebuilding from scratch would remove the draw of the legacy of the shooting that brings numbers of trespassers to the school every year. Over 2,000 intruders were stopped in 2018. In 2019,

Jefferson County Public Schools decided against tearing down the school

COLUMBINE MEMORIAL

7306 W. Bowles Ave, Littleton, CO 80123

Construction on the memorial began in August 2006. The site was completed in September 2007. The interior of the memorial is a Ring of Remembrance where plaques honor each of the people who were murdered. The exterior wall is the Wall of Healing where polished stone plaques bear inspiring quotes from people who were at the dedication. It also has a water feature of six flowing fountains. The memorial costs roughly $10,000 a year to upkeep. You can help by donating at https://www.columbinememorial.org/

WHY?

We know what happened to whom, where, and when. But why? Why did two young men from nice neighborhoods and solid families commit such a heinous, unrepentant act of violence?

The toxic combination that resulted in the Columbine High shooting involves many elements. "Why" is further complicated by the fact that the two gunmen are dead. In their videos and journaled rants they expressed a desire to kill and destroy. They accused society of being hypocritical, mean, biased, deceptive, and unappreciative even as they acknowledged they, too, embodied those traits.

To understand why the tragedy happened, it's essential to understand what led up to it. The answers can be found in the environment and culture the shooters were in, their personalities and mental predispositions, the people they were with, the media they took in, the ease at which they were able to make and get weapons, a desire to not grow up, a lack of adult attention to the growing threat, and the use and abuse of drugs and alcohol.

Eric Harris and Dylan Klebold spent their last two years of life immersed in a game of pretend that bled over into real life. Their characters: Bad-ass hitmen REB and VoDkA, who lived in a make-believe world that was a cross between *Natural Born Killers* and *Doom*. In that world, they were stronger, better, smarter, cooler, edgier, and more powerful than the jocks and hypocritical snobs they hated and envied. They wanted to be noticed and respected. They wanted to make the rules. They

335

convinced themselves the assault showed their superiority. It gave them total control in a final epic act of terrorism they hoped would motivate a "revolution" of like-minded individuals.

But the attack was supposed to happen a lot faster.

THE PLAN

The plan was to set time bombs in and around the city, the school, and their cars. In his NBK.doc Harris described it as a two-man apocalypse. It was far-fetched, like a pitch for an action film or violent video game, better suited to *The Matrix* than real life. He even created a *Doom* level based on Columbine featuring two heavily armed characters with unlimited ammo. It wasn't realistic, but he tried to make it happen. I say Harris did because evidence points to it being his passion project. While Klebold wrote about isolation, depression, and self-harm, Harris was plotting in his journals. Figuring out how to get weapons, make bombs, where to focus the attack. Harris wrote about hating the human race and who he wanted to kill. Klebold fixated on self-loathing and wanting to be loved. Harris was the idea man. Klebold was a willing soldier.

To distract authorities, they rigged time bombs off campus. After those detonated, time bombs inside the school cafeteria were supposed to explode. The gunmen wanted it to be like the Oklahoma City bombing. Computer modelling and field testing by investigators showed that, had the bombs gone off as planned, they would have seriously injured or killed most people in the commons. Structural damage could have caused a partial collapse of the cafeteria and library. Harris and Klebold stationed themselves at their cars flanking the main entrance, waiting to pick off survivors who ran out from the flaming wreckage. Then they would charge in and shoot anyone they saw, including their friends, if they happened to get in front of their guns. Who died didn't matter. The death toll did.

"We don't give a shit because we're going to die doing it." Eric said on one of the Basement Tapes. *"I don't give a fuck about anybody."*

But faulty timers and not understanding the safety features of propane tanks meant none of their time bombs went off right. The diversionary explosive behind the school partially detonated but instead of cinematic widescale destruction inside, the duffel bag bombs just sat there. The killers had to jump ahead in the plan. They threw bombs and shot people.

Brooks Brown said: *"It was about them living in the moment, like they were inside a video game. As long as they were rolling with the plan, the slaughter didn't seem real to them."*

At first it was exhilarating, gunning down targets for real. They whooped and laughed. Harris said on one of the Basement Tapes he planned to think of his victims as monsters from *Doom* so he could shoot them without remorse. But the more he and Klebold talked to people, the less they shot at them.

The people targeted weren't monsters. They cried, screamed, begged, and bled. The gunmen didn't even know many of them. Killing teen after helpless teen wasn't the same as running through a video game level defending against attacking beasts. They met little resistance. Police initially engaged them in a gunfight but shifted to cover fire when survivors fled the school. The last person the killers met face to face was Evan Todd. The terrified boy tried to reason with them. They threatened him at gunpoint but didn't kill him, even though Harris fired two shots at him earlier.

With nothing to keep their adrenaline pumping, it was likely difficult for Harris and Klebold to stay in character as REB and VoDkA. Reality set in. Roaming the building in search of victims was time-consuming and tiring—a bigger challenge than imagined. They tried several times to blow up the school, but nothing worked. While they could pretend that they were in a video game for a while, after nearly an hour of "living the dream" there was no climactic end in sight. The school wasn't

337

going to explode. SWAT wasn't going to come in guns blazing. Charging officers outside carried the risk that the shooters might be wounded, not killed. Then they would be arrested and stand trial for their actions. That was not part of the plan.

It took the SWAT team hours to reach the library where the gunmen were. By then they had committed suicide.

ENVIRONMENT

Klebold and Harris lived in an upper middle-class, predominantly Caucasian Christian suburb of Denver. Hunting and guns were commonplace. So much so, local high schools had to tell seniors not to bring firearms for yearbook photos. When asked about the shooters owning and firing guns, the mother of one of their friends told investigators she only saw them use BB guns, which "every boy owns, and every boy does". Tom Klebold, Dylan's father, was antigun yet even his son owned a BB gun at age 10 or 11. Both boys were raised in loving homes where they were permitted to have and do almost anything they wanted provided it didn't conflict with their parents' lifestyles.

As early as 1995 Harris wrote about guns for school assignments. His dad Wayne was a decorated air force pilot who earned several medals and awards, including one for small arms marksmanship. The Harrises were stationed at six different military bases before Wayne retired in 1993 due to cutbacks. In his journals Eric complained about moving. He hated being the new kid, always leaving friends behind and starting over at the bottom. He was particularly upset leaving Plattsburgh, New York, their last home before they moved to Wayne's birth state of Colorado after his retirement. Eric's parents enrolled him at Ken Caryl Middle School midway through 7th grade. Once again, he was the "new guy".

Dylan Klebold was born in Lakewood, Colorado. His family didn't move around as much—only once in 1990 to Deer Creek Canyon. He was a Boy Scout and went to good schools.

He played soccer, T-ball, and baseball. In 3rd grade he was placed in the gifted program, Challenging High Intellectual Potential Students (CHIPS) at Governor's Ranch Elementary. Though it seems like an advantage, it came with pressure and peer competition. He wasn't happy but he stayed in because he didn't want to disappoint his parents. In 7th grade he went to Ken Caryl Middle School where there was no gifted program.

When younger, Klebold was described as a shy, gentle person though he had a quick temper which would show when he competed or was embarrassed. Harris was described as shy and imaginative, smart and a good athlete. He was also known by his peers to be manipulative and aggressive, especially when he wanted or was denied something. After the gunmen became friends, Klebold developed a reputation for being surly and unpleasant. His academic drive declined. Early on, he was a student assistant in theatre and computer science at CHS. His sophomore year, Klebold assisted vocal teacher Lee Andres, Jr. When Andres asked him to help in his senior year, Klebold declined. Harris was polite to adults but prided himself on his lying. He had an ego that grew into an obsessive, aggressive superiority complex after he was prescribed antidepressants. He raged in his journals that he was better than others and wanted people to die. By 1998 he'd dropped sports and was fixated on computer games, weapons, and dark, violent subjects.

Parents are a child's template for what a person is. Even if the parent is the worst example of a human being, they are what a child believes every person is like. Similarly, school becomes a template for the world. Kids in traditional school spend 8 or more hours there, 5 days a week. It's where they learn what other children are like and how they fit into the bigger social picture. Students and faculty become representatives of what society is, even though it's not an inaccurate representation. Students in private schools and gifted programs often experience culture shock when they hit the real world because it's vastly different. Kids from tough schools come out ready to fight and treat others like competition or threats without provocation. School is a training ground for how we see the world.

339

In 1999, Columbine High was a relatively small school that reflected the values of the people who lived around it. Those who didn't fit the mold weren't given the social advantages of those who did. But there was duality there we see in many communities. For example, there are Christians who exemplify the Christ-like ideal of compassion and love, and then there are "performative" or "buffet" Christians, who pick and choose from Scripture what they want to follow. They lambast others, telling them they'll go to hell, but then gossip, cheat, and get wasted. There were people like that at Columbine among the popular crowd. Their social status despite their hypocrisy angered the gunmen. One of many things that did.

Almost anyone who has gone to school has dealt with a social structure like what's described at Columbine. The pecking order is a caste system ranging from popular kids at the top down to outcasts at the bottom. It's so common and relatable, film and television have covered the subject for decades. *Revenge of the Nerds. Mean Girls. The Breakfast Club. Head of the Class. Heathers. Carrie. School of Rock. Glee.* It's not unusual to feel taken for granted, left out, frustrated with the stupidity of others—especially as teens in school. It's also common to entertain vengeful, violent fantasies. Even Cassie Bernall, one of the victims who died, wrote about wanting to kill her parents and teachers when she was younger. But there's a big difference between fantasizing about violence and going through with it.

Columbine was/is sports oriented. Many of the teachers are coaches. Frank DeAngelis was a softball coach before he became principal. His successor Scott Christy has been with Columbine for 15 years. He was an athletic director before becoming principal, a role he's held for 7 years as of 2024.

In 1999, the pecking order at Columbine was like most schools in the United States: Those who excelled in athletics were in the top social tier. This is true of many middle schools, high schools, and especially colleges where athletes and coaches are given special privileges and budgets. The top tier at CHS also included the wealthy and those who professed to be Christian.

On the bottom tier were social misfits who didn't fit the standards. Most students were in the middle, "normal" kids from varied financial and cultural backgrounds and academic strengths. Ralph W. Larkin, author of *Comprehending Columbine*, compared this peer structure to a rhombus or diamond shape where the majority are in the middle while the minority are at the top and bottom. Although Larkin's book has some misinformation in it, this assessment seems accurate and applies to most primary and secondary school systems. What makes a kid popular or a "loser" varies by location, taking root as early as preschool and solidifying over the years. This tends to be more intense in smaller schools and communities.

The bottom tier of Columbine's social structure included Goths, stoners, those who went against or lacked school spirit, and those with developmental and physical disabilities. Kids who were considered "poor" also fell into this category, ironic because most students were from upper-middle class families. It was the *appearance* of wealth that mattered to the top tier: Keeping up with trends, being seen at the right events with the right people, etc. The athletic top tier was divided between charismatic leader-types and those who used their physical prowess to intimidate others. The two circles coexisted but were drastically different in attitude and reception by other students. Leader-types, the athletes, were friendly high-achievers who were popular because of their athletic ability, academic success, winning personalities, and school spirit. The bullies, called "jocks", were generally disliked and feared by other students. This same division exists in many schools under different names.

Jocks were known to dominate others in crude, aggressive, and violent ways. Males and females both were targets. Some individuals were picked on more than others. The bottom "outcast" tier was picked on most, though even the top tier was not exempt. And crap rolled downhill: People who were picked on tended to punch down on those they considered inferior to them. Harris and Klebold were near the bottom of the social diamond, Klebold because his role solidified over years spent with the same kids and Harris because he wasn't there when the social structure was forming. Harris and Klebold resented the top tier for their privilege and hypocrisy yet were unwilling to conform to the social norms to gain the status they envied. Neither was going to make it to the top and they didn't want to fall into the anonymous "normal" rank. They wanted to be special, but they wanted it to happen on their terms.

Despite being "outcasts" they weren't the friendless loners the media first made them out to be. They had connections at work who were willing to turn a blind eye when they set off bombs on top of and behind the pizza shop. They convinced several people to help them get weapons. At school, they had a pool of friends they bowled, gamed, and went to movies with. They made amateur film productions with them. There were teachers they assisted. Though they complained about their love lives, both knew girls who were interested in them. Harris was upset he couldn't get a date for prom, but he had a casual date with Susan DeWitt the same night. He took Katie Thompson out two weeks before the shooting. Klebold didn't consider Robyn Anderson his girlfriend, but he took her to prom. Her friend Monica Schuster told investigators Anderson was "very close" with both gunmen and wanted to be Klebold's girlfriend.

To others, Klebold and Harris appeared to be typical high school seniors, which was part of why their plans went undetected. Both were skilled at pretending to be "normal" for people who could make their lives hard. They took pride in how well they fooled others, especially their families.

Many have tried to pin the "why" on the shooters' parents. When I discuss Columbine with someone unfamiliar with the subject, that tends to be the first thing they suggest: Surely the boys—at least one of them—had a bad home life. But the Harrises and Klebolds were stable, upper middle-class families with no history of divorce. Those who knew them said the parents were family-oriented, good people. Dads were employed, moms were domestic. Klebold's parents were involved but not overtly affectionate with their children. Harris' parents were more strict but also more liberal with affection. Both families had high-achieving, popular older sons. It wasn't until the gunmen were arrested for breaking into a van in January 1998 that their parents couldn't avoid seeing the dark side of their sons. But a single break-in wasn't the end of the world. The parents agreed to let Dylan and Eric participate in a county diversion program for juvenile perpetrators of minor crimes. It was better than jail.

Klebold's parents had long, heartfelt talks with him about the incident. He expressed his anger with the system, society, and school, while they tried to drive home the importance of how his actions affected others. His mother Sue suggested he speak with a counselor, but Klebold adamantly refused. Harris' parents put Eric in therapy and an anger management program. His therapist prescribed him the SSRI Zoloft. When that resulted in his having an obsessive preoccupation with murder and suicide, the doctor switched him to Luvox (Fluvoxamine Maleate). Wayne kept a log of Eric's actions in a steno notebook, though his records were more defensive than insightful.

For generations, disaffected youths have talked about inflicting violence on their schools to vent their frustrations. In an era when home versions of violent video games showed uncensored graphic bloodshed without warnings and movies like *The Matrix* and *Natural Born Killers* glorified gun-toting outcasts who declared war on the system, the shooters had no shortage of inspiration to pattern their attitudes and wardrobes after. They loved violent games and films and spent a disproportionate amount of time absorbing and mimicking them. But while media influenced the gunmen, a more significant factor in "why" they went through with the assault seems to be the use of the mood-altering SSRI medications by Harris for over a year.

Research shows several people have had extreme negative reactions to the drugs, including homicide and suicide. Harris' friends noticed throughout 1998 he became increasingly more aggressive. His writing reflects this. Prior to the attack on Columbine, Harris deliberately stopped taking medication so he would be as angry as possible the day of the assault. He was up to 100mg daily. The washout period for the drug is around two weeks, so he still had lower midlevel amounts in his system during the shooting. It took the massacre and several lawsuits for pharmaceutical companies to acknowledge the risks despite disastrous previous outcomes of other patients. That family of drugs are generally no longer prescribed to young people and come with hefty warnings for adult use.

Luvox was given the warning label: *"Antidepressants increased the risk compared to placebo of suicidal thinking and behavior (suicidality) in children, adolescents, and young adults in short-term studies of major depressive disorder (MDD) and other psychiatric disorders. Anyone considering the use of Fluvoxamine Maleate tablets or any other antidepressant in a child, adolescent, or young adult must balance this risk with the clinical need."*

The drug was discontinued in 2003.

But what about Klebold? He wasn't on antidepressants. But he was a lifestyle copier. He was shy, awkward, temperamental, and unsatisfied with himself. He gained empowerment by aping Harris' aggressive behavior. He could adopt a stronger, edgier persona he liked and vent his frustrations to someone who agreed with him. He had the acceptance he desperately craved. After the van incident, Klebold wrote in his diary that he felt his life was over. The crime and the fact he liked porn led him to believe his soul was damned. Disregarding the Judeo-Christianity belief of Divine forgiveness, he decided nothing he did mattered anymore.

The teens fed into each other's worst, darkest thoughts. They condoned and echoed the negative views they had about the world and how they didn't fit into it. They talked themselves into believing they had evolved beyond normal humans ("zombies" they called them). After death they expected to level up someplace more appreciative of their awesomeness. They wanted to command the same sort of respect they had for the murderers in *Natural Born Killers*. But they were aware of the scrutiny they were under, so they acted normally around adults

344

who might interfere. This afforded them privacy and trust they wouldn't have had if they were causing overt problems. They did such a good job that they were released a month early from the court-ordered year-long diversion program. Both received a "good" prognosis from the officer who said of them:

"Eric is a very bright young man who is likely to succeed in life. He is intelligent enough to achieve lofty goals as long as he stays on task and remains motivated. ... He impressed me as being very articulate and intelligent."

"Dylan is a bright young man who has a great deal of potential. If he is able to tap his potential and become self-motivated, he should do well in life. ... He is intelligent enough to make any dream a reality, but he needs to understand hard work is a part of it."

It was all an act. While they wrote apology letters for breaking into the van, they were also writing hateful journals about how people deserved to be robbed. They pretended to prepare for the future as they hoarded weapons and gloated about how much fun it would be to kill everyone. When the diversion program ended, Harris' mood noticeably declined. He and Klebold grew more aggressive. They isolated themselves. The pressure to keep up the good guy mask was off. They had to get ready for their "NBK" doomsday.

The Harrises and Klebolds have been criticized for being unaware of their sons' activities. How could they not know the teens were making hundreds of bombs and stockpiling ammunition? How did they miss so many warning signs? Between the essays, the police reports, their clothes, the games and films they obsessed over… how could it not add up to something sinister? But most don't see their loved ones as a threat. Even those in abusive relationships tend to believe their abuser would never kill them. Parents think they know their children well enough to detect when they are having serious problems. If nothing else, they trust their child would talk to them before committing mass murder.

With as much misconduct as the pair logged, several people saw and heard bits and pieces, yet no one saw it all. While some knew Harris and Klebold could be mean, they didn't know the ruthless violence they were capable of. Some of their best friends were in the school during the shooting. No one was safe that day. Harris summed it up best in his academic planner with a quote from Shakespeare's *The Tempest*:

> *"Good wombs hath born bad sons."*

BULLYING

Bullying has long been present in school systems. In the USA, it can be traced as far back as the 1800s thanks to author Laura Ingalls Wilder. In her "Little House" books she described town kids teasing her and her older sister for being "country girls" because they came to school barefoot and had to share school supplies. Rich girl Nellie boasted and flaunted her wealth. She and Laura were constantly at odds. But Nellie wasn't just one girl. She was the composite of three different people Laura knew. Ironically Alison Arngrim, who played bratty Nellie on the television adaptation of *Little House on the Prairie*, said in her memoir *Confessions of a Prairie Bitch* that she was bullied by kids at school and abused by a relative before she starred on the show. Being able to kick, scream, and break things helped her cope with bottled-up trauma. In an interview with *Remind Magazine*, she said:

> *"Being able to release all of this anger, all of this rage…*
> *Anyone who has survived any kind of childhood abuse*
> *knows… Where do we put this displaced anger? Where*
> *do you put this rage? And this is what just kills people."*

Bullying at Columbine is a heavily debated topic. How is bullying defined? How did it factor into the shootings? Was it worse than anywhere else? Were the gunmen bullied or bullies?

Early news reports characterized Klebold and Harris as frightened victims pushed past their limit. The media ran photos from their freshman year when they were dressed preppy and looked innocent—before they went "dark side". The story was less scary if they were frail nerds making a stand in an abusive situation they couldn't escape. But that wasn't the case. People who knew them said they were harassed by jocks, but they also said Harris and Klebold were "mean and rude" aggressors who started fights. There is footage of Harris and his friends walking down a hall at Columbine when some jocks deliberately bump shoulders with them as they pass, just to be rude. This also happened to Aaron Brown, Brooks' younger brother… when Harris did it to him unprovoked. *"Fucking freshman,"* Eric snarled when Aaron didn't react.

Reporters focused on bullying as the sole reason for the rampage, which put the school on the defensive. Faculty said bullying was no worse at Columbine than any other school. Students interviewed tended to agree, even those who described bullying they experienced. They said there was elitism and classism at CHS, cliques and favoritism. There were "mean girls" and posers, posturing alpha males and mousy brainiacs. The same sources called the environment "stereotypical high school". The National Center for Education Statistics (NCES) has graphs that show bullying occurs mostly in the middle grades (4th-8th). Other NCES studies showed faculty thought there was less bullying than students did. Kids aren't as likely to pick on each other when an adult is near. I have spoken with people worldwide about bullying in school and heard similar stories.

I first faced bullying in daycare. Run by a church, they had an afternoon program for children of many ages. I was pre-kindergarten. It was my first time on a playground with bigger kids. The equipment was too big for me, so I went to the sandbox, an old tractor tire. I was stopped by a group of older girls who said "fat-faces" weren't allowed in the tire. They formed a human wall to keep me out. I had never encountered such hostility. Confused and intimidated, I wandered away to play by myself near the door for the rest of recess. It didn't occur to me to tell a teacher.

Victims of bullying often don't tell adults for a variety of reasons, including feeling that they're dealing with it alone. Even in schools where there are "Safe to Tell" programs, there's an instinct to bury the encounter and move on. School can be a lot like an understaffed prison. You're a long-term inmate locked up with others who aren't going anywhere. There are too few Correctional Officers, and they're spread too thin to know or care about any but the worst infractions. So, you group up. There's safety in numbers. Those without a group typically have the worst experiences.

By high school, everyone knows their place and it's difficult to change. Breaking into established ranks is even harder. In his book *On Writing* Stephen King shared his high school experience with kids who were bullied. One was a "loser" due to her family's low income and her bad hygiene. She was an inspiration for his novel *Carrie*. Kids at school teased her relentlessly. While he didn't harass her, King admitted he saw it happen and did nothing to stop it. After winter break their sophomore year, the girl came to school in new clothes with her hair styled. She looked wonderful, but the change came too late. In King's words:

"The teasing that day was worse than ever. Her peers had no intention of letting her out of the box they'd put her in; she was punished for even trying to break free."

She started the day with confidence. She was happy. She thought she would fit in. By the end of the day, she was crushed back down into a scurrying, timid mouse.

King went on to say:

"I never liked Carrie, that female version of Eric Harris and Dylan Klebold, but through Sondra and Dodie I came at last to understand her a little."

348

According to witness statements, bullying at Columbine fell within the norm. It's unfortunate it is a "norm", but that's how humans in close quarters do things. There is a similar pecking order in the animal kingdom established through proxy contests, socio-political maneuvering, and brute force. Males test one another with surprise attacks. They degrade, roughhouse, target genitals—whether they like each other or not. Females exclude, deride, and upstage one another. They compete for the best mate or the most lovers. These behaviors prepare them for adult competition over resources and provide a sense of identity within the group. Over the years schools have tightened rules, but kids find new ways to pick on each other. Peer harassment on social media for instance has seen a drastic rise.

In high school I saw several instances of bullying. Most happened when faculty weren't around. There was conflict after hours, too. One evening my buddies and I drove past a local high school. Some male tennis players were coming off the campus on foot. We didn't know them but as we passed, they threw balls at our car. My friend who was driving slammed on the brakes and whipped the car around. The boys ran back to the tennis courts. My friend would have kept circling the school because he and another guy wanted to "get them back"—even though there was no damage to the car. But we were low on gas, so they grudgingly gave up the hunt.

Worse happened to a girl who rode the same school bus as me. Unattractive and shy, she wore ugly, mismatched clothing. Kids at school avoided and made fun of her. On the way home one day, some rowdy guys threw spitballs at her. She ignored them. When they ran out of spit, they wadded up sheets of paper to throw at her. When she still didn't react, they threw hardback textbooks at her. No one defended her, not even the bus driver. Bullying involves victims and instigators. Frequently there are witnesses who stand by, afraid to speak up because they don't want to become a target. A small number cheer on the aggressors, but they are often the bully's friends. I believe most people on the bus just didn't want to be the next victim, including me. We knew if the driver wouldn't stop the boys attacking a defenseless girl, he wouldn't stop anything they did. And we all had to ride that bus the rest of the year.

My experiences were in Texas where schools emphasized sports and Christianity. The community I was in was a lot like Columbine. There was a veneer of competitive Godliness and affluence. My family had three cars: One for my mother, one for the family, and a nicer "business" car dad drove to work and church. As a child I played the party line but in high school I was an "outcast". Jaded and unimpressed by the show of wealth and fake holiness, I rebelled. I smoked with stoners in the alley and listened to heavy metal. I saw cheerleaders excused from tests for practice and watched our Arts programs get slashed to pump money into football uniforms and stadium lighting. When I tried to get Algebra tutoring, I sat there the whole lunch period listening to my teacher talk to basketball players about last night's game. She didn't even acknowledge me. Very little was as important in school as sports. But it's not just Texas or Colorado. This focus on athletics is at the heart of most U.S. educational institutions. It's what brings in money and fame.

One of the worst examples of this athletic classism was the case of Jerry Sandusky, former Penn State University coach. Sandusky coached there for 30 years. He was allowed special privileges even after his sudden retirement in 1999 such as having keys to the football facilities and a personal office. He was even allowed to hold sleepover camps for young boys on campus until he was caught raping one in the school shower. In 2011 Sandusky was convicted of 45 charges of child sex crimes he committed between 1994 to 2009. Worse, people knew he was up to no good long before 2011 and didn't turn him in. Instead, he was allowed to "retire" and prey on kids until someone with a soul caught him in the act and reported him.

At Columbine, athletes and jocks were given attention by everyone. Brooks Brown said in his book *No Easy Answers: The Truth Behind Death at Columbine* that he and his friends were often targets of harassment by jocks, which appears to be true according to witnesses. But Harris, who was once a friend of

350

Brooks, also violently harassed him and his family for months. Further in his book Brooks said seniors slicked the floors with baby oil and slung hapless newbies down the halls into other students in a game he called "bowling with freshmen". Principal Frank DeAngelis refuted this in his book *They Call Me "Mr. De"*, saying the hallways were carpeted before the shooting. Which is true. He also denied bullying was worse at Columbine than it was at any school. This also seems to be true, based on witness statements. While bullying and elitism persist, it was not unique to Columbine. Whether it was worse comes down to who is asked and what it's compared to.

Juvenile Diversion Chief Regina Huerter was tasked with creating a report about it in 2000 that shows the opinions of staff and students there. Prior to 1998, there was a group of jocks at CHS whom other students called "Steroid Poster Boys". They were a predacious pack led by Rocky Hoffschneider Jr. Many said they were allowed to get away with bad behavior others wouldn't have. Rocky was a wrestling and football star from a family who historically excelled at sports. Rocky's younger brother Dusty was also a wrestler and played on Columbine's 1999 football team but was known to be a nice guy. The Hoffschneider family is still involved in sports: Rocky went on to televised MMA. In 2024, there's a Hoffschneider on the Columbine football team and one in wrestling at the University of Wyoming, Rocky Sr.'s alma mater.

Trench Coat Mafia member Joe Stair told NBC on April 23, 1999, the jocks hated his friends and other outcasts. Stair graduated in 1998, the same year Rocky Hoffschneider and his circle did. Rocky and his group affected most students they encountered, though their contact with Harris and Klebold seems minimal. When Klebold's dad asked him if he was picked on, Dylan said no, and pointed out he was 6'4—not an easy target. He did say Harris was a target, though.

In his journals, Harris complains about being teased for his appearance, being left out, and not being complimented enough. Klebold writes about friends abandoning him and girls

351

not liking him, though he never tells them he likes them. Angry because they weren't given the respect and attention they wanted, they lashed out through their hateful writing and illegal "pranks". Yet the "missions" and abuse they inflicted were more dangerous and problematic than what they complained about. Their belief that they were left out also seems skewed when compared to their social lives. They gamed online and hung out with people who considered them close friends. They attended and hosted gatherings: Birthday parties, holiday parties, theatre cast parties. They even went to the after-prom party, celebrating with the same people they would try to kill just days later.

The guys in trench coats were bullied but they dished out the same hostility to others. They bullied and harassed Special Education students, freshmen, and girls. They told themselves they were better than others and resented that they weren't doted on and admired like the jocks were. Fear wasn't their primary motivation. Anger was. And while bullying played a part in this equation, it wasn't the only factor behind the shooting.

CHOICE

In their senior year Klebold and Harris wanted to intimidate others. Envious of the top tier and feeling unappreciated by their peers, they reimagined life with themselves as apex predators. On the Basement Tapes they made fun of their peers, ripping on their beliefs and mannerisms. During the attack they shouted about "four years of shit" they put up with, but they terrorized and killed people they didn't even know. They gloated in their journals and videos and said the reason behind the violent spree was because it's what they wanted to do with their lives. Other students aspired to become engineers or health care workers. The gunmen wanted to be murderers with the highest kill count, even if it meant killing their friends. The things they shouted during the massacre were likely to keep themselves angry and in character.

Klebold and Harris deliberately internalized their anger, hiding it so no one could interfere with their self-aggrandizing rage binges. They nurtured God complexes. In their world, they were powerful and unforgiving. A force to be reckoned with. Any who didn't respect their superiority deserved to suffer at their hands. They were entitled to do whatever they wanted: Underage drinking, owning illegal firearms, setting off fireworks outside someone's house. The world was theirs and they wanted to burn it down. This entitled mindset is seen more now, particularly after COVID thrust people into isolation. Videos now show public meltdowns over things as minor as chicken nuggets. In 1999 it was rare to see. Part of that is because cell phones couldn't record video and uploading was a pain, but there's been a shift in social norms. People have given themselves permission to say and do whatever they want, regardless of the consequences.

The gunmen grew their anger like a hobby, immersing themselves in the violent identities of REB and VoDkA. They knew it was wrong, so they kept it secret. They might also have been testing whether anyone would notice they were on self-destruct. Getting away with things gave them smug satisfaction, but it likely added to their sense of being ignored. And they nurtured that, too. They couldn't murder people if they were securely bonded to sources of love. To detach, they spent less time with friends and family and shut them out emotionally when they had to be near them. Self-radicalization. Sue Klebold said if she could go back, she wouldn't leave Dylan alone as much. She believed she was respecting his feelings and giving him space. Instead, it gave him time to stew in hatred.

Around December 1998 Harris and Klebold's social circle dissolved. Unaware that the gunmen were actively pushing them away, their friends started to avoid them because of their antisocial, dangerous actions. With Harris' hostility driving a wedge between him and the people he considered his posse his only constant was Klebold. And while Klebold socialized with many people, they described him as a doggedly loyal follower who went anywhere Harris did.

Except Klebold was moving to Arizona after graduation. He would be someplace new with unfamiliar people. A whole new world of potential rejection. He might have been living a dual life, too. Until they stormed the school, it was just roleplay. If "NBK" day didn't happen Klebold could go on to college. Nobody would know what he'd been pretending. Harris wanted to enter the military, but when his mother told the recruiter he was on antidepressants, he was sure his chance was blown. He never heard that he was denied. He assumed the drug or his failure to disclose it would rule him out. Harris didn't want to go to college and resented being pressured to plan for his future. Like Klebold he seemed to be roleplaying up until they got the guns. That's when he wrote it felt like the "point of no return". Time to prove he wasn't just a blustering edgelord.

It can be difficult to see a situation objectively, especially when hormones and substance use/abuse are factors. Both teens drank hard liquor. The antidepressants Harris took have been proven to increase hostility and violence in teens. His dosage was steadily increased over months by a doctor who has scored a 1-star rating on various platforms for the past 25 years. The drugs surely affected his thinking, especially since he was drinking alcohol while on it. He stopped taking the medication before the shooting. While SSRIs can cause homicidal and suicidal thoughts, sudden cessation makes things worse. Klebold copied Harris' behavior; as Harris spiraled, so did he.

The choices they made were influenced by their environment, culture, and personalities. The school rewarded jocks for their wins while turning a blind eye to their behavior. Evangelicals pushed a "good or evil" viewpoint, compelling youths to preach a holy attitude they couldn't live up to. The shooters' parents and friends trusted that despite warning signs there was nothing to worry about. Police didn't take the threat seriously. The gunmen saturated themselves in media that glorified violence. Hormones and alcohol played a part. Immersed in the dark personas they created, they made an echo chamber to validate and reinforce their feelings of anger, neglect, and rejection. But their violent fantasies might have remained just that if not for the effects Zoloft and Luvox had on Harris.

If Columbine was a prison for them, their sentence was up. In two weeks, they would have graduated and been free. But they would also be cut off from Columbine. No more rage highs. No more megalomaniacal power trips. No more justification to pretend to be bad-ass hitmen. They would be normal guys trying to figure out what to do with their lives. They waited until school was almost over so they could pretend as long as possible before they had to grow up. They didn't kill because they were afraid. They were playing *Doom* for real.

Even people they liked were disposable. They planted the cafeteria bombs near a table where jocks sat, which was just a few feet away from where the Trench Coat Mafia sat. Krista Hanley, a friend of both gunmen, was standing in the lunch line right next to one of the bombs. Jessica Holliday, who was in the library during the massacre, also knew the gunmen. Her older brother Derek (an assistant principal and athletic director at Columbine in 2024) was close friends with Kevin Harris. At one point Jessica considered standing up and telling the shooters to stop, but she knew it wouldn't work. She told the *Rocky Mountain News*:

> *"Nobody could have stopped them. Nobody. They didn't have a reason for shooting somebody. They just shot. I think no matter what anybody would have done, if someone had stood up and tried to stop them, that person would have gotten shot."*

Klebold and Harris killed because they chose to. They knew they weren't measuring up to standards they and others put on them. Rather than work to better themselves, they wanted to bring others down with them using hatred, racism, and violence. They spent over a year intentionally enraging themselves just to get in the mental state just to do it. Their underlying thought process seems to have been: "I don't like myself. I want to destroy myself. Being around others reminds me of what I don't like about me. So, I want to destroy them too."

355

In the end, the gunmen chose to do something awful that they admitted would hurt their families and friends. They knowingly left them to be villainized and hated by the world. They made a series of bad decisions so they could feel omnipotent, which led to their unheroic deaths. They gained the notoriety that they wanted but they can't enjoy it.

That said, some of "why" they decided to go through with this horrible crime will never be understood. We don't have access to the answers. And while the "why" might seem important to stopping a similar tragedy in the future, it has become clear over the years that the thing we should be asking isn't "Why did this happen?" but "What should we be doing differently?"

WHAT SHOULD YOU DO?

Where to start?

Carl Sandburg said: *"Time is the most valuable coin of your life."*
Gandhi said: *"Be the change you want to see in the world."*

How we spend our time directly affects our life experience. While our problems can make it tempting to lash out at others or to give in to discouragement, does it improve our lives when we do? Or make the experience worse? Instead of letting the bad things drag you down, channel that negative energy into something productive and worthwhile. It won't fix everything, but it will give you the satisfaction of knowing you've done something that matters.

But where to start? Change is needed in many areas, such as the way schools and corporations are run, the way the media deals with crime, how the mentally ill are managed, the way our culture handles toxic behavior and the use of technology, how our justice system and government work, and more. It can be overwhelming to pick a place to get started.

The simplest, most direct change begins with the individual. It starts with each of us becoming more vigilant, more tuned in, more engaged in society. We need to be aware of what is going on around us—in the moment and in the bigger picture. We need to connect with people. Isolating ourselves makes strangers of us all.

357

If you're thinking of harming yourself or others

Don't do it.

Seek help. No matter how upsetting your situation is, how trapped or angry you feel, it is a temporary moment in your life. It will change. Whether it changes for better or worse depends a lot on you.

When we're in a bad situation, especially one that has gone on for a long time and will continue to, it can distort our world view. It can feel as though that's all there is to life. But escaping a life path doesn't have to lead to violence or self-destruction. Instead of pumping energy into hate and feelings of worthlessness or resentment, try this:

- **Love yourself.** One thing many killers have in common is that they disliked or even hated themselves. Everyone has flaws and shortcomings. Forgive yours. Then you can work on changing those things you don't like about yourself. Treat your inner self as though you were your own child. That's double duty: You must love and protect yourself but also teach and correct yourself. There are books and counselors to help if you need to learn how.
- **Find your voice.** Before making plans to harm yourself or others, talk to people and keep talking. Seek out *positive* influences to help you feel good about yourself. Avoid negative, toxic environments and people; they'll only make things worse. There are folks out there who care enough to help you navigate your problems, so you can grow into a stronger, happier you. Surround yourself with positive messages and goals. A good goal to start with is: Make something good come from your struggles.
- **Change your life.** This can be as basic as changing jobs or schools or taking a break from social media, or as complex as moving to another country. You aren't a prisoner of your current path. Talk to your family so they know what you're dealing with and why change is needed. If they won't work with you, consider changing

on your own if you're of legal age. If you're already on your own, it's even easier. Moving someplace else and starting a whole new life is better than going "postal" at school or work. As long as you're alive, there's chance for positive change. You just need to make it happen. There's a whole world out there. Discover it. Every life is different. You'll find a better one if you look for it. If you're a minor, it may feel like forever at the time, but you will eventually be an adult and able to make your own decisions. Setting healthy goals now and working toward them will help you start out on solid footing when you can move on.

- **Get busy doing something constructive**. Being occupied with a hobby or task is a great way to put your mind on something other than what's bothering you. Volunteer at a children's hospital or animal shelter. Create music or art. Go hiking. Write a book. Help build a house for a family in need. Start a business or a charity. Use your emotions to fuel a worthwhile project. You might be surprised at what you can achieve.

- **Get in tune with your thoughts**. People are smothering themselves with input and not taking time to process what they're experiencing. Some keep earpods in constantly even when they sleep because they start to think when they don't have input. The reason thoughts race when a person unplugs is because they have a backlog of processing to do. Take time to digest what you see and feel day to day. Analyze your opinions and beliefs. You can't avoid pitfalls if you're not thinking for yourself.

- **Darkness breeds darkness**. When we're upset, playing angry music and watching/reading violent media may validate our feelings, but it doesn't help us get past them. While it's good to recognize and accept your feelings, stewing in them is unhealthy. If you find yourself routinely doing things that make you mad or fuel depression, change your behavior. Seek out things that will trigger happiness instead, even if (and especially if) you don't feel like it. Happy is a choice.

If you feel bullied, outcast, or ignored

Everyone feels this way at some point. How we handle those feelings is important. There are plenty of helpful books about how to manage our emotions, written by people who have been through some of the worst experiences imaginable. You can search the internet for highly rated titles. But to summarize.

Communication is key. Try to talk to the people you are having a problem with. If you think friends are ignoring or "ghosting" you, try to connect with them one-on-one and have a real talk with them. Approach the matter with an open mind and with love, not accusation or anger: It's possible they're unaware of how you are feeling. If you value their friendship, isn't it worth it to try and fix things? Something as simple as: "I've noticed we're not spending much time together lately. Can we change that?" can get the ball rolling.

If you're not friends yet and want to work your way into a social circle, watch how they interact. Are you meeting them on their level? Chatting one-on-one with some or all of them about why you're not fitting in could help. If you talk with them and get nowhere, it could be they're just not meant to be your group. Accepting this will allow you to move on and find folks you click with. There are always more people to meet.

If you're being bullied, you can try to talk to the person or people, but you might find you need help to put a stop to it. Follow proper channels for reporting the situation. If they won't listen, keep going up the line of command. Talk to your family and friends about what you're experiencing and what you're doing about it. Document everything. Get authorities, lawyers, or the news involved if necessary to call attention to the problem. It's not ideal, but neither is a mass shooting.

Regarding being "outcast": Most people want to feel like they belong. Some are just better at hiding their struggles. Life often involves pretending like you fit in until you do. Fake it till you make it. Some of the biggest social outcasts later became world-famous artists, authors, and leaders in business and politics. Who you're around will only have as much impact as you allow. And there's no greater revenge than living well. Albert Einstein was expelled from school at 9 years old because he couldn't speak fluently. Everyone knows who he is now. As a testament to his struggles, he said: *"Success is a failure in progress. Someone who has never failed cannot truly be a successful person."*

If you routinely find it difficult to connect with others, it might be helpful to talk to a therapist—one who will listen to you. Perhaps you have antisocial traits or tendencies that can be worked on if you're made aware of them. Self-help in general can do wonders: Take a public speaking or storytelling class to gain confidence. Exercise can help us feel better about our bodies. Psychology class teaches us to recognize our negative behavior patterns. Dr. Joe Dispenza wrote a book, *Breaking the Habit of Being Yourself*, which can help you define issues and work on them. You can never go wrong with self-improvement, even if it's just brushing your teeth every day. At the end of the evening, you can feel good about that one step you took to love yourself.

If you're infatuated with the shooters

Chances are you relate to their apparent motivations or backgrounds. Perhaps you've been bullied or snubbed. Maybe you were neglected or ignored to the point where you felt like nobody cared. Unfairness in life and hypocrisy frustrate you. These are all relatable feelings many people experience. But understanding and empathizing with a relatable situation does not make the gunmen's actions right. It doesn't make them sympathetic antiheroes. They killed people they didn't even know, not to right a social wrong but to get a higher death count.

Some people who are infatuated with the gunmen chase those feelings to platforms that reinforce this infatuation or fictionalize who the killers were. This includes forums and "fanfiction" archives where the personalities of the shooters are overwritten by individuals who scripted or roleplayed their own

361

versions of what they thought Harris and Klebold were like. Roleplay and fiction are not reality. The gunmen were real people. The shooting was a horrible slice of nearly two decades of their lives. The nuances of who they were and what they were like have been distilled to a jumble of items. Anyone's life can be romanticized if you cherry-pick details and invent the rest.

Shift your focus to someone in your own life you didn't like. Pick a person you thought was weird or cringey or clingy or was prone to doing things that embarrassed, annoyed, or scared you. Someone you deliberately avoided because they made you uncomfortable. Can you put aside your personal experience and apply the same infatuation to them?

If you know someone who might be at risk

When dealing with a person who could have issues or cause them, it can be difficult to know when to act. Most people want a smooth existence. They don't want to make waves, rock boats, or sound false alarms. Nor do they want to tangle with an unstable person. The easiest route for many would be to avoid the individual who makes them uncomfortable. But avoidance that doesn't make the problem go away. It just takes it off the radar.

When does personal discomfort with a person become something reportable? There's not a meter for that. We must be alert to the actions and attitudes of others around us. It's one thing if your friend exclaims in frustration that he's going to kill his brother for messing with his stuff. It's another if that friend regularly "jokes" about hurting people for fun or revenge and talks mostly about guns and killing.

Again, communication is key. Talking to the person who's showing warning signs can be a good place to start if you're friends. Ask them if they're seriously thinking about harming others or themselves and why. If they're truly a friend, you should be able to talk with them. Let them know you care about them and don't want to see them make choices that might hurt them or ruin their lives. If they're not a friend, connect with whoever is next in line: Siblings, parents, school staff, bosses, authorities. Talk to your friends and peers about their experiences with the person. Communicate the situation to others and compare notes. Knowing what's going on means a better chance to stop tragedy before it starts. I have resources in the front and back of this book if you need to reach out for help.

Thoughts for parents

Intervention requires recognizing when your child is having problems. It can be difficult to know what they're doing and experiencing day to day. School staff might be trying to communicate, but they can't keep track of what every child does for eight hours, five days a week. And kids tend to do a poor job of self-reporting. You can ask, but the typical conversation about "How was school?" often dead ends in "Okay." Even asking specific questions can result in a false sense that everything is "normal". It may not be deliberate evasion; kids often don't think to tell others what they're going through. Some may not realize how bad things are or they may not want to upset or burden their parents. Some feel they can handle it, even if the results show otherwise. Trouble can creep up so slowly, it may not register until things get dire.

So, at what point do we start worrying? Especially if the person isn't talking about their problems?

The better you know your child, the easier it is to tell what is going on with them. You'll know what's characteristic. If you see them withdraw and change their wardrobe or behavior drastically, take note. This is especially true if they are getting into dark or violent interests. Find out what's behind the change and stay connected. Let them know you're concerned, that you love them and want to help. Talk to their teachers and friends. Get the bigger picture from those who are with them the most.

Making secure bonds with our kids early on is vital. Keep nurturing those relationships with regular communication. Cross thresholds. Hang out with your child in their room occasionally. Ask them what they've been doing online and off. Talk to them about their friends. Stay in the loop about things they like and do. Keep them in touch with what's going on in your life and what your goals are. Find areas where you can connect.

I'm going to go one step further and suggest something taboo: Snoop around your kid's room when they're not home. Until they're an adult with their own house, anything they're doing in their room is your responsibility. You need to know what's happening under your roof. You don't necessarily have to do anything about it, but you should know what's in your home or on your computer. Psychologists have written books to help you talk to your children about porn, drugs, toxic social media, internet addiction, etc. Get help if you need it.

Having a secure bond with your kid won't mean you always know everything, but it will help when you need to discuss concerns with them. If communication breaks down, family counselors are there to help. Health insurance may cover the cost of therapy. Just be leery of anyone in the profession who tries to steer you to drugs immediately. Do your own research before agreeing to any sort of medication routine, particularly for minors whose brains are still growing and changing. It's optimal to try talk therapy first. Know your options.

Ways for everyone to make a POSITIVE impact

It's not hard to make the world worse. It's just as easy to become a hero, too. This is true whether you're doing well or wrestling with problems of your own. In fact, it can be more rewarding to do good when you're struggling. It's difficult to dwell on your problems when you're handing a gift to a child cancer patient or taking a rescue dog for a romp. There are many ways to have a positive impact on the world, to do something people will respect and be grateful for. So many things you can do will make you feel good about yourself and have lasting impact.

- *Schools.* They need all kinds of help, from peer support to volunteers. The Theatre and Arts programs especially need all the help they can get.

- *Charity.* As with schools, charities are always in need of assistance. Collecting donations, dressing up as superheroes for hospitalized kids, talking to parents of ill children, helping with repair and running of shelters, caring for a lonely animal… you see the impact you're having. To be sure a charity is legit, check out https://www.guidestar.org/. It's a free online service, like the BBB, which shows who's who in the charity world.

- *Politics.* If you're over 18 in the USA, you might have noticed on your ballot that some roles have only one person running for office. Some have none. There are many city and government jobs available, more than they have candidates for. School board positions often have openings. In my state in 2024, only one person ran for State Representative. When only one person runs, that person wins by default. We need more than default candidates if things are going to improve.

- *Outreach.* There's no substitute for bonding with others, whether they're your kid, your brother, or your coworker. A few basic questions and words of kindness can go far if you keep at it. There are many organizations available for people who need help. Teen hotlines, suicide hotlines, support groups, senior centers, library programs, grief support… there are so many ways to connect. You can use your own experiences to help others get through their tough times.

The important thing is to get busy doing good. If hatred and depression are a downward spiral, then activism and charity are an upward one. The more you do, the better you'll feel. When you make something positive come from your negative experiences, the world becomes a better place because you're in it. There is no cap on how much change you can affect by being you. This is your life, your stage. Do something amazing with it.

APPENDIX A:
MAPS & PHOTOS

Columbine High School — lower level

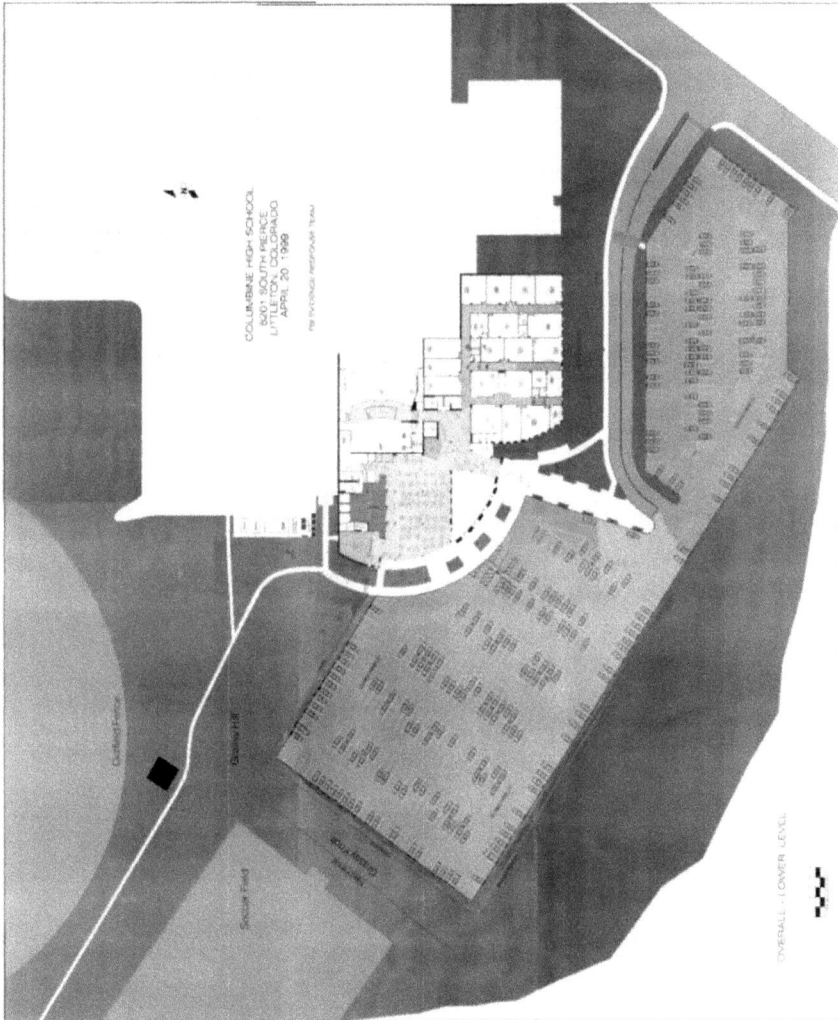

Better quality: http://www.acolumbinesite.com/columbine/maps/clow.jpg

Columbine High School — upper level

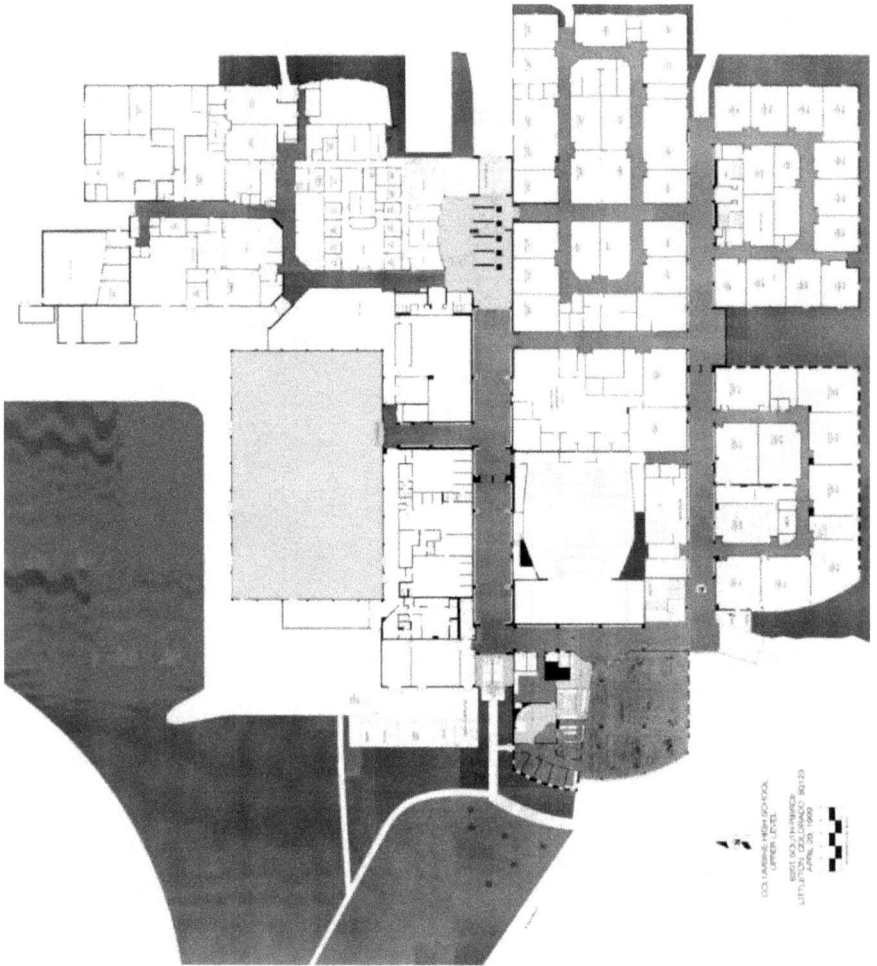

Better quality: http://www.acolumbinesite.com/columbine/maps/cup.jpg

Columbine High Cafeteria

Better quality:

http://www.acolumbinesite.com/columbine/maps/CAFEBW.png

Columbine High library

Better quality:

http://www.acolumbinesite.com/columbine/maps/LIBRARYBW.png

Aerial Views

371

Rachel Scott's rose

Columbine signs

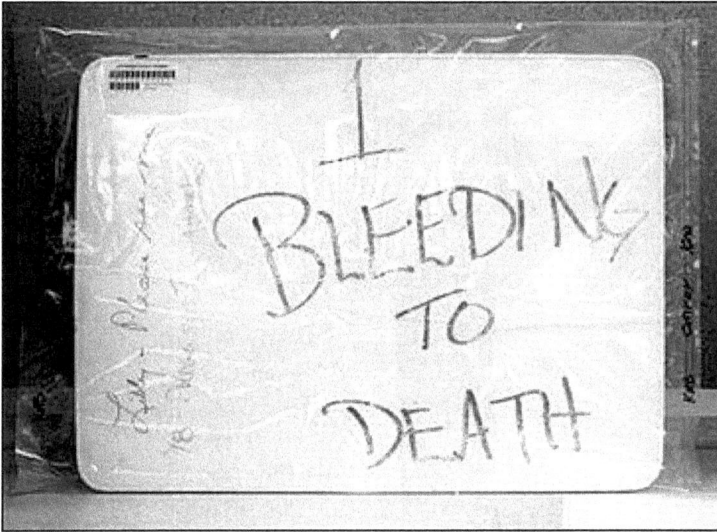

Columbine library memorial wall

APPENDIX B:

RESOURCES

A Columbine Site http://www.acolumbinesite.com

- Daniel Mauser official site http://www.danielmauser.com
- Rachel's Challenge https://rachelschallenge.org
- Craig Scott official site https://www.craigscott.org
- Krista Hanley official site https://kristahanley.com
- Crystal Woodman Miller official site https://www.crystalwoodmanmiller.com
- Amanda Stair Duran official YouTube channels https://www.youtube.com/@amandaduran7898
- https://www.youtube.com/channel/UCnnhdqm3Xhq9y1exAjd vSyw
- *I Asked, God Answered: A Columbine Miracle* by Mark Taylor
- *Walking in Daniel's Shoes* by Tom Mauser
- *No Easy Answers: The Truth Behind Death at Columbine* by Brooks Brown
- *She Said Yes: The Unlikely Martyrdom of Cassie Bernall* by Misty Bernall
- *Dawn Anna* - 2005 film by Robert Munic, Arliss Howard, and James Howard. Directed by Arliss Howard.
- *The Inside Story of Columbine* by Randy Brown
- *The Journals of Rachel Scott: A Journey of Faith at Columbine High* by Beth Nimmo
- *Over My Shoulder* by Kacey Ruegsegger Johnson https://kaceyruegseggerjohnson.com
- *A Mother's Reckoning* by Sue Klebold
- *They Call Me "Mr. De"* by Frank DeAngelis
- *Comprehending Columbine* by Ralph W. Larkin, PhD
- *Echoes of Columbine* – FBI documentary https://www.youtube.com/watch?v=KyxjvqjHxec
- *Ripples of Columbine* – Rocky Mountain PBS https://www.youtube.com/watch?v=BXPfePcxaZw
- *Denver Post* Columbine coverage https://www.denverpost.com/tag/columbine-shooting
- Project HOPE http://www.projecthope.com
- Columbine High School https://columbinehs.jeffcopublicschools.org
- Columbine Memorial https://www.columbinememorial.org
- The Rebels Project https://www.therebelsproject.org
- Frank DeAngelis Academic Foundation https://www.chsaf.org/
- Channel 7 Denver KMGH

- 9 News Denver
- 20/20
- 60 Minutes / 60 Minutes II
- ABC
- AOL
- Alan Prendergast
- APB News
- Arizona Republic
- Adam Kyler
- Anne Marie Hochhalter
- Austin Eubanks
- BBC News
- Boulder News
- Boulder Weekly
- Friends of Brian Johnson
- CBS
- CNN
- Colorado Bureau of Investigation
- Columbine Review Commission
- The Daily Camera
- Dailymotion
- Dave Cullen
- Dawn Anna
- DejaNews
- Denver7
- The Denver Post / Denver Post Online
- El Paso County
- Federal Bureau of Investigation
- Fox News
- Frank DeAngelis
- Good Morning America
- Instituto Columbine
- Jeff Kass
- Jefferson County
- JCAA
- The Mauser family
- Mark Taylor's family
- MSNBC
- New York Times

- Newsweek magazine
- Nicole Nowlen
- NPR
- NRA
- Oprah
- Pat Ireland and friends
- People magazine
- Research Columbine
- Rocky Mountain News
- Salon.com
- Sean Graves
- Slashdot
- The Smoking Gun Archive
- TED Talks
- TIME magazine
- The Tomlin family
- USA Today
- Washington Post
- WBS
- Westword
- Yahoo!
- Safe to Tell: 1-877-542-SAFE (7233)
- Suicide and Crisis Lifeline SMS: 988
- Suicide Prevention Resource Center https://www.sprc.org
- We Are Safer Together https://wearesafertogether.com/
- JeffCo DeAngelis Center https://deangeliscenter.org
- Yellow Ribbon Suicide Prevention https://yellowribbon.org/

About the Author

I have spent the past 25 years researching and writing about Columbine. I wrote and maintain the Internet's largest site about the event, http://www.aColumbineSite.com, established April 21, 1999. In one year, the site sees over 1,000,000 visitors and is available free anyone to use worldwide.

In 2023, I earned an associate's degree in arts with emphasis on film and forensic science. As of this publication I am pursuing a bachelor's degree majoring in journalism with a minor in film.

In addition to being credited by amazing authors in several best-selling books about Columbine, my writing has been referenced by Columbine families and by law enforcement and EMS for their official disaster-readiness plans in the USA, Australia, Malaysia, and more. I've assisted journalists, teachers, students, authors, playwrights, and film directors with their Columbine projects. I've also spoken at events and appeared in short educational films about the subject. This is my fourth nonfiction book and my second book about Columbine.

I am certified by the IBCCES. I'm a member of the AFI and the Clara Barton Society and assist several charity organizations that work with survivors of trauma and abuse. I've volunteered at community events run by law enforcement, first responders, and schools for over 20 years, including the Crimes Against Children division of the Phoenix police department. In 2009, the Fort Wayne police department honored me with a certificate of appreciation for assisting them in developing their crisis training program. In 2024, I attended the private memorial service at Columbine High that marked the 25th year following the tragedy and the 8th year of Columbine's Day of Service, an inspiring community operation put into motion by the Columbine families. While there, I was gifted with the Columbine Challenge Coin.

If you found this book helpful, please leave a 5-star review at Amazon. It helps others find it.

https://amzn.to/3NNSBCl

Semper memento — always remember.

www.ingramcontent.com/pod-product-compliance
Lightning Source LLC
Chambersburg PA
CBHW070905100426
42737CB00047B/2616